KITCHEN
CONVERSATIONS

Books by Joyce Goldstein

Back to Square One

The Mediterranean Kitchen

Kitchen Conversations

Joyce Goldstein

*Robust Recipes and Lessons in Flavor
from One of America's Most
Innovative Chefs*

William Morrow and Company, Inc.
New York

Library of Congress Cataloging–in–Publication Data

Goldstein, Joyce Esersky.
    Kitchen conversations : robust recipes and lessons in flavor from one of America's most innovative chefs / Joyce Goldstein.
        p.   cm.
    Includes index.
    ISBN 0-688-13866-7
    1. Cookery.   I. Title.
TX714.G649   1996
    641.5—dc20

96-13592
CIP

Printed in the United States of America

First Edition

1 2 3 4 5 6 7 8 9 10

BOOK DESIGN BY PENTAGRAM

In memory of Maggie Waldron,

who understood the value of a good kitchen conversation

Acknowledgments

Big **thank-yous** are in order for the following wonderful people: *Evan Goldstein* for his worldly wine wisdom, for knowing his mother's food really well, and for training my granddaughter's palate so that at the age of two she understood the concept of "tart"

Kit Hinrichs of Pentagram for his brilliant design and infinite patience and to *Kashka Pregowska-Czerw* for her diligent execution of the design work

Maureen Lasher for her writing and diplomatic skills

Gail Kinn, who asked really good questions

Ann Cahn, for meeting the challenges involved in getting from manuscript to finished book

Barry Reder for good advice and his theory of boxes

David Nussbaum for his critical skills and sense of humor

Tom Shelton of Joseph Phelps Vineyards for inviting me to cook the recipes from this book at many special dinners

Lisa Ekus for support and encouragement

Greg Drescher, Dun Gifford, and Sara Baer-Sinnott of the Oldways Preservation and Exchange Trust for sending me back to Greece, Turkey, Spain, and Italy to pursue recipe research and test the accuracy of my taste memory

Photographer *Jock McDonald* for capturing me in action

Alain Rondelli for his friendship and critical taste buds

Bill Foley of Westchester for his patience and typesetting skills

And to the superb staff of Square One Restaurant, who kept the ship of state afloat when I had to hole up in the office to face the computer: *Ed Hancock, Lesley Hoelper, Kirsten Miller, John Bill Jones,* and *Sandy Martin*

But **most especially thanks** to *Gary Woo, Julia Drori, Matt Banks,* and *Jennifer Millar,* who tested the recipes and offered their expertise and fine palates so that the recipes really work and so you won't panic as you stand at the stove.

Contents

Introduction
How This Book Came About

My life as a chef is the result of a career change. I was an artist and a scholar first, growing up in a time when travel was less financially taxing, and when costs of daily living were less burdensome. Living for many years in New York, then moving to San Francisco, I had ample opportunity to dine out in all manner of restaurants to learn about food. On my tiny savings I traveled through Europe after graduate school, lived in Italy for a time, and ate out as often as possible. I read cookbooks voraciously because I knew there was so much more to experience and learn. (I still do.) I taught myself to cook through trial and error. I experimented on friends and family. Despite my responsibilities in graduate school or while raising three children, I made time to read, to practice, to experience, and was able to develop a strong taste memory because I would constantly taste new dishes and then go back to my kitchen to try to reproduce them.

If truth be told, I have a large account of recipes in my memory bank. But it is a long-established account, B.R. (before the restaurant), most of it based on past experience. It is a fact of my A.R. (after the restaurant) life that in the past fifteen years I have been able to travel abroad less and less, in search of The Great Meal or The Perfect Dish. Every once in a while, because of a conference or scheduled class, I have the blessed occasion to squeeze a few extra days of travel into my already overcommitted schedule. When this opportunity arises, I eat as many meals as I can fit into one day and one body. I try to dine with as many friends as possible so I can taste many more dishes in a brief but hedonistic orgy of eating. I buy innumerable cookbooks to add to my library and send or schlepp them home. I return to work physically exhausted but mentally reenergized, full of ideas and tastes. Before memory fades, I transcribe dining notes madly. I play food detective and try to research dishes I have eaten but couldn't obtain a recipe for at the time.

When I am running a professional kitchen, I am excited about dishes whose tastes I know in my mouth and my mind, about recipes I have eaten and loved. Whenever I cook I have a taste in mind. My cooking process is the means to get to that goal, to achieve that taste, that taste of memory. But how do you explain and describe the tastes you are looking for in a dish to those who have never experienced them?

As a chef and teacher my responsibility is to convey my excitement about food to the young people working with me, or to my cooking class students, and teach them how to taste. Most cooks know just what they have learned at school, on the job, or from reading food magazines. They know how to shell and devein shrimp, but may not know how to intensify the taste by searing. They've studied how to plate artistically composed salads, but didn't learn how to assess when lemon juice might be better than that trendy vinegar. They've practiced how to make fresh pasta, but didn't understand how much sauce it would take, and what kind, as opposed to dried pasta. They've tasted fresh herbs to identify them, but didn't realize that if one tablespoon of tarragon was fine, substituting a bunch of tarragon could destroy a delicate dish. My job is to turn technocrats into tasteocrats.

This book is the result of talking with people about food, explaining with language (a difficult means of expression for something so sensual and emotional), while tasting what I am aiming for with a recipe, and how to get there. I want you to learn how to bring flavors to their peak, or how possibly to rescue a dish if it has gone astray, to recognize when it is approaching success and when the dish is in balance, to stop and savor it when it is "right," and to learn to remember its taste so you can make it again. And again. I want to share my tasting experiences and Kitchen Conversations with you.

Who Is This Book For?

When you are a beginning cook you often feel that you are working in a haze, handicapped by your lack of experience, and occasionally driving without a license. You know you could do so much better if only you knew more. (Or had someone with more cooking experience looking over your shoulder.) When a dish comes out well, you are pleased but often feel it was just beginner's luck. The second time you cook the dish it might not be as good and you don't know why. You'd love to know how you can get it to come out better or at least as consistently good as the first time. You don't want cooking always to be a game of chance.

After you have been cooking for a while, you reach a point where you are comfortable with your skills. You generally succeed with the tried-and-true dishes in your repertoire. But sometimes when you try a new recipe, the dish seems flat. Or it tastes as if something is missing. Only you don't know what it is or where to go with it.

How is it that some cooks know what is missing in a dish? Why did they pick nutmeg and not cinnamon? Why did they up the garlic instead of the oregano? How do they know how to correct errors in seasoning and when to stop? It would be so comforting if you had someone there in the kitchen to discuss the recipes with you so that you could answer these questions! Then your cooking could rise above the simply competent, and you'd learn to achieve a really fine balance of flavors and even exhibit, dare we say it, a "personal style."

Whether you are a beginner, a moderately capable cook, or even a technically proficient and experienced cook who does not adjust flavors well or taste as accurately as you'd like, this book will help you. Our Kitchen Conversations will address flavor elements in the recipes, how they can be heightened, or pushed back, or made to get along with others. Through aware tasting and cooking practice, you'll be able to approach new recipes with greater confidence because you'll understand how the taste elements work. You will learn to recognize those flavors you like and feel comfortable with, and how to modify and balance those that you are learning to like. You'll learn how to taste so that you achieve better balance and greater satisfaction with your cooking. You will become a person with a well-tuned palate.

Training the Palate

As a chef I am fascinated by taste. Taste is not finite or static. The first bite is not like the last. Some tastes are cumulative, and build on repetition. Some depend on good strong first impressions. When I cook I become a culinary juggler, playing with the balance of flavors. I've got so many balls in the air. Taste, texture, temperature, and aroma. While cooking I am constantly striving for balance and symmetry, seeking the proper proportion of taste elements to delight my palate.

Many of us cook and eat out of taste habit. Can we educate our palates to be more broad-minded and learn to work with ingredients so that we understand their taste properties? Can we train our palates to know how to bring the dominant flavors to maximum intensity without sacrificing balance in a dish? Can we monitor our progress while cooking so we know to stop when the dish has achieved balance? In fact, can counterpoint and balance be taught? Can tasting be trained? Yes!

If you want to become a better cook, if these questions of taste and balance reflect some of your own hopes and aspirations, I believe this book will help you in achieving your goals.

Having been a chef and cooking teacher for many years, I believe that most palates are trainable. If a palate were not trainable, how could anyone have a "favorite" dish or remember how that favorite tasted? In fact, if palates were not trainable, it would be almost impossible for me to run a restaurant, unless I wanted to cook all the food myself! Obviously, different chefs have distinctively different palates. That is how we distinguish their food from someone else's. And why we like one restaurant's cuisine better than another's. The job of the chef is to train the staff to reproduce his or her personal palate, his or her "signature" style. The job of the kitchen crew is to learn to re-create that taste. How do they do it?

A really skillful restaurant cook can prepare something over and over again so that it is easily recognizable to the regular patron whose "favorite" it is. It's also that way in families. If your Aunt Ruth's pea soup was your favorite soup, you'd want her to make it the same way for you every time. If it was always different, it would be just another pea soup, not your favorite. Like an accomplished restaurant cook, Aunt Ruth can reproduce the soup perfectly every time. Both can follow a recipe and have it come out consistently "right," even when raw ingredients may vary. On any given day, a tomato may be sweet or acid, a squash sweet or starchy. Well-trained cooks know what to do to get back to the "right" taste. How do they do it?

Let's try to find out. In the restaurant kitchen the cooks and chefs taste the food together and have the advantage of dialogue. They have a Kitchen Conversation and discuss each dish. They assess what it "needs," where the "hole" is in the flavor, what they might do to "round it out," or "bring it up," or push some element back. They talk about balance, fullness, top, bottom, and midrange tones.

A chef is blessed when he or she finds a "soulmate" or "natural," someone who not only learns quickly but whose taste buds are similar to the chef's. The chef can trust this person to reproduce a recipe because they both like the same amount of vinegar in the vinaigrette, because the sense of the "right" amount of oregano is the same for both of them. They "agree" when the garlic is too mild and should be brought up, and know when that pinch of sweet nutmeg is missing. It's that way at home when you find a cookbook you love. You and the author are on the same wavelength.

It is through repetition, constant tasting, and re-tasting that a palate is trained. Also, by comparative tasting and experiment. One day you try the sauce with red wine vinegar, then balsamic, then lemon juice, then lime or orange juice until you know which is the "right" acid to balance out the flavors and bring the dish to its maximum potential. One day you add allspice instead of cinnamon, another time nutmeg, to see which sweet spice is the right accent for the sauce. Did you really want oregano, or should you try milder thyme or sweeter mint to work with the orange juice next time?

Part of one's palate training is to be able to identify those individual flavor elements that make up the dish, and then decide where their place is in the "landscape." Which is to be foreground, background, undertone, accent? What is to be bold? Subtle? Once you identify the components and their position in the dish, then you can keep working to refine the final taste.

Cookbooks can provide recipes, menu suggestions, and cultural background material, but most don't provide the opportunity for dialogue with a culinary companion. I hope that our Kitchen Conversations will inspire you and help you to become a more intuitive cook, trained to taste, so you can become less dependent upon following every recipe down to the last syllable and quarter teaspoon. Then you can have real fun and adventure in the kitchen.

How We Experience Taste

Some of us have more sensitive palates than others. There are physiological differences in our personal taste buds; we don't all taste food in the same way. Some people tolerate more salt; others are quite sensitive to foods that are strongly salted. While most of us love foods that are sweet, a few recoil at excessive sweetness. Some of us love foods that are tart. (I don't know what I would do without lemons!) But pleasantly sour to me could be mouth-puckering to you. What might be vibrant to one person could be flat to a person used to "bigger" tastes. And some people taste foods as if through a fog, as their palates are not well tuned. Others, as in the fairy tale of the princess and the pea, can detect the one sprinkle of thyme in their stew or the drop of almond extract in the fruit compote! The more you taste, the more you sharpen your senses. You even increase your ability to taste old favorites in a new way. You will recognize more easily when flavors work for you and when they don't.

Part of my work as a chef is to understand what my guests really love to eat so I can give them pleasure. (I was that way as a mom too.) After talking with people about food "likes and dislikes," I've learned that the most idiosyncratic and personal physiological element is texture. Some love foods that are creamy and custardlike; others may be turned off by a runny egg yolk. Some love gelatinous textures; others shiver at the shimmer of aspic and bavarians. Rarely have I heard someone say they hate sour or salt or sweet or bitter per se. But they will admit to not liking certain herbs and spices, or too much heat. Some think one chili pepper is hot enough, while others need ten chiles to feel the heat. Just as we can build up tolerance for the amount of heat we can take, so can we learn to love flavors that at first seemed off-putting, like cilantro or anise, saffron or salt cod. Rather than breeding contempt, familiarity can make an odd food into an old friend.

Besides physiological differences, personal palates are influenced by our family's food habits and by ethnic and cultural flavor traditions. Our taste preferences and dining patterns are formed by what we eat at home, or by our community food environment. What is being grown, cooked, and served at the time we are growing up. And who is cooking it for us.

Upbringing strongly affects palate development. People who were raised on white bread and peanut butter most assuredly taste things differently than those who were raised on couscous and harissa or pasta and bitter greens! If you grew up in an Italian household, the flavors and smells that are familiar to you will not be as evocative to or easily recognized by those brought up in an English or German or Japanese home.

We can, of course, learn to broaden our palates and learn to enjoy all sorts of ethnic specialties from other cultures. This requires a certain open-mindedness, a culinary sense of adventure, and a willingness to try, afresh, unusual or new dishes. The more you taste, the more you can taste. Dining out and travel help us to expand our flavor spectrum.

Everything you taste for the first time can be considered "exotic." The taste memory is flexible and has lots of room to acquire many new and exotic flavors. If you grew up in Iowa, radicchio may be exotic to you, but not if you grew up in Italy. At first taste you may like it, or you may hate it. The more you taste it, you may come to love it. And the more you taste it and understand its properties, the better you will be able to use it in your cooking. Achieving your own sense of balance is the key. But learning how to balance is an acquired skill. That comes from practice, tasting, cooking, tasting again.

Mediterranean Flavors

When exploring something as subtle as taste awareness and the development of a personal palate, it's best to keep our culinary horizons well focused and cooking techniques relatively uncomplicated. Therefore, in this book I have chosen to limit our taste explorations to recipes based on the Mediterranean palate. Why

Basic Tastes and Mediterranean Flavors

Bitter		Sour	Salt	Sweet	
endive	turnips	lemon	salt	honey	fennel
escarole	raw onions	lime	anchovies	sugar	peas
radicchio	radish	orange	pancetta	almonds	green beans
arugula	thyme	grapefruit	sun-dried tomatoes	hazelnuts	cinnamon
bitter greens	mustard	wine	cheeses (Parmesan, feta, pecorino, Gorgonzola, etc.)	pine nuts	nutmeg/mace
walnuts	cucumbers	vinegar		mint	allspice
rosemary	pepper, black, hot	pomegranate		tomatoes	cardamom
garlic		tomatoes	prosciutto	basil	coriander
eggplant		dill	olives	caramelized onions	cloves
oregano		capers	clams		cream
watercress		yogurt	salt cod	fresh fruits (some may be sweet and sour): cherries, apples, plums, nectarines, apricots, berries, peaches, pears, melons, bananas, figs	coconut
cilantro		asparagus	salted capers as opposed to brined capers		corn
cumin		leeks			hard squashes like butternut, acorn
saffron		grape leaves			
sage		lemongrass			yams, sweet potatoes
ginger		sorrel		dried fruits: (raisins, figs, dates, prunes, apricots, etc.)	
turmeric		fresh fruits (some may be sweet and sour): apricots, peaches, berries, apples, plums, nectarines, cherries, etc.			balsamic vinegar (sweet and sour)
cabbage				peppers (roasted, unroasted, red and yellow)	oranges (sweet and sour)
Brussels sprouts					
cauliflower				scallops	
broccoli				shrimp	
artichokes				crab	
spinach				lobster	
chard				mussels	
zucchini				beets	
green peppers				carrots	
tarragon					

focus on the Mediterranean? Most obviously, because I love the food! (And the public's enthusiastic acceptance of this cuisine tells me I am not alone.) Most Mediterranean recipes are based on long-established culinary traditions. The signature tastes and combinations of tastes are easily recognizable and remembered. Flavors are direct and forthright. The basic ingredients of Mediterranean cooking are familiar, readily available, and not too many are combined in a recipe. Who doesn't love tomatoes, eggplant, peppers, onions, and garlic? Citrus fruits, figs, grapes, and wine. Olives, nuts, and dried fruits as accents. Cheeses. Herbs such as mint, basil, dill, oregano, and thyme. Grains such as pasta, rice, polenta, couscous, cracked wheat, and bread.

Besides having familiar and delicious tastes, Mediterranean cooking is based on simple culinary techniques, so we are not stopped in our tracks before we begin. We don't need lots of fancy equipment or special professional knife skills. It's great home cooking. In this book you'll be able to use the recipes for dining pleasure and develop your palate at the same time!

Basic Tastes

Every day we sit down at the table and food is placed in front of us. A dish looks appetizing and we take a taste. After the first bite our mental food computer goes to work. We like it, or we don't like it. *Why?* What is happening in our mouth that tells us to proceed carefully or with gusto?

Our mouth is equipped, by nature, with taste buds that deal with four basic elements: sweet, sour, salt, and bitter. And combinations of these elements. But tasting is a complex act. It is more than recognition of the properties in the dish. It is more than simply understanding our tolerance for these flavors, our personal taste preferences. Tastes can be colored by other sensations that we like or dislike. Spiciness or heat: the bite or burn of hot chiles. Aroma: the perfume of basil or mint. Texture: the crunch of nuts, the slipperiness of oils or fats, the sponginess of mushrooms and eggplant, the chewiness of meat fibers, the gelatinous qualities of mousses, the creaminess of custard or pureed potatoes. Scent, temperature, and texture complicate our reactions to these basic tastes, and can even seduce us into liking a dish we might not have enjoyed on its taste merits alone.

Let's look at the Four Basic Taste Components

☛ **Sweet** is easy to like. Sugar, honey, fruits, coconut milk, cream, almonds, sweet potatoes, beets, corn, roasted peppers, ripe tomatoes. Sweet is a treat, a reward, and a tempering agent for foods that are hot, sour, or salty. A pinch of sugar rounds out a tomato sauce that is too acidic. Honey tempers a marinade and adds a certain caramelization and crustiness to meat and poultry when cooked. Sweetness works to tame chiles especially when paired with the acid of lemon or lime. A bit of sugar in a tart citrus vinaigrette adds the balance that makes it taste "right." Sweet-and-sour dishes have a history going back to Roman times. They remain in our culinary repertoire because the interplay of tastes is intriguing and appealing to our palates.

☛ **Sour** makes the mouth in our mind pucker. You'd think we wouldn't find it so appealing. Sour is acid. It can come in the form of wine or fruit vinegar, raw or aged. It can be fruit- or citrus-based, the juice or zest of lemon, lime, orange, or grapefruit. Sour is a major player in achieving flavor balance. It helps cut fat in sauces like vinaigrettes, hollandaise, béarnaise, mayonnaise. Sour enlivens and lightens starches. The classic gremolata added to risotto for example. Or tomato added to a pilaf. And it plays up sweetness by cutting it. A bit of lemon added to peach jam, or balsamic vinegar sprinkled over fresh berries heightens their sweetness.

☛ **Salt** is more than just a table condiment. The body needs it. It can come to us in the form of anchovies, bacon, prosciutto, smoked fish, oysters, clams, cheeses, capers, olives, foods in brine. We like it. Witness our passion for corn or potato chips, pretzels, and salty French fries. Salt adds sparkle to starchy foods. It brings out the seasonings in a dish that lie dormant until the proper amount of salt brings them to the surface of our palate. As you gradually keep adding salt to the finished dish, you start to taste the cinnamon or cumin that you put in earlier.

☛ **Bitter** is a taste most of us think we don't like. Perhaps it is the emotional connotation of the word. It sounds unhappy. Yet increasingly we are attracted to the bitterness of endive, arugula, radishes, radicchio, mustard greens, walnuts, and the tannins in wine. We especially enjoy bitter when it's used as a counterpoint to bland and creamy foods, or mingled with fat, such as the oil in a vinaigrette. Or combined with heat, such as hot pepper flakes or horserad-ish. Or sweetened by caramelization or a bit of honey or sugar. Bittersweet, more than a poignant mood, is a most attractive food combination because of culinary counterpoint, the interplay of opposites achieving balance. Learning how to balance tastes enables us to eat foods that would be overpowering or unpleasant if not tempered with the other taste elements.

The Recipes

When we go to the museum and look at a Monet painting, we can experience it two ways. When we get up close to the canvas, we see brush strokes of indi-vidual colors. When we back away, lo and behold, these strokes merge and become an image of water lilies. Cooking is like painting. We have flavors that we add in varying proportions or strokes. When we sit down to taste the finished dish it has become a harmonious whole, a round and balanced dish. We can pick out the individual flavors, but it is the whole that ultimately interests us and satisfies our palate.

Which brings me to how the recipes are organized in this book. Rather than arranging the chapters by the taste components salt, sweet, sour, and bitter, which makes meal planning an intellectual and tactical obstacle course, I've chosen to arrange the chapters conventionally by menu categories: salads, soups, fish, meat, vegetables, desserts, etc. It is in fact the way most of us approach meal planning and cooking at home. I've bought some fish, let's see what's in my larder. Now let's see what's in the fish chapter. Aha, here's the dish I'd like to try tonight. Do I have radicchio? Olives? Rosemary? Artichokes? Potatoes? And, by the way, while preparing this recipe for fish with radicchio, olives, and rosemary, if I make mashed potatoes, I could study how bitter and salt work together and can contrast with bland and creamy.

Or I have salmon, oranges, mint, and thyme. I think I'll make the Greek-inspired fish, if there's a little ouzo in the house. What to serve with it? Sweet fennel to echo the anise taste of ouzo? Tart greens to cut the sweetness? Bland rice? Rice with pine nuts? Pine nuts and raisins? Do I want to stress the sweet accents of this dish or play them down?

What is unconventional about this book is that within each chapter the recipes are organized in such a way that they demonstrate how different flavor combinations constitute and change a dish. Some explore variations on a theme. What happens when olives become foreground rather than background in a dish or sauce? How do they change when they get paired with citrus rather than tomato? What happens when you substitute almonds for walnuts? Or hazelnuts? Will feta cheese taste the same when paired with green peppers or with melon in a salad?

Some recipe groupings play with flavor contrasts such as sweet and sour or bitter and sweet. Or look at taste similarities. Do you really want to serve fresh fennel with a dish that has fennel seed in the sauce? How many kinds of bitter can you put in a dish before it goes over the edge and becomes unpleasant rather than intriguing? How many sweet spices can you add without making a savory dish too sweet? You'll learn how cooking techniques affect how spices taste in a dish. Will grilling change the taste of spices in a marinade more than braising? Or baking?

Following each recipe you'll find a section called Kitchen Conversation, where we talk about what to look for in the flavor of a dish so you'll know if it tastes "right." Certainly this is a subjective conclusion. But after tasting, tasting, and tasting the dish and analyzing the balance of its ingredients, you'll reach a point where you'll say, that's it! I'm happy with the dish. The flavors harmonize and are in balance. So stop.

You Mean After All This Work, Now We Have to Pick a Wine?

After so many flavor decisions, the thought of having to make one more may just be one too many. When faced with the question of what wine to serve with which dish, we are going to ask a pro, Evan, My Son the Sommelier, to guide us in a few appropriate suggestions that will harmonize with our recipes. Look for his Wine Notes at the end of the recipes after our Conversation.

Evan Goldstein's Wine Guide

Matching wine and food by fundamental taste components is nothing new. Many wine and food gurus around the world have espoused such a rationale for several years now. However, no two individuals have done as eloquent a job in explaining this marriage as David Rosengarten and Joshua Wesson in their acclaimed book *Red Wine with Fish*. For those of you who find this matchmaking aspect of the meal the most appealing, this book is a must. The following interpretation is my personal version and variation on this theme.

Basic Taste in Wine

Following the groundwork laid out by my mother in the preceding pages, I would offer that wine flavor and your perception of it are also based on primary tastes. It is critical that you understand there is a significant difference between taste and flavor in wines. Wine aficionados, wine makers, many sommeliers, and, alas, even chefs talk about wine in terms of flavor: the chocolate quality of a Cabernet, the green-olive flavor of a Sauvignon Blanc, or the clove and nutmeg in a glass of Gewürztraminer. And while it may be true that you can in fact detect these flavors, they are reiterated aromas and olfactory clues. A bad cold, annual hay fever, or other nasal congestion will make it quite difficult to distinguish between a fillet of sole and shoe sole, to say nothing of anise or tarragon. These flavors give us much to talk about, but have little to do with what will make that wine go with a specific dish or not.

With that flavor-is-relatively-unimportant caveat stated, it becomes paramount to understand that tastes drive wine and food together in the same manner that we choose our friends: We seek out similar or like-minded companions who share our interests or we find out that opposites can attract and that we can be equally content with those whose personalities contrast with our own. It is on those two premises that the lion's share of taste-based food and wine matches do and do not work. So let's explore basic tastes.

Sweetness

Wines can be sweet in several ways. In the case of very sweet dessert wines this is most obvious and has a rule, which I shall expand upon shortly. Wine can also be off-dry, which is to say it may have a trace of sweetness, such as many Rieslings, Chenin Blancs, and lighter-style Muscats. Off-dry levels of sweetness are wonderful foils for moderate levels of heat (cayenne, red pepper, etc.), actually taking the edge off the heat. In addition, off-dry wines can mirror a slight sweetness in dishes, such as fruit salsas or sauces with fresh or dried fruit (raisins, dried apricots, cherries). Dry wines that are produced from exceptionally ripe grapes might give the illusion of being sweet, even though they aren't, and can often reference slightly sweet dishes in a similar manner. The issue of dry wines with sweet foods can be problematic. My recommendation here is (1) do not serve very sweet wines with nonsweet dishes, and (2) when you do serve dessert-style or very sweet wines, ensure that the food in question is at a parallel level of sweetness or just a touch below; the dessert wine must be sweeter or the wine will come off as sour. Finally, sweetness in wine can be fun to contrast against salt: Sauternes with salty Roquefort or similar blue cheese and port with English Stilton. This concept requires a lot of experimenting, however, as not all of these types of marriages end up happy!

Salt

Fortunately for those of us who watch our sodium intake, wine does not contribute to it. "Cooking wines" off the shelf in a grocery store have added salt, which may interact with the salt levels you use in preparing a dish. But here we are paying more attention to how a "regular" table wine plays to the sodium in the dish. Our perception of salt needs to be reduced rather than exaggerated, so I offer the following thoughts: First, acidity, the tart factor in wines, cuts salt. Whites and sparkling wines as a rule contain higher levels of acidity, and therefore generally fare better than those that are less tart, e.g., most red wines. Second, tannin in red wines, that chalky perception you sense when drinking reds, exaggerates salt, so be forewarned when making your selections. Third, alcohol, like tannin, accentuates salt and often accompanies those same tannic reds, yet one more reason to pay attention when making choices. Finally, sweet wines, as I mentioned earlier, can work nicely with some salty dishes, but can as often confuse and damage one's enjoyment of them. The key in all cases is play around but pay attention!

Tartness

The acidity level in wine, or tartness factor, is the single most important issue in matching wine with food. There are many ways in which acidity plays into one's selections. First, acidity in wine contrasts by cutting through foods that are rich, either by the nature of ingredients or sauces, and by refreshing the palate, and it is similar when it matches with items that are tart (vinaigretted salads and such).

In addition, I like wines with high acidity to mitigate oil, such as that of deep-fried foods or pizza, or to lighten the flavor of fish that contain high levels of oil. I like to think of acid in wines as the gastronomic equivalent of the yellow highlighter pen we use to mark textbooks or other reading materials when we want to make text stand out. Wine can achieve the same effect in food by "bringing out" flavor through the wine's acidity. It would be safe to assume subsequently that wines that are low in acid are going to be more difficult to match than those of healthy acidity. In fact, a wine that may seem too tart on its own may make the most logical of choices when pairing with food. As you explore, this fundamental building block's vital role will be evident.

Bitterness

We associate bitter flavor in wine specifically with tannin. The tannin in wine is very much like that found in oversteeped tea, bitter and astringent. Its source is twofold: fruit tannins generated from the skins of grapes, specifically those of ample red wines, and wood tannins derived from a wine's spending time in oak barrels. Longer maceration of wine along with the skins will amplify the fruit tannins, while extended barrel aging, especially in newer barrels, will accentuate the wood tannins, which are the more acrid of the two. When tannin and bitterness are present in wines, it is safest to match them with foods that share like-minded, or in this case like-flavored, personalities. Foods that have been grilled, charred, blackened, or that contain implicitly bitter ingredients (sautéed broccoli rabe, arugula, and other bitter greens) are candidates for bitter wines. I'll go into the physiological effects of tannin separately, but suffice it to say that when you anticipate tannin, from a taste standpoint, you can expect bitterness.

There are other factors that need to be considered when analyzing a wine's affinity for a style of food that are unique. Wine can possess physical characteristics that make it more or less likely to go with a specific dish.

Alcohol

Wine's alcoholic content, because of the fermentation that converts the inherent grape sugar at harvest into alcohol, provides a sense of body and weight in the wine. As a general rule, the more generous the wine in alcoholic content, the more full-bodied our perception of that wine. One can make a parallel with the fat content in dairy products. As you increase that fat, say from nonfat milk to half-and-half, your perception of the density and texture changes. A milder wine (7 to 10 percent alcohol) is significantly less weighty and textured on the palate than one of 13 to 14 percent. A good rule of thumb is to match wines and foods of equal "weight." A rich meat preparation, or a fish or poultry dish that incorporates cream, is often well suited to full-bodied wines, while a thick-textured Chardonnay with a light, simple piece of fish may often be overkill.

In addition, as you increase the alcohol in wine, you limit your choices. Alcohol is amplified by food and specifically by salt and by spice/heat. If you are serving meals that incorporate either of those two flavors, be advised that wines will appear more alcoholic, "hotter" in winespeak. Especially with foods that require a modicum of refreshment from the wine (cayenne, jalapeño, or even fresh-cracked black pepper), you may feel as if you've thrown alcohol onto the fire! Salty foods do a similar dance with the alcohol in wine. Medium-bodied wines, and even lighter-bodied wines, are infinitely surer bets than big, inky California Zinfandels, ample Rhône wines (red or white), and fat Chardonnay from Australia.

Oak

It is almost impossible to imagine wine without barrel aging (we can all vividly imagine wineries with their row after row of sweet-smelling oak barrels). Many a vintner would say that from a flavor standpoint, it's impossible to create a wine without oak. Many of the flavors we associate with our favorite wines are barrel-generated. The toast, vanilla, and caramel tones in Chardonnay or the smoky, coffee bean aromas in Pinot Noir are attributable to oak aging rather than to the grape.

These oaky flavors are exaggerated by food. If you love the taste of oak, you'll be thrilled; if not, you may find many a bottle tasting like someone had jammed a two-by-four into it. Oak becomes a segregated component with food. If you have ever found yourself describing a wine as being too oaky, you probably agree with that assessment. I like to work with wines that are either lower in oak, absent of oak (made in stainless steel tanks or very old barrels that impart no flavor), or extremely well-balanced. When working with very oaky wine, play to the match of similar flavors (toast, vanilla, char, caramel, etc.) or to the bitter basic taste (see section on Bitterness).

Finally, oak does provide smoothness and roundness of mouthfeel, and can work well with dishes of similar textural personality. Oak is like visits by family and friends, nice but best in small doses!

Dissecting a Dish

Now that we have a basic grasp of how to define a wine's ability to go with food, it is essential that you know how to break down a dish so that you know what wine hook to hang your hat on. While the recipes in this book are as different as fingerprints, the rationale in understanding them from a wine standpoint remains the same: Look for stand-out features and characteristics. It comes down to asking yourself a series of questions about the dish and then determining which query is the key.

Ingredients

When you put together a meal, what you are cooking is important. One night you may feel like having fish, while on another evening a big steak may call to you from the butcher's window. It goes without saying that the type of wine you'd choose to go with trout is the polar opposite to what you might select with Chateaubriand. But realize too that within the broad generalization of fish and shellfish, you have an equally large palette to work with. Some fish are fishy (anchovies, mackerel, and bluefish, for example), while others are very mild (sole, trout, and cod). Meat comes in colors, red and white. Some red meat is pungent, like lamb, while beef can often be on the blander side. White meat (pork and veal) is different in personality, often reacting more like chicken, with a more neutral character than an aged rib-eye. Poultry, too, may range from mild (chicken, quail, and Cornish hens) to gamy ("real" pheasant, squab, and wild duck). Then throw in that curveball category of offal (sweetbreads, liver, and such), and you've really got a more complex issue than just "what's for dinner?"

Methods of Preparation

Although the ingredient issue is a big one, it's only one part of the formula. The ingredient's nature may dictate what wine you select, or it may not. Often the manner in which the ingredients are prepared will have even more bearing. Flavorful marinades will transform the way a primary ingredient tastes so that the flavor becomes a mere shadow of the original elements. Of course the cooking method will almost always play the most vital role.

Some types of cooking impart minimal flavor, such as steaming, poaching, or boiling; others are very dominant. Smoking, grilling, charring, and pan-blackening are ways of preparation that will have a significant influence on the resultant taste profile of a dish. Smoking can add sweet elements, as well as a strong, smoky pungency. Grilling will add a bitter, slightly acrid taste and a textural crust that also will be bitter in nature. Sautéing is fairly neutral and has more to do with the ingredient profile. That's also the case with the three most neutral cooking methods: steaming, poaching, and boiling. Braising, roasting, baking, and even deep-frying fall somewhere in between some and minimal influence.

To Sauce or Not to Sauce

When sauce is involved, the sauce should dictate the match. Varied in personality, sauces may be cold, room temperature, or hot. They may be vinaigrettes, salsas, chutneys, or reductions. They may contain herbs, spices, fruit, or any combination thereof. Some have cream or butter, while others may be based on stock, flavored infusions, or even wine. Whatever the case, they tend to dominate the show. Every sauce can be analyzed and broken down (no pun intended) into its basic taste components. From that dissection, one can make a wine judgment.

For example, vinaigrette-based variations share the common base of acid. Whether it's vinegar, infused or not, or lemon juice, there is a tart foundation. Rather than selecting a wine that works with all of the ingredients, find one that matches against sourness, for that is the basic personality of the dish. For chutneys, sweetness may dominate; whereas for a salsa, charmoula, or pepper sauce, heat will be the characteristic with which you should work. The basic principles for matching to the basic tastes in various sauces should be followed. Whether to sauce or not to sauce *is* up to you, but when you do, the sauce *is* the question.

The Wine Chart

In order to maximize your options, I have put together a table that divides the world of wine into a series of stylistic categories. Underneath each category heading, there is a list of wines representing different countries, grapes, and interpretations, but sharing a thread of personality, which joins them together in this vinous familial context.

While not every wine known to the Western world is represented, there is enough variety that happiness should be found by both the novice wine drinker, for whom some of the more general selections will be apropos, and those with more developed palates whose thrill-seeking may even find a wine or two they are unfamiliar with. Obviously the main decision maker may at the end be the establishment where you shop, as the availability of wine varies from state to state, town to town, and (we hope) country to country!

How to Make Use of the Wine Notes

The basis of each of the recommendations is to provide you with some building blocks with which you can consider matching wines to individual recipes. As with all disciplines of an aesthetic nature, there are no correct or incorrect choices, only personal preferences. And while I have made some suggestions in both more general and more specific fashions, the choice is ultimately yours and you should feel free to dive into uncharted waters in the spirit of freedom and experimentation. That notwithstanding, those of you who are less secure in your vinous bravado can take comfort in having both my recommendations and the logic behind them spelled out for you.

Refer to the diagram of the Wine Notes on the opposite page– including Pairing Pointers, Categories, and Specific Recommendations–to learn how the format can be used to enhance your eating and drinking pleasure. In keeping this format consistent from recipe to recipe, I hope that you'll find it easy and comfortable to work with and will make use of our recommendations. Again I firmly support following your heart and pursuing it wherever it takes you. Let's hope that more often than not we'll end up in the same place or at the same dining table! Good eating and good drinking!

Guide to the Wine Notes

Pairing Pointers
are the basic
issue(s) in choosing
wine for the recipe.

Specific wines
highlighted in
each category are
those that I think
will work particu-
larly well with
the recipe.

Wine Notes

Pairing Pointers: *The key components are salt (anchovy), earth (garlic), and bitterness (frisée). A leafy light red or pungent light- to medium-bodied white would be ideal. Earthier sparklers would be fun too.*

Categories: 2, 4

Specific Recommendations:

2: *Sauvignon Blanc—rustic, pungent—European* ◼
Sparkling wine—not Champagne—Spain, France

4: *Pinot Noir—earthier style—USA, France* ◼
Cabernet/blends—lighter, with Merlot, Cabernet Franc

Categories of wine
from the Wine Chart
have been selected
to provide you with
a broad spectrum to
pick from. You may
want to mix and
match or have more
than one type at
table. There may be
a mixture of red,
white, and sparkling
wines with recipes
where appropriate.

Wine Chart

Category 1A

Light, dry white, sparkling, or rosé wines. Lower alcohol. No or very light use of oak. Clean and refreshing.

Arneis, Tocai, *etc.* *(N. Italy)*

Müller-Thurgau *(Germany)*

Brut Champagne *lighter style*

Chardonnay *(N. Italy)*

Cortese *(Gavi, lighter style)*

French/Spanish sparkling

USA Brut sparkling

Pinot Grigio *(Italy, Oregon, light)*

Prosecco & Italian sparkling

Riesling *(USA, dry)*

Riesling *(Germany, dry)*

Chenin Blanc *(France, dry/light)*

Garganega *(Soave, lighter style)*

Chenin Blanc *(USA, S. Africa)*

Alvarinho *(Vinho Verde)*

Muscadet *(France)*

Pinot Blanc *(Italy, France)*

Rosé/blends *(USA, France, light)*

White/blends *(USA, Europe, light)*

Other Italian *(Orvieto, Frascati)*

Category 1B

Like 1A but with off-dry levels of sugar.

Riesling *(USA)* off-dry

Riesling *(Germany, France)* off-dry

Muscat *(Italy)*

Chenin Blanc *(France, USA, S. Africa)*

Champagne, *extra dry*

Gewürztraminer *(USA)*

Rosé/blends *(USA, France)*

White/blends *(France, Spain, USA)*

Category 2

Medium, dry white, sparkling, or rosé wines. Moderate alcohol. No, light, or moderate use of oak. Reasonably rich.

Brut Champagne *richer style*

Albariño *(Spain)*

Chardonnay *(Chile/Argentina)*

Chardonnay *(Tuscany/Piedmont/Spain)*

Chardonnay *(Australia/NZ/SA, lighter)*

Chardonnay *(California, lighter)*

Chardonnay *(Pacific NW/NY)*

Chardonnay *(Burgundy, medium)*

Sauvignon Blanc *(N. Zealand, lighter)*

Sauvignon Blanc *(USA, lighter style)*

Sauvignon Blanc *(France)*

Cortese *(Gavi, richer style)*

Chenin Blanc *(France, dry/full)*

Riesling *(Australia, dry)*

Viura, Verdejo, *etc.* *(Spain)*

Semillon *(USA)*

Garganega *(Soave, richer style)*

Gewürztraminer *(USA, Germany)*

Rosé/blends *(USA, France, richer)*

White/blends *(USA, Europe, richer)*

Vernaccia *(Tuscany)*

Category 3A

Full, dry white or rosé wines. Moderate to ample alcohol. Little to significant use of oak. Quite rich.

Chardonnay *(Australia/ NZ/SA)*

Chardonnay *(California)*

Chardonnay *(Pacific NW/NY)*

Chardonnay *(Burgundy)*

Riesling *(France, dry)*

Gewürztraminer *(France, USA)*

Muscat *(France, dry)*

Semillon/blends *(Australia)*

Semillon/blends *(USA, full)*

Marsanne *(USA, France)*

Grenache Rosé *(USA, France)*

Sauvignon Blanc *(USA, full)*

Sauvignon Blanc *(NZ, full)*

Pinot Gris *(France, full)*

Pinot Gris *(USA, full)*

Viognier *(USA, France)*

White/blends *(Europe)*

Category 3B

Dry, fortified white wines.

Sherry *(dry styles)*

Madeira *(dry styles)*

White port *(dry)*

Category 4

Light, dry red wines. Lower alcohol. No or very light use of oak. Fresh, effusive fruit. Little, if any, tannins.

Rosé Champagne, *lighter style*

Pinot Noir *(Burgundy, lighter)*

Pinot Noir *(USA, lighter)*

Pinot Noir *(other, lighter)*

Gamay *(Beaujolais, lighter)*

Dolcetto & Barbera, *lighter style*

Cabernet /blends *(NE Italy)*

Cabernet/blends *(E. Europe)*

Cabernet /blends *(France, simple)*

Cabernet /blends *(USA, simple)*

Corvina *(Valpolicella, lighter)*

Merlot *(France, simple)*

Merlot *(NE Italy, simple)*

Merlot *(S. America, simple)*

Merlot *(E. Europe)*

Carignan/blends *(Provence, light)*

Nebbiolo *(USA)*

Sangiovese *(Tuscany, light style)*

Sangiovese *(Cent. Italy, lighter)*

Pinotage *(S. Africa, lighter style)*

Napa Gamay *(USA, lighter)*

Gamay Beaujolais *(USA, light)*

Various Spanish *(Valdepeñas..)*

Various Italian *(Breganze)*

Category 5

Medium, dry red wines. Moderate alcohol. No, light or moderate use of oak. Reasonably rich. Light to moderate tannins.

Rosé Champagne, richer style

Pinot Noir (Burgundy, richer)

Pinot Noir (USA, Richer)

Pinot Noir (other, richer)

Gamay (Beaujolais, richer)

Dolcetto & Barbera, richer style

Cabernet /blends (Chile, Argentina)

Cabernet /blends (S. Africa, NZ)

Cabernet /blends (Bordeaux, light)·

Cabernet /blends (California, light)

Cabernet /blends (Pacific NW, light)

Cabernet /blends (Australia, light)

Cabernet Franc (Loire Valley, other)

Nebbiolo (Piedmont, light/medium style)

Sangiovese (Italy, USA, Argentina)

Tempranillo (Spain, lighter style)

Various Portuguese (Alentejo, Dão)

Syrah /blends (Australia, lighter)

Syrah /blends (California, lighter)

Syrah /blends (France: S. Rhône, lighter)

Carignan /blends (France, Spain)

Zinfandel (USA, lighter style)

Merlot (NE Italy, S. America, richer)

Merlot (USA, France, lighter style)

Napa Gamay & Gamay Beaujolais (USA)

Category 6

Full, dry red wines. Moderate to ample alcohol. Noticeable to significant use of oak. Quite rich. Ample tannins.

Nebbiolo (Italy, richer)

Sangiovese (Italy, richer)

Cabernet /blends (France)

Cabernet /blends (Calif.)

Cabernet /blends (USA)

Cabernet /blends (Australia)

Tempranillo (Spain, rich)

Malbec (France, USA)

Various Portuguese (Port, Dão)

Syrah/blends (USA)

Syrah/blends (France)

Syrah/blends (Australia)

Carignan/blends (France)

Carignan, etc. (N. Africa)

Pinotage (S. Africa)

Corvina (Italy: Amarone)

Merlot (France, richer)

Merlot (USA, richer)

Mourvedre (France, USA)

Zinfandel (USA, richer)

Petite Sirah (USA)

Category 7

Dessert style and sweet wines. Varied levels of alcohol and oak.

Riesling, late harvest or botrytis *(Germany)*

Riesling, late harvest or botrytis *(USA)*

Riesling, late harvest or botrytis *(France, other)*

Semillon/blends, late harvest or botrytis *(France)*

Semillon/blends, late harvest or botrytis *(USA)*

Muscat, late harvest or fortified *(France, Australia, USA)*

Muscat, dessert style or sparkling *(Italy)*

Chenin Blanc, late harvest or botrytis *(France)*

Chenin Blanc, late harvest or botrytis *(USA, other)*

Various Italian *(Vin Santo, Recioto styles, etc.)*

Port *(wood: tawny, ruby, LBV)*

Port *(vintage)*

Port style *(USA, Australia, other)*

Other fortified *(France: Banyuls, etc.)*

Tokay *(Furmint) (Hungary)*

Champagne *extra dry & demi-sec*

Sparkling wines *extra dry & demi-sec*

Madeira *(sweet styles)*

Sherry *(sweet styles)*

SALADS

SALADS

A salad or appetizer is often the first bite a hungry diner eats after being seated at the table; it is the first impression of the meal to come. Many people think that if they throw some greens in a bowl and pour on some dressing, they've achieved a Great Salad. How wrong they can be. What appears to be a no-brainer actually requires a series of correct decisions and attention to fine details for success. Salad leaves must be clean and dry. If the leaves are wet the dressing will be diluted and will not cling properly. The balance between oil and vinegar or oil and citrus must be strong enough to stand up to assertive greens, or, if the greens are delicate, not so strong as to wipe them out. Salt and pepper may need to be added even if there is some in the vinaigrette. The greens can become soggy if they are overdressed, and conversely, what's the good of having a great vinaigrette if not enough is added to coat the leaves? In fact, the vinaigrette may be perfectly seasoned, but if you forgot to stir or shake it well before dressing the greens, the salad will taste flat because the vinegar and seasonings settle to the bottom of the container. And these are just details and decisions for a simple green salad!

In a way, making salads is somewhat like Chinese stir-fry cooking. Prep is time-consuming as there are so many parts to be readied, yet the dish is assembled in minutes. In the final stage of completion there is little room for error. Prep for stovetop cooking may not be proportionately as time-consuming, but the cooking process allows for development of flavor and leaves the cook more time to make amends for errors and adjustments in seasoning.

The misconception that salads are simple to make is not only held by many home cooks, but even follows into the restaurant environment. When most cooks apply to work in a restaurant they think that the salad or pantry station is the easy entry position, lacking culinary excitement, and that all the glamour is on the hot line. Making fine salads is an art. Not only is it filled with culinary and creative pleasures, it is important for palate development and learning how to taste. You work with sour, salt, bitter, and sweet flavors in astounding and subtle ways. Learning to play with these elements in a vinaigrette, then experimenting to see which vinaigrette will complement the greens and other salad components and bring out their flavors without overpowering them, is a critical balancing act. After you master the art of making salads, you will have a better, more well-tuned palate.

The chapter that follows is filled with a variety of light and leafy salads, some simple greens, some with fruit, cheese, or nuts. Others are first courses that could be called big salads or turned into main-dish salads by the size of the portion. They include seafood and fish, poultry, rice, and bread. Finally, there are appetizer spreads for bread, a few sandwiches, and savory first-course pastries that are all part of what I'd call the pantry or salad station.

Important flavor trends to watch for are how the acid changes in vinaigrettes from citrus to vinegar; how cheese is used for salty accents; how nuts are used for texture and flavor complexity; and how to intensify the flavors when placing foods on or between slices of bread.

Melon, Feta Cheese, Watercress, and Mint

*I*n Turkey a most refreshing meze is a slice of sweet melon paired with a slightly tart white cheese. While some of us are accustomed to thinking of fruit and cheese as dessert, I found this combination a striking way to stimulate the palate at the start of a meal, but one that is not familiar to American diners. So I took it one step further, and I combined the melon and cheese with watercress and mint to bring it into a more familiar salad format.

Serves 4

Mint Vinaigrette

Infusion

¹/₄ cup fresh lemon juice

¹/₄ cup chopped fresh mint

²/₃ cup pure olive oil

2 tablespoons red wine vinegar

1 teaspoon sugar, if needed

¹/₄ teaspoon salt

Salad

4 small bunches watercress, stems well trimmed

24 to 32 mint leaves, cut in half if large

1 small ripe cantaloupe or **¹/₂ ripe Crenshaw melon,** cut into thin wedges, about 2 inches long

³/₄ pound feta cheese or **fragrant sheep** or **goat cheese,** crumbled coarsely

For the mint infusion, combine the lemon juice and chopped mint in a small saucepan and bring up to a boil. Remove from the heat and allow the mixture to steep for 10 minutes. Strain the infusion into a mixing bowl. Whisk in the remaining ingredients to make the vinaigrette.

Toss the watercress and mint leaves with half the mint vinaigrette. Distribute on 4 salad plates. Toss the melon with the remaining vinaigrette and place atop greens. Top with crumbled cheese.

Kitchen Conversation

Here's bitter watercress, sweet, fragrant melon, and salty cheese, all happily held together by the fragrant lemon-mint vinaigrette. Feel daring? Throw another bitter element into the mix and add ¹/₂ cup toasted chopped walnuts. They not only add texture to the salad, but the toasty quality of the nuts intensifies the sweetness of the melon and helps the cheese lie back a bit.

Wine Notes

Pairing Pointers: *There are so many options. You can play off the salt and sweet while maintaining awareness of the tartness factor. A wine with tremendous structure and a current of acidity running through it is essential. Watch out for too much sweetness in the wine, as it will do battle with the salty cheese.*

Category: 1A

Specific Recommendations:

1A: *Brut Champagne—lighter style* ■ *Italian white—Frascati, Tocai, Arneis* ■ *Chenin Blanc—dry, light, and crisp*

Salad Surprises

Instead of only using chopped herbs as a flavor accent in a salad, try adding a few whole leaves for a wonderful and tasty surprise. I love to toss whole mint or basil leaves into mixed green salads. Italian parsley also lends a different kind of brightness. (See the Parsley and Escarole Salad with Grilled Tuna, page 32, or the Italian Parsley Salad, page 30). Herbs also brighten a sandwich (see Persian-Inspired Chicken Salad Sandwich, page 82).

Spinach Salad à la Grecque

*T*he classic spinach salad that American diners love is really Greek inspired. The tang of the feta cheese and the richness of the kalamata olives are essential for flavor balance. Adding the beets and beans makes this salad more substantial, almost a meal in a bowl. While you could dress the salad with a Greek-inspired Oregano Garlic Vinaigrette (page 50), the mint is lighter, and more tart and refreshing. Spinach is the ideal green for this salad (especially if you can find small tender leaves), as it is only mildly bitter. But you could use assorted lettuces or the more neutral romaine.

Serves 6

Mint Vinaigrette

Infusion

$1/4$ cup fresh lemon juice

$1/4$ cup chopped fresh mint

$1^1/4$ cups pure olive oil

$1/4$ cup red wine vinegar

2 tablespoons fresh lemon juice

$1/2$ cup chopped fresh mint, tightly packed

1 teaspoon honey

$1/2$ teaspoon salt

For the infusion, combine the lemon juice and chopped mint in a small saucepan. Bring up to a boil and remove from the heat. Let steep for about 10 minutes. Strain into a mixing bowl. There will be about $1/4$ cup. Add the remaining ingredients and whisk together for the vinaigrette.

2 small red onions, sliced thin

2 cups cooked white beans (optional)

12 cups baby spinach, well washed and dried, or

assorted lettuces

6 large or **12 small beets**, cooked

3/4 pound feta cheese, crumbled coarsely

1 cup kalamata olives

Marinate the onions in ¼ cup of the mint vinaigrette for about 15 minutes to soften them and lessen their bite. Place in a salad bowl. If using the beans, toss them in ½ cup vinaigrette to marinate for about 30 minutes.

If the spinach leaves are large, remove all stems and tear the leaves into smaller pieces.

Cut the large beets in half and then into ¼-inch slices. If the beets are small, cut them into quarters or eighths.

In a large salad bowl, toss the marinated onions, greens, and beets (and beans if using) with the remaining vinaigrette. Distribute on 6 large salad plates and sprinkle with the feta cheese and olives.

Kitchen Conversation

In a salad of this complexity, with so many diverse elements of texture and taste, the vinaigrette is the key to tying all the components together. Lemon juice is not sour or deep enough in flavor to stand up to the tart spinach and raw bitter onions. Vinegar alone is too strong for the mint and sweet beets, and can overpower their sweetness and weaken the punch of the cheese. The honey adds roundness and balance and echoes the sweetness of the beets. Diced or sliced cucumbers could be used in place of the more filling white beans. They are mildly bitter and add cool crispness.

Wine Notes

Pairing Pointers: *Fairly classic from a wine standpoint. Play the green elements of the salad to the forefront and make certain that your selection can cut the salt as well as pick up the tart components.*

Categories: 1A, 2

Specific Recommendations:

1A: *Garganega—Soave White blends—France, Italy—earthier style*

2: *Sauvignon Blanc—grassier style Vernaccia—fresh, earthy*

Yesil Domates Batisi Turkish Green Tomato Salad with Feta Cheese

I ate this tart and tangy salad at a buffet dinner where there were at least fifty dishes to sample from various regions of Turkey. This recipe, reportedly from Izmir, along the Aegean coast of Turkey, really caught my attention. We rarely utilize green tomatoes, except for pickles, and I thought this was a novel and tasty way to serve this underappreciated food. Serve slightly warm or at room temperature.

Serves 6

4 tablespoons olive oil

3 onions, chopped

1 tablespoon finely minced garlic

6 large green tomatoes, very coarsely chopped, about 6 cups

1 cup vegetable or **Basic Chicken Stock** (page 115)

3 to 4 tablespoons extra virgin olive oil

Lots of salt

Freshly ground black pepper

1 cup crumbled feta cheese

2 tablespoons chopped fresh dill

Warm the olive oil in a large sauté pan. Add the onions and cook over moderate heat until translucent, about 8 to 10 minutes. Add the garlic, tomatoes, and stock and cook, covered, for 15 minutes until the tomatoes are softened.

Do not overcook. Stir in the olive oil. Season to taste with salt and pepper. Place on a serving platter and top with crumbled feta cheese and dill. Serve slightly warm or at room temperature.

Kitchen Conversation

I love the tanginess of the tomatoes and how it is tempered by the salty, creamy feta. Freshly ground black pepper is an essential element of this salad, as it brings a very subtle heat. The dill adds its own grassy perfume, which complements the tomatoes. As a change of pace, try oregano for a deeper taste.

Wine Notes

Pairing Pointers: With these tomatoes we seek a wine to be a vivid "highlighter" to bring out the tart, clean flavors of the salad. The simpler and sharper the wine, the better.

Categories: 1A, 2

Specific Recommendations:
1A: *Muscadet—current vintage, as fresh as possible* ■ *Chardonnay—light, crisp, floral—Italy and France*

2: *Sauvignon Blanc—green, leafy styles* ■ *Viura, Verdejo—refreshing, fragrant, exuberant*

Cheese in Salads

Adding cheese to a salad does two things. It provides another kind of salt and it adds interesting texture. Crumbly mild goat cheese or salty feta cheese, slightly pungent Gorgonzola or Roquefort, waxy Gruyère or fontina, each changes the balance of the equation. Cheeses pair especially well with bitter elements like toasted walnuts.

Green Pepper and Feta Cheese Salad

I n Greece or Turkey you will find variations of this tangy salad. While such assertive flavors, bitter and salt, could be on a collision course, here they are held in check by a powerful vinaigrette. Serve with bread as part of a meze assortment.

Serves 4 as a salad and 8 as part of a meze assortment

2 large green peppers, seeded and with thick ribs removed, cut in $1/2$-inch dice, about 4 cups

4 tablespoons olive oil

2 teaspoons dried oregano

$1/2$ teaspoon hot pepper flakes or **minced jalapeños** to taste

$1/2$ pound feta cheese, cut in $1/2$-inch pieces

Freshly ground black pepper

Lemon juice or **red wine vinegar** to taste

Sauté the peppers in olive oil with the oregano and hot pepper for just about 2 minutes. Cool.
Combine the diced peppers and cheese in a bowl.

Add black pepper and a bit of lemon juice or vinegar to taste.

Kitchen Conversation

Two assertive flavors take center stage. There is nothing shy about bitter green peppers or salty feta cheese. So you need enough peppery heat, garlic, oregano, and a touch of acid to keep them in balance. Try lemon juice first and if it is too mild (depending upon how assertive your peppers and cheese are), then add a few drops of red wine vinegar.

Wine Notes

Pairing Pointers: Although different in personality, this dish demands a wine stunt double to that Turkish Green Tomato Salad on page 10. Rather than complicate the sharp, zippy personality of the salad, roll with it and pick a wine with a similar personality.

Categories: 1A, 2

Specific Recommendations:

1A: Pinot Blanc— current vintage, as fresh as possible, no oak ■ Chardonnay— light, crisp, floral—Italy, France

2: Sauvignon Blanc—green, leafy styles ■ Garganega—Vernaccia—refreshing, fragrant, exuberant— Italy

Mandorlata di Peperoni Sweet-and-Sour Sautéed Peppers with Almonds, Raisins, and Tomato

*T*his colorful dish of sautéed peppers comes from the Southern Italian province of Basilicata. While peperonata is usually served at room temperature as part of an antipasto assortment, or as a side dish to accompany boiled beef, it also can be tossed with cooked pasta for a piquant dish, or used as a sauce over grilled fish or sautéed chicken breasts. In summer use strips of fresh peeled tomatoes, but in winter months you may use tomato puree.

Serves 4 to 6

2 yellow bell peppers

2 red bell peppers

2 small red onions

4 to 5 tablespoons olive oil

3 tablespoons vinegar

1 tablespoon sugar

6 tablespoons rich tomato puree or **4 large tomatoes**, peeled, seeded, and cut into strips

3 to 4 tablespoons raisins, plumped in hot water

3 to 4 tablespoons slivered blanched almonds, toasted

Salt to taste

Cut the peppers in half lengthwise and remove the stems, seeds, and thick membranes. Cut into long strips about ½ inch wide.

Cut the onions into slices about ⅓ inch wide.

Warm the olive oil in a very large sauté pan over medium heat. Add the onions and cook for 8 to 10 minutes, then toss in the pepper strips and fresh tomatoes, if using, and cook for 8 minutes, stirring occasionally. Add the vinegar, sugar, and tomato puree, if using, and cook for about 5 minutes longer.

Add the raisins and almonds, and adjust the seasoning. This dish should have a nice balance of tartness and sweetness. The vegetables should be tender but not mushy.

Pugliese Peperonata

H ere's another variation on the peperonata theme, this time from a neighboring province of Southern Italy, Apulia. Rather than playing with sweet and sour, this version has an element of heat and the herbaceous quality of parsley.

Serves 6

3 red bell peppers

3 yellow bell peppers

Olive oil as needed

3 onions, sliced ¼ inch thick

2 cloves garlic, minced

3 large peeled tomatoes

¼ cup chopped parsley

1 small fresh hot pepper, minced

Wash the peppers, cut in half, remove the seeds and thick ribs, and slice them into ½-inch strips. Heat the olive oil in a large sauté pan and cook the onions over moderate heat until softened, about 5 minutes. Add the peppers and sauté, stirring often, for about 8 to 10 minutes. Add the garlic, tomatoes, parsley, and hot pepper, and simmer the peperonata for about 20 minutes over very low heat. Season with salt and pepper.

Kitchen Conversation

Sweet and sour is very different from sweet and hot. The mandorlata di peperoni is sweet but not cloying. The vinegar and onions give depth, and the raisins and almonds provide intermittent sweet high notes. In the Pugliese version, the sweetness of the peppers is not highlighted by sugar or any other sweet elements, and there is no vinegar to change the balance. If the tomatoes are more sweet than tart, add a little red wine vinegar to round this out. But remember to salt first.

Wine Notes

Pairing Pointers: *This is a very challenging dish. The two variations need different wines. In the* mandorlata di peperoni *you want to play off the sweet and sour with refreshing acidity and, if you want it, a snap of transparent sweetness in the wine. In the Pugliese variation, the hot pepper merits the sweetness, as it will hold the heat in check while picking up the remaining flavors.*

Categories: 1A, 1B, 4

Specific Recommendations:

1A: *Muscadet—youthful*

1B: *Riesling—earthier Germans are best, kabinett level*

4: *Barbera—exuberant fruit, acid backbone—Italy, California*

Puntarelle e Peperoni Chicory (Curly Endive) and Roasted Peppers with Anchovy Garlic Vinaigrette

I n Rome in the spring a variety of chicory called Catalogna *appears in salads all over the city. If you walk through the open markets, you can watch people trimming it. It is cut lengthwise in a special way, then chilled in ice water so that it forms curls resembling tiny green snakes. Puntarelle salad is served with a vinaigrette loaded with anchovy, which adds a saltiness that blends perfectly with the bitter greens. To play sweet opposed to bitter, toss strips of roasted peppers with the greens, but don't cut down on the anchovies. They are the salt needed for perfect balance.*

Serves 4

4 small heads curly endive (frisée)

2 roasted red bell peppers, stemmed and seeded

Anchovy Garlic Vinaigrette

1 tablespoon finely minced garlic

3 tablespoons finely minced anchovies

¹/₂ cup pure olive oil

¹/₂ cup extra virgin olive oil

¹/₃ cup red wine vinegar

Freshly ground black pepper

Trim the stem end off the curly endive and separate it into leaves. Wash well and then dry. Cut the roasted peppers into strips ⅓ inch wide.

To make the vinaigrette, combine the garlic and anchovies in a small saucepan with the pure olive oil and warm slightly over low heat. Remove from the heat and whisk in the virgin olive oil and vinegar. Season with black pepper. Put the endive and peppers in a bowl. Toss with the vinaigrette.

Kitchen Conversation

I realize that frisée or curly endive is not puntarelle, but it is as close as we can get. And its shape is visually spiky and attractive. If you like, first taste this salad minus the sweet red peppers. It will help you to understand the power of anchovy used as salt. Then toss in the peppers. See how they change the balance? You may want to up the black pepper and the vinegar.

Wine Notes

Pairing Pointers: *The key components are salt (anchovy), earth (garlic), and bitterness (frisée). A leafy light red or pungent light- to medium-bodied white would be ideal. Earthier sparklers would be fun too.*

Categories: 2, 4

Specific Recommendations:

2: *Sauvignon Blanc—rustic, pungent—European* ■ *Sparkling wine—not Champagne—Spain, France*

4: *Pinot Noir—earthier style—USA, France* ■ *Cabernet/blends—lighter, with Merlot, Cabernet Franc*

Olive Oil

If they asked me I could write a book about olive oil. Except that others have. The difference between extra virgin and pure is night and day. Pure has minimal olive taste and is good for sautéing or frying where flavor is not a factor. Extra virgin oils have diverse personalities. Some have a bitter or peppery back bite that stands up well in salads. Others are fruity and almost sweet. Still others have a nutty taste. Taste the oil before using. To showcase a good oil, swirl a little into a cooked pasta while it's hot and smell its perfume. Or spoon a bit on hot cooked vegetables. If the olive oil is very intense, cut it with some pure oil when making mayonnaise, aioli, and certain vinaigrettes, or it will overpower all the other tastes.

Chick-pea Salad with Roasted Peppers and Olives with Two Vinaigrettes: Spanish and Moroccan

*I*n the Mediterranean, many of the same ingredients are used from country to country. It is in the use of spices and herbs that national differences emerge. Originally this was a Spanish salad, with the chick-peas and peppers tossed in a garlic vinaigrette. But one day my mind took the ferry to Morocco and added a North African–inspired vinaigrette to the same ingredients. I am going to give you both recipes so you can travel at will.

Serves 8

Salad

1¹/₂ cups chick-peas, soaked overnight in the refrigerator

1 small onion

2 bay leaves

2 cloves garlic

1 teaspoon salt

3 large sweet red peppers, roasted, peeled, and seeded

Drain the chick-peas and rinse. Place in a medium saucepan and cover with fresh cold water. Bring up to a boil. Simmer for 2 minutes. Let rest for 1 hour. Drain and cover with fresh cold water. Add the onion, bay leaves, and garlic, and bring up to a boil. Reduce the heat and simmer, covered, for about 15 minutes. Add salt and continue to cook for another 15 to 20 minutes, or until done. Drain.

Cut the roasted red peppers into large dice.

Toss the chick-peas and peppers with the vinaigrette, and let marinate for a few hours. Adjust the seasoning again. Add olives at serving time.

Spanish Vinaigrette

¹/₂ cup sherry vinegar

1 cup olive oil

¹/₂ cup virgin olive oil

1 clove garlic, minced

Salt and freshly ground black pepper

4 tablespoons chopped parsley
or 1 tablespoon dried oregano

¹/₂ cup Spanish arbequino olives

Moroccan-Inspired Vinaigrette

¹/₂ teaspoon cayenne pepper

2 teaspoons toasted ground cumin

¹/₂ teaspoon freshly ground black pepper

1 tablespoon paprika

¹/₂ cup fresh lemon juice or mild red vinegar

3 cloves garlic, finely minced

1 cup olive oil

¹/₂ cup chopped cilantro

Salt to taste

¹/₂ cup ripe black or green Moroccan olives

For the Spanish vinaigrette, whisk together all
of the ingredients.

For the Moroccan vinaigrette, combine the spices
and lemon juice. Add the garlic and then whisk in
the oil and cilantro. Adjust the seasoning.

Kitchen Conversation

Want to play with this salad? Just make a normal vinaigrette without the Moroccan spices and see how the salad changes. Do the peppers taste fleshier and richer, less tart? Leave out the salty olives and what happens? Sweet peppers, bland chick-peas. Needs something, doesn't it? Without the olives you will probably have to increase the herbs, vinegar, and maybe even the salt.

Wine Notes

Pairing Pointers: The keys are the smokiness of the peppers and the salty component of the olives. Chick-peas are a bland canvas calling for a generous wine. The Spanish vinaigrette requires a more fragrant wine; the Moroccan needs a little more oomph!

Categories: 2, 3A, 5

Specific Recommendations:

2: *Spanish: Viura, Verdejo—play the local angle* ■ *Moroccan: white or rosé blend—rich, spicy—Southern France, Spain*

3A: *Spanish: Chardonnay—full, rich, smoky—Australia, USA* ■ *Moroccan: Grenache rosé—USA or Rhône Valley*

5: *Spanish: Tempranillo—local—adds an intangible quality of harmony* ■ *Moroccan: Zinfandel—lighter style with olivy, herbal flavors*

White Bean Salad with Shrimp or Tuna and Two Vinaigrettes: Sun-Dried Tomato and Rosemary Garlic

White bean salads are often part of an antipasto assortment or served as a first course. The most popular of these salads is the classic combination of tuna and white beans with lots of chopped red onion and parsley. Here is another take on this combination of seafood and beans, using a deep-flavored sun-dried tomato vinaigrette with sweet basil. Or try a more pungent and resinous rosemary garlic vinaigrette.

Serves 6

1 cup white beans

6 cups water

Salt and freshly ground black pepper

1 cup olive oil or as needed

1/2 cup red wine vinegar or as needed

2 tablespoons finely minced garlic

1/2 cup chopped sun-dried tomatoes, oil packed preferred

2/3 cup finely chopped red onions

1/2 cup chopped fresh basil

1 pound medium shrimp, shelled and deveined, or
1 pound tuna, broiled or grilled until medium cooked

Put the white beans in a pot with cold water and bring up to a boil. Boil for 2 minutes, then remove from the heat and let rest for 1 hour. Pour off water and add 6 more cups cold water. Bring up to a boil and simmer the beans until tender but not soft. Add 1 teaspoon salt halfway through cooking time. Drain the beans and transfer to a mixing bowl. While warm, dress with 1/3 cup of the olive oil, 1/4 cup of the vinegar, and salt and pepper.

Warm the remaining 2/3 cup olive oil in a sauté pan and heat the garlic and sun-dried tomatoes for just a minute or two. Add half this mixture (1/3 cup) to the beans and mix well.

When the beans are cool, add the chopped onions. Season with salt and vinegar to taste. Combine the rest of the sun-dried tomato oil with the remaining 4 tablespoons of vinegar for a sun-dried tomato vinaigrette for shrimp or tuna.

To cook the shrimp, sauté in the reserved sun-dried tomato vinaigrette or broil and then toss with the vinaigrette before placing atop bean salad.

To cook the tuna, brush lightly with some of the sun-dried tomato vinaigrette and broil for 4 minutes on each side, or until medium cooked but not dry. Cool. Break up into pieces. Toss with the remaining vinaigrette before placing atop the white beans.

continued

Just before serving fold in ¼ cup chopped basil and top with the cooked shrimp or tuna that have been tossed in the sun-dried tomato vinaigrette.

Rosemary Garlic Vinaigrette for White Bean Salad

½ cup extra virgin olive oil

1½ tablespoons finely chopped rosemary

1½ tablespoons finely minced garlic

4 tablespoons wine vinegar plus more to taste

Prepare the beans as directed above.

To make the vinaigrette, warm olive oil in a small saucepan with the rosemary and garlic. Simmer for 3 minutes. Steep for 30 minutes. Strain.

After cooking the beans, dress while warm with this rosemary garlic vinaigrette. When cool, add the chopped onions and vinegar to taste as well as salt and pepper. This bean salad is especially nice with grilled tuna or cooked shrimp dressed with the remaining rosemary garlic vinaigrette, served atop a bed of arugula. In summer garnish with cherry tomatoes if desired.

Kitchen Conversation

Beans are bland and creamy, a perfect vehicle to absorb a variety of savory vinaigrettes. They really need a dice of raw red onions to spark them both from the texture point of view and also taste. Even if you think you are afraid of the onions, don't skimp. Their bite will soften in the vinaigrette. And please don't mince them to dust. They are supposed to add texture.

Wine Notes

Pairing Pointers: The white beans are a nonfactor here, providing only an earthy, starchy canvas for us to work with. I prefer reds or rosés when working with sun-dried tomatoes, as they tend to dominate all the other ingredients. While you should be aware of the sweetness of the shrimp, play to the tomatoes. For the rosemary garlic vinaigrette, stay with whites.

Categories: 2, 4, 5

Specific Recommendations:

2: *Chardonnay—French Chablis, Maçon, or Chalonnais*

4: *Dolcetto—fresh and earthy*

5: *Napa Gamay or Gamay Beaujolais*

Mushroom, Walnut, and Spinach Salad
with Mustard Vinaigrette ✓

Many Mediterranean countries pair mushrooms and nuts. In Italy hazelnuts are the complement for assorted mushrooms. In Spain almonds are often part of the duet. In this Greek-inspired salad, walnuts are combined with spinach in a spicy mustard vinaigrette. This is very nice served with tiropetes, the classic cheese-filled filo pastry.

Serves 6

Mustard Vinaigrette

1 teaspoon dry mustard

2 tablespoons red wine vinegar

1 tablespoon prepared Dijon mustard

3 tablespoons fresh lemon juice

³/₄ cup olive oil

Salt and freshly ground black pepper

3 tablespoons chopped dill (optional)

Make a paste of the dry mustard and vinegar. Add the rest of the vinaigrette ingredients and whisk together. Season to taste. Add the optional dill.

Salad

1¹/₂ cups thinly sliced mushrooms

1 cup toasted walnuts, very coarsely chopped

＊ **6 cups small spinach leaves,** well washed and dried

(1 Bunch) large leaves } if small not obtainable

＊ *Packets of Baby Spinach 2 × 6 oz or 171 gm or the equivalent weight in loose leaves.*

Toss the mushrooms with ¼ cup of the vinaigrette and marinate for 10 minutes. Toss the walnuts with some of the vinaigrette and marinate for 10 minutes. At serving time, toss the spinach with the remaining vinaigrette, and fold in the mushrooms and walnuts.

Kitchen Conversation

For those in quest of understanding vinaigrettes and who are following the acid trail, here is a case where both lemon and vinegar are needed to balance the bitterness of the dry mustard. The vinegar alone would be too strong for the mushroom, spinach, and walnut mixture. Vinegar has a tendency to dominate. The lemon softens the vinaigrette and makes for better balance. The mushrooms are mildly pungent and earthy, and delicate in texture, a fine contrast to the crunchy nuts.

Wine Notes

Pairing Pointers: Walnuts and mushrooms provide texture. The mustard vinaigrette augments the earthiness and bitterness. White wine is the call here.

Categories: 1A, 2

Specific Recommendations:

1A: *Pinot Grigio—Italy, California ▪ Sparkling wines, Prosecco—France, Spain*

2: *Sauvignon Blanc—green flavors, austere structure ▪ Viura, Verdejo—fresh, rustic—Rueda, Rioja*

Toasting Nuts

When nuts sit in the pantry or, preferably, are kept in the freezer in order to prevent rancidity, their flavors go dumb. It is advisable to toast them in a 350 degree oven for 8 to 10 minutes to revive them. Heating activates the oils that carry the nut flavor.

Add ± 1 TBS(lean)
Sugar to Mustard
Vinaigrette

Mushroom, Scallop, Hazelnut, and Arugula Salad
with Orange Balsamic Vinaigrette

Scallops are sweet and very rich with a sensual, almost fleshy texture. Contrast them with mild, crisp mushrooms and sweet, toasty hazelnuts, then toss with bitter arugula in a warm vinaigrette, and you have a very complex and seductive salad. To make the balance work you need a note of citrus in the vinaigrette (we use the sweetness of orange to play up the sweetness of the scallops) and mild balsamic vinegar, also sweet. Be sure to salt this enough or it will all fall flat.

Serves 4

Orange Balsamic Vinaigrette

¹/₃ cup hazelnut oil

²/₃ cup olive oil

2 tablespoons balsamic vinegar

2 tablespoons sherry vinegar

¹/₃ cup fresh orange juice

2 tablespoons grated orange zest

Salt

Salad

1 cup white or **brown mushrooms,** thinly sliced

¹/₂ cup toasted hazelnuts, coarsely chopped

About 4 loosely packed cups small arugula

Salt and freshly ground black pepper

16 large or **24 small scallops,** trimmed of tough muscles

To make the vinaigrette whisk all the ingredients together in a bowl. Toss the mushrooms and hazelnuts in a bowl with about ½ cup of the vinaigrette. Salt to taste. Place the arugula in a large salad bowl and salt lightly.

Sprinkle the scallops with salt. Warm the remaining vinaigrette in a large sauté pan and sauté the scallops quickly for about 3 minutes, or until they become opaque but are still quite soft and tender, even quivery. Add the nuts and mushrooms to the arugula, then add the scallops with their vinaigrette to the salad bowl and toss. Serve while the scallops are still warm.

Kitchen Conversation

There are lots of different sensations here. Temperature contrast of warm scallops and vinaigrette against cool arugula leaves. Soft texture of scallops against crisp arugula and crunchy nuts. Sweet shellfish, nuts, orange, balsamic vinegar against bitter arugula and neutral or slightly nutty mushrooms. Balsamic vinegar is not enough to balance this salad. It's too mild and sweet. You need a little more depth of flavor, which the sherry vinegar provides. Don't forget to salt.

Incidentally, in case you were wondering why we didn't sauté the mushrooms along with the scallops, we tried it but found that the mushrooms lost presence, as they softened too much over direct heat in the vinaigrette. We preferred them crisp. But why don't you try it and see which you prefer.

Wine Notes

Pairing Pointers: *This is a fun wine match. The textures (scallops, nuts), the sweetness (scallops, balsamic, orange) provide a perfect stage for waxy, unctuous white wines.*

Category: 3A

Specific Recommendations:

3A: *Chardonnay—big, ripe* ■ *Semillon/blends—opulent Graves or Australian Chardonnay* ■ *Viognier—France, California*

Warm Vinaigrettes

These are especially nice when you want the salad leaves to wilt slightly and absorb the dressing. By warming the vinaigrette you highlight the perfume of the vinegar. Balsamic vinegar or sherry are particularly fragrant when warmed. I love to use vinaigrette to sauté shellfish quickly before adding them to a salad, as this infuses them with the vinaigrette flavors, rather than just staying on the surface.

Belgian Endive, Fennel, Mushroom, and Walnut Salad Two Ways: with Gruyère and Lemon Mustard Cream or Gorgonzola Cream Vinaigrette

et's try another salad that plays with the theme of mushrooms and nuts. Take the basic combination of endive, fennel, mushrooms, and walnuts, and try two vinaigrettes, one a French-inspired lemon mustard cream and the other an Italian-inspired Gorgonzola cream. In the French version we are playing a delicate balancing act between bitter endive, bitter but toasty walnuts, crunchy, anise-scented sweet fennel, mildly salty Gruyère, tart lemon, and the bite of mustard with mild cream and neutral mushrooms. When this one works, it is a poem.

Serves 4

Lemon Mustard Cream

2 tablespoons strong Dijon mustard

3 tablespoons fresh lemon juice

6 tablespoons olive oil

2 tablespoons cream

Salt and freshly ground black pepper

Salad

4 small or **2 large heads Belgian endive**

2 small bulbs fennel

1/4 pound mushrooms, about 2 cups, sliced 1/8 inch thick

1/2 pound Gruyère cheese, sliced thin, cut into slivers 1/4 inch wide and 1 inch long

1 cup toasted walnuts, coarsely chopped

To make the lemon mustard cream, whisk the mustard and lemon juice in a small bowl. Gradually add the olive oil and cream. Add salt and pepper to taste.

Remove the root ends from the endive and separate the leaves. Cut the fennel bulbs in half, remove the tough outer leaves, cut out the core, and slice thin. **C**ombine the endive leaves, fennel, mushrooms, and Gruyère in a large salad bowl. Toss with the vinaigrette. Top with chopped walnuts.

In the Italian variation, we omit the Gruyère from the salad and put cheese in the sauce. We have changed the equation because Gorgonzola is saltier than Gruyère. And the sharpness of the mustard is gone. So now we're dealing with bitter nuts, sweet fennel, and salty cheese. Here the walnuts become a crucial element, keeping the salt in check.

Gorgonzola Cream Vinaigrette

½ cup olive oil

¼ cup crumbled Gorgonzola dolcelatte

¼ cup cream

1 tablespoon fresh lemon juice or to taste

Pinch salt

Freshly ground black pepper

To make the Gorgonzola vinaigrette, pulse all of the ingredients in a food processor but don't over-process. If too thick, thin with water.

Kitchen Conversation

This salad is a study in textures. Crisp fennel, crisp-tender endive and mushrooms, crunchy walnuts, and smooth Gruyère cheese. I love the way bitter endive and fennel dance together. If you can't get fennel you will miss a certain exotic anise-flavored sweetness. But you can use celery, which is milder, less sweet, and doesn't have a licorice taste. With celery the bitter walnuts take on greater importance and need to be controlled because the anise is not present to sweeten the mix. Since the celery is blander than the fennel, you may want to play up the lemon by adding more juice and maybe some grated lemon zest to hold the bitter walnuts and endive in check. Incidentally lemon is much better in both these vinaigrettes than vinegar. Vinegar brings out an unpleasant bitterness in the cheese, cutting the more pleasing salty aspects.

Wine Notes

Pairing Pointers: While the introduction of Gorgonzola ups the salt, it does not dramatically affect the choice of wine, especially if it's dolcelatte Gorgonzola. If the cheese is more salty than sweet, play up the acidity. The endive's bitterness is mitigated by the cheese, so I choose to work with good acidity and moderate richness.

Category: 2

Specific Recommendations:

2: *Cortese—a fuller style of Gavi* ■ *Sauvignon Blanc—light oak okay, texture* ■ *Chardonnay—leaner, flinty, French (Chablis, Chalonnais)*

Italian Parsley Salad
with Pecorino Cheese and Walnuts

The first time we served this salad at Square One, a guest asked the waiter, "The parsley salad, it's not made with parsley, is it?" This concept seems a bit unusual for the average American diner. So why try? Because on my last visit to Istanbul I ate a truly delicious salad that made me want to try using parsley as a salad green again. The salad was served as part of a meze assortment, and also as an accompaniment to a very rich lamb sausage. I loved the clean taste of the parsley dressed simply with lemon juice and olive oil, but how could I get others to love it as well? The salad might be a hard sell as is ("It's not parsley, is it?") but perhaps if it had some crunch and . . . if it were Italian . . . ! ☛Here is my Italianized variation, which I serve successfully, accompanied by a crostini of chopped roasted eggplant or peppers. For a less ethnically consistent accompaniment, try Turkish eggplant puree (page 60) or Ajvar (page 58) on grilled bread.

Serves 4

2 tablespoons fresh lemon juice

5 to 6 tablespoons fruity olive oil, depending upon tartness of lemons

3 cups or **6 small handfuls Italian flat-leaf parsley,** stems removed, torn into bite-sized pieces or very coarsely chopped

1/2 cup toasted walnuts, chopped coarsely but not too fine

1/2 cup grated pecorino cheese

Whisk the lemon juice and olive oil together in a small cup or directly in the salad bowl.

Toss the parsley, walnuts, and pecorino cheese in this citrus vinaigrette.

Distribute on 4 salad plates. Serve with grilled bread topped with roasted eggplant puree or a puree of roasted peppers seasoned with garlic.

Kitchen Conversation

It is parsley and it's delicious, isn't it? Clean, crisp, only slightly bitter but nicely assertive. The pecorino adds an interesting element of salt; the walnuts add bitterness and texture. (You might want to try almonds or hazelnuts in this salad, but I think that they will pale next to the more assertive walnuts, which hold their own so well against the salty cheese and intense greens.)

Lemon juice is the crucial acid to balance these feisty elements. Vinegar is too deep and heavy. (Try vinegar and see how it makes the cheese taste weirdly sour and the parsley too bitter.)

Good fruity olive oil is also important. A neutral, pallid oil will not bring anything to the party.

Wine Notes

Pairing Pointers: *Green, clean, and lively. You are looking for a wine that mimics the personality of the salad, yet has enough personality of its own not to get lost.*

Categories: 1A, 2

Specific Recommendations:

1A: *Chardonnay—Northern Italy, Alto Adige, Friuli* ■ *Alvarinho—Portugal—Vinho Verde* ■ *Muscadet—France*

2: *Chardonnay—French Chablis, Mâconnais, or lighter American* ■ *Pinot Blanc—California* ■ *Sauvignon Blanc—New Zealand—no oak, others with grassy style*

Parsley and Escarole Salad
with Grilled Tuna, Capers, and Pine Nuts

*A*s you may have noticed, I'm not one to leave a good food idea alone. I need to play with it in different ways until I am satisfied that I understand its possibilities. The idea of parsley in salads continues to pique my culinary imagination. Here's yet another way to use this forthright green, paired with bitter escarole and grilled tuna in a tart caper vinaigrette.

Serves 4

Caper Vinaigrette

1 tablespoon finely minced garlic

4 tablespoons capers, rinsed and coarsely chopped

¹/₄ cup fresh lemon juice

³/₄ cup olive oil

Freshly ground black pepper

Salt if needed

For the vinaigrette, combine the garlic, capers, lemon juice, and olive oil in a bowl, and whisk together. Add pepper and salt to taste. Remember that capers are salty.

Salad

1 pound tuna fillet, broiled or grilled to medium doneness, broken into 1¹/₂-inch bite-sized pieces

1¹/₂ cups torn Italian parsley, stems removed

2 cups escarole, cut into bite-sized pieces

¹/₂ cup toasted pine nuts

¹/₄ cup chopped fresh mint (optional)

Sprinkle the cooked tuna with a little salt and pepper and toss with a little of the vinaigrette. Marinate for 10 to 30 minutes. Toss the parsley and escarole with the remaining vinaigrette and distribute on 4 salad plates. Top with tuna, mint, if using, and toasted pine nuts.

Kitchen Conversation

This parsley salad takes a different turn. It picks up a taste partner in escarole. Instead of salty pecorino it has brine-salted capers. Meaty tuna lends weight to the salad and contrasts with the lightness and bitterness of the greens. Instead of the bitter walnuts, pine nuts add a little bit of sweet relief after the bitter, sour, and salt. Again, lemon juice cuts through the strong flavors in a lighter way than does vinegar. You might want to try a little chopped mint on this salad for another sweet note to support the pine nuts. If you are not in a minty mood, try basil and see if you like it.

Wine Notes

Pairing Pointers: The tart, salt, and earthy aspects of this salad crave an "old world" wine with bold flavor and austere structure. While the bitterness of the nuts provides an opportunity for a trace of oak, it's not license for full-blown woody wines.

Category: 2

Specific Recommendations:

2: *Garganega (Soave), Vernaccia (Tuscany)* ■ *Sauvignon Blanc—France's Loire Valley, Sancerre, Pouilly-Fumé*

Shrimp, Greens, and Tarator Vinaigrette

*T*arator is a classic Middle Eastern sauce for shellfish, fish, and cooked vegetables. Thinned with water and olive oil, it makes a very interesting vinaigrette. Tarator can be made hours ahead of time, but it will probably need additional water because it thickens as it stands. Any combination of romaine, watercress, spinach, parsley, and mint contrasts nicely with the fleshy shrimp. Top with more toasted nuts, cucumber, and feta cheese if you like.

Serves 6

Tarator Vinaigrette

1¹/₂ tablespoons finely minced garlic, 4 to 5 large cloves

1 cup toasted walnuts

4 tablespoons sesame tahini

4 to 5 tablespoons fresh lemon juice or to taste

¹/₂ cup water or as needed to thin the dressing

¹/₂ cup olive oil

Salt and freshly ground black pepper to taste

Salad

1¹/₂ pounds medium shrimp (prawns), shelled and deveined

4 cups watercress or **romaine**

1 cup torn Italian parsley, stems removed

¹/₂ cup fresh mint leaves

1 English cucumber, peeled, seeded, and sliced or diced (optional)

¹/₂ cup chopped toasted walnuts (optional)

³/₄ pound feta cheese (optional)

To make the vinaigrette, put the garlic, walnuts, tahini, and lemon juice in the container of a blender or food processor. Pulse to combine. Add the water and olive oil until a smooth and heavy creamlike consistency is obtained. Season with salt and pepper. **P**oach the shrimp in water or wine until cooked through, about 4 minutes. Drain shrimp and refrigerate until needed.

To serve, toss the shrimp with ½ cup of the vinaigrette. Toss the watercress, parsley, mint, and cucumber, if using, with the remaining vinaigrette. **P**lace the greens on 6 salad plates. Top with the shrimp, additional chopped walnuts, and crumbled feta if desired.

Kitchen Conversation

We're playing with the balance of bitter, sweet, and sour. As the shrimp are stars in the salad, their sweetness holds its own against the bitterness of the greens and walnuts. If you find that the bitter is too strong, increase the lemon in the vinaigrette; if you want to highlight the sweetness, increase the mint and add a bit more salt or up the feta cheese.

Wine Notes

Pairing Pointers: *This salad provides an interesting wine opportunity, as you can go in several directions —the obvious whites and even light reds. One can work with the richness of texture, play off the bitter angle, or play with the sweeter elements.*

Categories: 3A, 4

Specific Recommendations:

3A: *Sauvignon Blanc—fuller and sharp styles—USA, New Zealand/ Australia* ■ *Semillon/blends—USA* ■ *Chardonnay—French Puligny-Montrachet, California's Napa Valley, Washington State*

4: *Barbera—Piedmont* ■ *Sangiovese—Tuscany, Central Italy* ■ *Gamay Beaujolais—earthier rather than fruitier*

Shrimp, Radicchio, Spinach, Raisins, and Pine Nuts with Warm Balsamic Vinaigrette

At La Rosetta, a Roman restaurant specializing in seafood, I was served a salad of tiny, tiny calamari and radicchio. I was so delighted by the taste of sweet raisins and pine nuts mixed with bitter greens and shellfish that as soon as I returned home I decided to experiment with this theme. Shrimp seemed like a natural for this combination of tastes. To accent their appealing sweetness, I added orange juice and zest to the balsamic vinegar. This vinaigrette also would be delicious with scallops, and would give a decided lift to cooked chicken or turkey.

Serves 4

Orange Balsamic Vinaigrette

3 tablespoons balsamic vinegar

2 tablespoons sherry vinegar

²/₃ cup olive oil

2 tablespoons grated orange zest

¹/₄ cup fresh orange juice

Salt and freshly ground black pepper

Salad

2 large heads radicchio, cut in half and then sliced into about ¹/₂-inch strips

4 cups small spinach leaves

1 pound shrimp, 20 to 24 per pound, peeled and deveined

¹/₂ cup toasted pine nuts or **almonds**

¹/₂ cup golden raisins, plumped in sherry or Marsala

Assemble the vinaigrette by whisking together all of the ingredients in a bowl. Transfer the vinaigrette to a large sauté pan. Place the torn salad greens in a large bowl. Sprinkle them lightly with salt.
Sprinkle the shrimp with salt and sauté over moderate heat in the vinaigrette until barely cooked, about 3 minutes. Add the pine nuts and plumped raisins, and toss with the shrimp for a minute longer. Add to the greens and mix well. Serve at once.

☛Note: You can make this salad ahead with pre-cooked shrimp and simply warm them in the vinaigrette; however, for maximum flavor it is best to cook the shellfish directly in the vinaigrette, then add them while warm to the greens. It only takes 3 minutes, so relax. Tender sweet scallops cook even more quickly than shrimp and are best when still quivery. Sauté them but a minute or two.

If you decide to use cooked chicken or turkey, cut the meat into ½-inch strips, each about 1½ inches long, and warm them in the vinaigrette along with the pine nuts and raisins for just a minute or two. **Variation:** Incidentally, this sweet-and-sour vinaigrette is spectacular spooned over warm steamed asparagus.

Kitchen Conversation

Sweet shrimp, raisins, and pine nuts, bitter radicchio, and mildly bitter spinach are joined together harmoniously by the warm citrus-scented vinaigrette. Sweet flavors dominate; the orange juice and sweet wine used for plumping the raisins accentuate the sweetness of the balsamic vinegar as well as permeate the shrimp with their perfume. However, the vinaigrette needs the deep flavor of the sherry vinegar so that it isn't too sweet and light to temper the greens. While pine nuts and raisins are a classic Roman and Arabic combination, you might want to try almonds to see what happens.

Wine Notes

Pairing Pointers: *Staying with the sweeter elements of this salad would be my choice. A razor-edge balance of zesty acidity is needed to play off the sweetness. If the wine is the least bit cloying or heavy, it won't work.*

Categories: 1A or 1B

Specific Recommendations:

1A: *Sparkling wines, dry but with high dosage (sweetness level)*

1B: *Riesling—Pacific Northwest or German halbtrocken or kabinett* ▪ *Chenin Blanc—Loire Valley*

Radicchio, Mint, Beets, Oranges, Pine Nuts, and Raisins with Warm Balsamic Vinaigrette

*M*atisse would have loved this incredibly beautiful salad with its streaked red and white radicchio, dark red beets, golden oranges and pine nuts, and green mint leaves. Here bitter radicchio is cheerfully tamed by the sweetness of beets, mint, raisins, pine nuts, and balsamic vinegar and sweet-tart citrus.

Serves 4

Balsamic Vinaigrette

7 tablespoons olive oil

3 tablespoons balsamic vinegar

1¹/₂ tablespoons sherry vinegar

Salt and freshly ground black pepper

Salad

2 heads radicchio, cut in wide strips

4 tablespoons raisins, plumped in water, orange juice, or Marsala

4 tablespoons toasted pine nuts

4 small cooked beets, cut in eighths or thinner

40 mint leaves (torn if very large)

2 oranges, segmented (20 to 24 segments)

Assemble the vinaigrette by whisking together all of the ingredients in a bowl. Put the radicchio in a salad bowl. Pour the vinaigrette into a sauté pan and add the plumped raisins and pine nuts. Warm them for a few minutes, then add to the radicchio and toss while warm. Add the beets and mint, and toss again. Place on 4 salad plates and top with the orange segments.

☛Note: For instructions on cooking beets, see page 40.

Kitchen Conversation

Here we are playing with many kinds of sweet: beets, mint, raisins, pine nuts, and the tart sweetness of oranges. You might wonder why we didn't dress this salad with just orange juice and olive oil. Orange juice is just too sweet and mild to brighten the salad by itself. You need the sour of vinegar for depth/bottom to keep it from becoming too cloying or wimpy. If you're in an experimental mood, try a little grated orange zest in the vinaigrette. This salad is lighter than the one with shrimp on page 36, but the flavor theme is similar. The raisins will take on two different qualities of sweetness if plumped in orange juice (sweeter) or Marsala (a deeper tone).

Wine Notes

Pairing Pointers: *Your wine should echo the sweet elements (orange, raisins, balsamic vinegar) with ripe fruit or a kiss of residual sugar. Earthiness (beets) and bitterness (radicchio) also need to be taken into consideration.*

Categories: 1A, 1B, 2

Specific Recommendations:

1A: *Alvarinho—Portugal—Vinho Verde—crisp*

1B: *Rosé blend—with a snap of sweetness—France, USA, Spain*

2: *Gewürztraminer—earthy, rich fruit—USA*

Beet and Radicchio Salad
with Warm Pancetta Vinaigrette

*T*his salad is very beautiful, with a palette of dark and light reds. It is based on a familiar and well-loved flavor combination: bittersweet. However, it's interesting to see what happens when we add a third element to the classic counterpoint, changing the balance to a triad of sweet, bitter, and salty. Roasting beets intensifies their earthy flavor; boiling them reduces that root vegetable taste. Try both techniques and see which you prefer.

Serves 4

Salad

2 large or **4 small beets**

3 medium heads radicchio, or about 4 cups leaves

¹/₂ cup crumbled goat cheese or **croutons spread with goat cheese**

¹/₂ cup toasted walnuts, chopped (optional)

Cook the beets by roasting, covered, in a 350° oven until tender, or by boiling in water on the stovetop. The amount of time will vary according to the size of the beets, stovetop, 20 to 40 minutes, oven, 30 to 60 minutes or longer if very large. Test for doneness with the point of a knife or fork. Peel the beets while lukewarm and set aside until cool. Slice them into rounds or wedges if small, or half rounds if large. Toss with a little olive oil. Put the beets and radicchio (and the walnuts if using) in a salad bowl. Salt them lightly.

Warm Pancetta Vinaigrette

5 ounces pancetta, cut ¹/₄ inch thick, sliced crosswise into ¹/₄-inch strips

³/₄ cup olive oil

3 tablespoons balsamic vinegar

2 tablespoons red wine vinegar

Freshly ground black pepper

Salt to taste

Cook the pancetta in a small saucepan or sauté pan over medium heat until the pancetta has rendered its fat and is slightly crisp. Add the olive oil and vinegars, and season to taste with salt and pepper. Be careful not to oversalt, as some goat cheese can be quite salty. However, the dressing needs to be slightly salty and rather peppery to pick up the sweetness of the beets and pancetta.

Toss the beets and radicchio with the warm vinaigrette. Distribute on 4 salad plates. Top with crumbled goat cheese or serve with goat cheese on croutons.

Kitchen Conversation

Vinegar and black pepper are keys to balance the bitter, sweet, and salty components of this salad. The vinegar adds bottom tones and depth. The black pepper plays up the sweetness of the beets and pancetta. The meaty pancetta adds depth of flavor and its own crunchy sweetness. The walnuts, if added, contribute another kind of crunch and an undertone of bitter. I love goat cheese on top, but if this is too salty a combo for you, you can serve the cheese on the side, all the milder for having been spread on toasted bread.

Wine Notes

Pairing Pointers: *From a wine perspective, the bitterness of the radicchio, the earthiness of the beets, and the rich, sweet quality of the pancetta fat are the key elements. Pepper is also a bitter barometer. Bitter flavors validate a wine with some tannin, while the beets and richness demand an earthy wine. Both whites and reds could work here.*

Categories: 2, 4, 5

Specific Recommendations:

2: *Semillon—USA or lighter-styled Australian*

4: *Merlot—lighter style—Italy, France*

5: *Pinot Noir—fruity, earthy, moderately rich, good acidity*

Tonno e Ravanelli Tuna and Radish Salad

T he combination of flavors in this Milanese recipe is simple and clean. Meaty tuna, the sharp bitterness of radishes, and a tart citrus-based vinaigrette. If you can find Spanish black radishes, use them instead of the classic reds. Just slice paper thin and soak in ice water to crisp. Then toss with the vinaigrette. If you can't find fresh tuna, you may use canned, preferably packed in olive oil. This is a nice beginning for a rich meal, or an ideal dish for a summer antipasto assortment.

Serves 4

Lemon Vinaigrette

¹/₂ cup olive oil

¹/₄ cup fresh lemon juice

Salt and freshly ground black pepper

Salad

1 pound fresh tuna

3 large bunches radishes, sliced paper thin

¹/₄ cup chopped Italian parsley

2 to 3 cups torn romaine or **other crisp, mild salad greens** (optional)

For the vinaigrette, combine the olive oil and lemon juice with the salt and pepper.

Broil or sauté the tuna until it is cooked through but moist. Not rare, not tough and dry.

Break the tuna into bite-sized slivers.

Toss the tuna, radishes, and parsley with the vinaigrette.

Serve as is or atop some lightly dressed greens.

Kitchen Conversation

Here's a snappy little salad, clean and tart in taste. The lemon is a perfect foil for the meaty fish and lively bite of the radish. Vinegar would be too strong for the tuna and would bring out the bitterness of the radishes. Radishes also work well with smoked trout, smoked salmon, or sturgeon, as they cut through their richness.

Wine Notes

Pairing Pointers: Select a wine that mimics the bright, zesty, and tart flavors of this dish. Don't fight it. Be careful to avoid all traces of oak.

Categories: 1A, 2

Specific Recommendations:

1A: *Chardonnay—floral, lively—Northeast Italy* ■ *Pinot Blanc—with no wood—Italy, California, France*

2: *Sauvignon Blanc—clean, zesty* ■ *Rosé/blends—Burgundy, Provence, USA*

The Acid Test of Vinaigrette

When making vinaigrettes or dressings for salads, acidity is the key in achieving flavor balance. Not all salad ingredients have big taste. There are times when you want the thin, high note of sour that only lemon can give. Other times, especially in fruit-based salads, lemon might need to be cut with orange juice or sugar for roundness of tone. And at different times of the year, lemons can be sweeter. So taste them before using.

Conversely, there are salads where lemon would get lost. That is when you need vinegar or a combination of vinegars or a mixture of vinegar and lemon to balance the salad components. Until you know these things intuitively, it is wise to dip a leaf into the vinaigrette to see if the acid is strong enough to stand up to the greens or if you need added punch. Balsamic vinegar is sweet and nutty. Asian rice wine vinegars are mild. Certain Champagne-based vinegars are tart and high. Red wine vinegars can be deep and flavorful or sharp and tannic. Please taste them before you pour. All vinegars are not created equal.

For an experiment, dress nutty arugula leaves with a simple dressing of olive oil and lemon juice. Now try a vinaigrette with olive oil and vinegar or some combination of vinegars. Do the same with bitter Belgian endive. Then assertive, bitter radicchio. Then mildly bitter spinach. Then mild romaine. Add sliced fennel or cheese, or apple slivers, and see how the balance changes.

Tuna Carpaccio with Radishes, White Beans, and Mustard Shallot Vinaigrette

ere's another way to play with tuna and radishes that will make a very impressive, tasty, and easy first course. The bitter slivers of radish and sharpness of good Dijon mustard are tempered by the bland white beans and the silkiness of the raw tuna. Now set up a counterpoint with the nutty, bitter arugula leaves, and you have an interesting interplay of taste and textures. The tuna can be pounded thin and refrigerated. The beans can be cooked ahead of time and the vinaigrette holds quite nicely.

Serves 4

Salad

4 2-ounce thin slices sashimi-quality tuna

12 radishes, sliced paper thin

2 bunches small arugula

1 cup cooked white beans (see page 208)

Mustard Shallot Vinaigrette

3 tablespoons Dijon mustard

8 tablespoons olive oil

4 tablespoons fresh lemon juice

3 tablespoons finely minced shallots

Salt and freshly ground black pepper

Place each slice of the tuna between sheets of lightly oiled baker's parchment or wax paper and pound very gently to uniform thinness. Refrigerate in the paper until needed.

Place the radishes in ice water to crisp. Trim the stems off the arugula. Make the mustard shallot vinaigrette by whisking together all of the ingredients in a bowl. Toss the cooked white beans with ¼ cup of the vinaigrette.

To serve, toss the arugula with ¼ cup of the vinaigrette and place in a circular pattern on 4 salad plates. Remove the paper from the bottom side of each tuna slice and place the fish carefully atop the arugula. Carefully remove the top piece of oiled paper and push the tuna down onto the plate. It is crucial that you sprinkle the tuna lightly with salt or it will taste flat. Drizzle the remaining vinaigrette on top. Distribute the white beans around the tuna and sprinkle the radish slices on top.

Kitchen Conversation

Is the vinaigrette tart and sharp at the same time but not too overpowering? Has it thickened and emulsified, adding a creamy mouthfeel? Please don't forget to salt the tuna or the dish will be out of balance and the vinaigrette and radishes will overwhelm the fish. Actually, a key ingredient here is the shallots in the vinaigrette. Their crunchy, earthy onion sharpness helps hold everything in balance by picking up the crunch of the radishes and enlivening the creamy but bland white beans. If you can't feel them or taste them, add a few more.

Wine Notes

Pairing Pointers: *The addition of white beans and mustard to the tuna and radish combo means we need a richer and earthier wine than in the recipe on page 42. But the basic rationale is the same.*

Categories: 2, 3A

Specific Recommendations:

2: *Sauvignon Blanc—a little oak for richness okay* ■ *Chardonnay—light oak, fresh, citrusy*

3A: *Pinot Gris—richer, light, no oak—Oregon, Alsace* ■ *Marsanne—California, Australia, Rhône Valley*

Smoked Trout, Beets, and Cucumbers with Mustard and Herb Vinaigrette

*Y*et another way to use a mustard vinaigrette on fish. This one uses red wine vinegar, which is a little more assertive and complements the rich and smoky flavor of the trout. This salad is very nice paired with creamy fava bean puree and pita bread. Or you could serve it atop a bed of romaine lettuce or watercress.

Serves 4

Salad

2 smoked trout

4 small cooked beets

1 English cucumber

2 large heads romaine, torn (optional)
or **4 bunches watercress,** stems removed

Mustard Vinaigrette

2 tablespoons Dijon mustard

2 tablespoons red wine vinegar

6 tablespoons olive oil

¹/₄ cup chopped fresh dill

¹/₄ cup chopped scallions

Salt and freshly ground black pepper

Remove the skins from the trout, carefully remove all the bones, and break the trout into 2-inch pieces. **S**lice the beets into half rounds, about ¼ inch thick. **C**ut the cucumber in half lengthwise and scoop out the seeds. Slice on the diagonal ¼ inch thick. Lightly salt the slices just before tossing the salad.

Make the vinaigrette by whisking the mustard and vinegar together in a small bowl. Whisk in the olive oil gradually, add half the herbs and salt and pepper to taste.
Toss the trout and cucumbers with most of the vinaigrette. Top with the beets and remaining herbs, and drizzle with the rest of the vinaigrette on a bed of romaine or watercress, if desired.

Kitchen Conversation

Because the smokiness of the trout is so assertive, the vinaigrette needs a strong bottom. Here's where the wine vinegar will deliver the punch that lemon cannot. The bitter mustard enforces the power of the vinaigrette and makes the sweet beets seem even sweeter. The cucumbers provide a cool counterbalance between the smoky trout and the sweet beets. Be sure to salt the cucumbers first, then test a piece of cucumber in the vinaigrette along with the dill and scallions, to make sure you taste its cool bitterness underneath. If you do not, add more oil and salt until they hold their own against the mustard and vinegar.

Wine Notes

Pairing Pointers: *In selecting wine for this recipe, the vinaigrette is of less importance than the other ingredients, especially the smokiness of the trout and the refreshing crunch of the cucumbers. Pick up the smoke with a rich and smoky white wine.*

Category: 2

Specific Recommendations:

2: *Sauvignon Blanc (Sancerre, Pouilly-Fumé)* ■ *Garganega—earthy, smoky style, refreshing acidity* ■ *Riesling—richer style—Alsace, California, Australia*

Gazpacho Bread Salad

*T*he word *"gazpacho" is Arabic for "soaked bread." Here, in a Spanish variation of panzanella, an Italian tomato and bread salad, the bread is soaked in a tangy tomato vinaigrette, then tossed with tomatoes, peppers, cucumbers, and a little onion, reminiscent of the summer soup we all know and love. But chunkier.*

Serves 8

Tomato Vinaigrette

Makes about 4 cups

1/2 medium red onion, cut in pieces

2 large cloves garlic, peeled and cut coarsely

3 large ripe tomatoes, peeled and seeded, about 1 1/2 cups puree

6 tablespoons red wine vinegar

1/2 cup extra virgin olive oil

Salt and lots of freshly ground black pepper

For the vinaigrette, puree onion, garlic, and tomatoes in a blender or processor. Add vinegar. Transfer to a bowl and whisk in olive oil. Adjust seasoning. Think intense.

Bread Salad

6 cups French or **Italian bread,** crusts removed, cut in 1/2-inch cubes

3 cups diced tomatoes

2 cups diced cucumbers, peeled and seeded

2 cups diced red and green bell peppers

1/2 cup finely minced red onion

1/2 cup chopped parsley

Marinate bread cubes in half the vinaigrette for 30 minutes.

To serve, toss marinated bread with rest of chopped vegetables and remaining vinaigrette.

Kitchen Conversation

It pays to keep in mind that bread is bland and will absorb much of the vinaigrette, so the vinaigrette has to be very punchy. Remember to salt the vegetables before adding them to the bread mixture. If the peppers are too assertive or bitter, increase the tomatoes and vinegar.

Wine Notes

Pairing Pointers: *Because of the tartness of the tomatoes and because the vinaigrette is mostly absorbed by the bread, I'd select a red or rosé. Lively whites will work, but not as well.*

Categories: 4, 5

Specific Recommendations:

4: *Pinot Noir—lighter with sharp acidity* ■ *Various Spanish, Italian—Navarra, Valdepeñas, Breganze*

5: *Tempranillo —less woody, vibrant fruit, crianza styles* ■ *Pinot Noir—ample style, low oak*

Paella Salad

*I**n summertime rice salads are very popular in Italy and Spain. This is a room-temperature variation on a classic Valencian rice dish, paella. Instead of using Spanish short-grained rice, I prefer fragrant basmati, as the rice holds firm in a vinaigrette a great deal longer than does short-grain or any other long-grain rice. This makes a wonderful lunch or light summer supper dish.*

Serves 6

Chicken

6 boneless, skinless half breasts of chicken

1/2 cup olive oil

5 tablespoons red wine vinegar

4 tablespoons dried oregano

2 tablespoons freshly ground black pepper

4 tablespoons finely minced garlic

Salt

30 medium-sized shrimp

White wine or **water**

1/2 teaspoon crushed saffron filaments, steeped in 1/4 cup water

2 cups basmati rice

3 cups water

Marinate the chicken in the oil, vinegar, spices, and garlic for at least 4 hours or overnight. Broil or grill for 2 to 3 minutes per side. When cool, cut the chicken into strips that are about 2 inches long and 1/2 inch wide. Set aside.

Oregano Garlic Vinaigrette

2/3 cup olive oil

3 tablespoons dried oregano

1 tablespoon finely minced garlic

2 to 3 tablespoons red wine vinegar

Salt and freshly ground black pepper

2 bell peppers, red or green or both, cut in 1/4-inch dice

1 red onion, finely diced

1/2 cup peeled, seeded, diced tomatoes

1/2 cup olives (optional) for garnish

Poach the shrimp in wine or water until they turn pink, about 3 minutes. Refrigerate until needed.
In a small saucepan, put the saffron in water and bring up to a simmer. Remove from the heat and set aside to steep.

Wash the basmati rice, drain, and place in a medium saucepan. Cover with 3 cups water and the saffron infusion, and bring up to a boil. Add salt, lower heat, and cover the pan. Cook over low heat for 12 to 15 minutes until all water is absorbed.

While the rice is cooking, make the oregano garlic vinaigrette. Warm the olive oil in a small sauté pan over low heat. Add the oregano and garlic, and warm for a minute or two to release their flavors. Remove from the heat and add the vinegar, salt, and pepper to taste.

When the rice is cooked and still warm, toss with most of the vinaigrette. Add the diced peppers, onion, and tomatoes to the rice. Toss well. Season with salt and pepper.

Toss the chicken and shrimp with the remaining vinaigrette.

Distribute on 6 salad plates or place all of the rice salad on a large platter. Top with the strips of chicken and cooked shrimp. Garnish with olives if desired.

Kitchen Conversation

Rice is passive and bland and will absorb the vinaigrette, as in bread salad, so make the vinaigrette aggressive. The marinade in the chicken needs to be equally intense, as the chicken is mildly flavored. Into this passive-aggressive mix go the sweet shrimp, sweet peppers, and tart-sweet tomatoes for added excitement. Remember to salt and taste the rice to readjust its seasoning after it has rested for a while. You know how it is with passivity; you need to agree to be aggressive for balance.

Wine Notes

Pairing Pointers: *I treat this salad as if it were a paella, but with a bit less richness and more acidity. The flavor profile is almost identical: pungency, sweetness, and tartness, demanding a wine with a bold, angular personality.*

Categories: 2, 4

Specific Recommendations:

2: *Albariño—honest, refreshing—Rias Baixas ■ Chardonnay—earthier, angular—France, Spain, Australian blends*

4: *Pinotage —medium body with substantial acidity ■ Sangiovese—good fruit, lean structure—Italy, Argentina, USA*

Cerkez Tavugu Circassian Chicken Salad in Romaine Leaves

*T*his is not a timid chicken salad, but one with an edge of excitement. Bland poached chicken is sparked by the heat of cayenne and the richness of walnuts. Because its flavor is so intense, Circassian chicken is usually served in small portions as a meze. I like it scooped up in romaine leaves or combined with a salad of cucumbers and lettuces.

Serves 6

3 whole chicken breasts (with bones), each weighing about 1 pound, cut in half but with bones left in

4 cups water or **Basic Chicken Stock** (page 115) as needed to cover

1 onion, chopped

1 carrot, peeled and cut in chunks

Thyme sprig

1/2 bay leaf

2 tablespoons butter

1 onion, chopped

1 tablespoon minced garlic

3 tablespoons sweet paprika

1 teaspoon cayenne

Salt and freshly ground black pepper

2 slices bread, crusts removed, soaked in water and squeezed dry

3 cups toasted chopped walnuts

2 cups reduced Basic Chicken Stock (page 115)

2 tablespoons fresh lemon juice

2 tablespoons walnut oil

12 romaine leaves

1/4 cup chopped Italian flat-leaf parsley

A few walnut pieces for garnish

Put the chicken pieces in a saucepan with water or stock to cover. Add the onion, carrot, thyme, and bay leaf, and bring up to a boil. Reduce the heat and simmer until the chicken is tender, 15 to 20 minutes. Remove the chicken from the broth and set aside. Strain the broth and put into a saucepan. When the chicken is cool enough to handle, remove from the bones and add bones to the reserved stock.

Simmer the stock until it is reduced to 2 cups. Strain and discard the bones.

Shred the chicken with your fingers into strips that are about 1 1/2 inches long. Transfer to a bowl and set aside.

Melt the butter in a sauté pan and add the onion. Cook over medium heat until the onion is tender, about 8 minutes. Then add the garlic, 2 tablespoons paprika, and cayenne, and cook for 3 minutes longer. Season with salt and pepper to taste.

Place the bread crumbs and walnuts in the container of a food processor. Pulse to combine. Add the onion mixture and the reduced stock, and puree until smooth. Adjust seasoning and add the lemon juice. Toss the chicken with most of the sauce.

Warm the walnut oil and 1 tablespoon paprika in a small sauté pan. Pour over chicken. Spoon a few tablespoons of this chicken salad in each romaine leaf. Garnish with chopped parsley and toasted walnuts. Or place the chicken salad on 6 salad plates lined with romaine leaves, drizzle with walnut-paprika oil, parsley, and nuts.

Kitchen Conversation

Childhood memories of boiled chicken still send a shiver up my spine. But this salad takes boiled chicken and transforms it, enrobing it in a rich and spicy sauce. The walnuts and bread absorb liquids as the dressing sits, so make the sauce looser than you'd ordinarily want for a dressed chicken salad. Be sure to salt the cooked chicken as well as the sauce. In Turkey Circassian chicken salad is served on a plate by itself. However, I think the romaine adds much-needed relief, as it provides a cool, crisp contrast to the dense texture of the salad. The final drizzle of walnut-paprika oil intensifies the walnut flavor and adds a dramatic note of color.

Wine Notes

Pairing Pointers: *The sauce dominates. Reds and rosés are best, but too big a wine will overwhelm.*

Category: 5

Specific Recommendations:

5: *Syrah blends—not too intense—France, California* ■ *Nebbiolo—Gattinara, Nebbiolo d'Alba* ■ *Pinot Noir—substantial, spicy*

APPETIZERS

APPETIZERS

Ricotta Infornata *Baked Ricotta,* **57**

Ajvar *Spicy Roasted Eggplant and Pepper Spread,* **58**

Turkish Roasted Eggplant Puree with Yogurt and Walnuts, **60**

Atascaburras *Salt Cod and Potato Puree on Toast with Walnuts,* **62**

Baccalà Mantecato alla Veneziana *Cream of Salt Cod,* **64**

Spicy Fried Chick-peas, **66**

Ricotta Infornata Baked Ricotta ✓

Baked ricotta is so simple you may wonder why there needs to be a "recipe." Although this is a classic Italian dish, the first time I ate it was at a giant buffet lunch for a group of chefs and food writers, prepared by chefs Catherine Brandel and John Ash up at Fetzer Vineyards. This simple little "throwaway" item has remained in my memory. ☞*What you need is fresh ricotta cheese, sweet and soft in texture, not the congealed and gelatinous supermarket variety. Bake it and serve with toast or bruschetta. I love it with rosemary bread or walnut bread. But any good bread will do. Of course you can add chopped fresh herbs to the cheese but often, as taste memory reveals, the simplest preparation can be the best.*

Makes 2 cups; serves 8 as an appetizer

1 pound fresh, soft ricotta cheese

Salt and freshly ground black pepper

Extra virgin olive oil

Grilled or **toasted bread**

Preheat the oven to 300 degrees. Stir the ricotta cheese with a fork and add a little salt and pepper to taste. Pack it into a lightly oiled 4-cup ceramic crock. Drizzle the top with olive oil. Bake for about 15 minutes, or until warm and a little quivery. Serve with grilled or toasted bread.

Kitchen Conversation

Now you know how ricotta can be demure and sexy at the same time. Serve it warm and listen to everyone purr. With rosemary or walnut bread, the purring will be louder.

Wine Notes

Pairing Pointers: *Simplicity is the answer. Either show off the sweetness of the ricotta or highlight a flavorful wine by not showing off the ricotta.*

Categories: 3A, 5

Specific Recommendations:

3A: *Chardonnay—a rich-textured, ripe example ■ Pinot Gris— Oregon, Alsace—richer than Italian Pinot Grigio*

5: *Gamay—with pedigree—Cru Beaujolais ■ Merlot—softer, less tannic style, with rich fruit*

Ajvar Spicy Roasted Eggplant and Pepper Spread

his roasted eggplant and pepper spread is very popular along the Adriatic, in the former Yugoslavia and in the other Balkan countries. It is reminiscent of Moroccan and Tunisian salads, also served with bread, or as a room-temperature salad accompaniment for meat and fish dishes. Ajvar can be mild or quite spicy. The sweet peppers can be red, yellow, or green. The choice of hot peppers is up to you. In Greece and Turkey I tasted long, skinny green peppers that had a subtle kick. Our poblanos (pasillas) are similar in that they can be mildly to moderately hot. Jalapeños generally are hotter, but even they vary in degrees of intensity. Nibble a bit of the peppers first and then add as much heat as you like. Some Bulgarian versions of ajvar have tomatoes added to the mix; in fact, this book has a recipe for ajvar made only with baked or blanched green tomatoes, walnuts, and garlic (page 324)!

Serves 6 to 8 as an appetizer spread

2 pounds eggplant, 3 medium or **2 large**

1 pound sweet, fleshy bell peppers, about 3 large or 4 medium, red, yellow, or green

1 to 2 hot peppers (2 hot jalapeños or **1 large pasilla and 1 jalapeño)**

¹/₂ small onion, grated or pureed in processor or blender

1 tablespoon finely minced garlic

6 to 8 tablespoons extra virgin olive oil

2 to 3 tablespoons vinegar or **fresh lemon juice**

Salt and freshly ground black pepper

Char the eggplant on a griddle over direct heat or under the broiler, turning often, until tender all the way through. Alternately, prick the eggplant with the point of a knife (to prevent its exploding in the oven) and roast in a hot oven until tender, turning occasionally for even cooking. Peel carefully, remove as many seeds as possible. Chop the flesh coarsely. Drain in a colander and squeeze lemon juice over the eggplant if you want to keep it pale in color.

Roast the sweet and hot peppers over a flame or under the broiler until well charred on all sides. Place in a plastic container or paper bag. After 20 to 30 minutes, peel the peppers, remove the seeds, and chop coarsely.

Combine the eggplant and peppers in a bowl. Add the grated raw onion (or sauté onion briefly in olive oil) and garlic. Gradually add enough olive oil to bind and vinegar or lemon juice to taste. Season with salt and pepper. This mixture keeps well in the refrigerator for a few days, but bring it to room temperature for serving.

Kitchen Conversation

The sweet or heat of the peppers, the bitter of the eggplant, and the sour of lemon or vinegar are held in balance by the richness of the olive oil, so use a good one. Lemon has a higher note of sour than vinegar. Vinegar has more bottom; it offers a deeper kind of sour. You may need a combination of lemon and vinegar for the right balance. And the amount of heat from the peppers will affect how much salt and sour you add. You will keep adding these elements until they taste right for you. There is no one right or wrong way, only your way. Don't forget the salt. The eggplant will drink it up, so you may have to keep adjusting it over time. Remember to taste this with bread so you see how it stands up.

Wine Notes

Pairing Pointers: *Select a wine of ample acidity that is forward enough to stand up to this bold spread. If you make the spread "hot" it would be interesting to contrast the heat with a snap of sweetness.*

Categories: 1B, 2

Specific Recommendations:

1B: *Kabinett Riesling—Germany, Mosel* ■ *Chenin Blanc—France, Montlouis* ■ *Muscat—off-dry—Tunisia*

2: *Vernaccia* ■ *Sauvignon Blanc—California* ■ *Chardonnay—Chile*

Turkish Roasted Eggplant Puree with Yogurt and Walnuts

*H*ere is another tangy eggplant spread but one with a crunch of walnuts. The tang in this case comes from yogurt instead of vinegar. Pair this Turkish eggplant puree with pita bread for a good party hors d'oeuvre or part of a meze platter.

Serves 4 to 8 as part of a meze platter

2 large eggplants

3 tablespoons fresh lemon juice

3 tablespoons olive oil

3 cloves garlic, finely minced

1 cup drained yogurt

3 tablespoons chopped fresh dill, mint, or cilantro

2 jalapeños, minced very fine

Salt and freshly ground black pepper

$1/3$ cup toasted walnuts, chopped

3 tablespoons chopped Italian parsley

More lemon juice to taste if needed

Broil the eggplants or grill on a griddle, turning frequently, until charred all over and very soft, 15 to 20 minutes. Place in a colander or perforated drainer tray. Let stand until cool enough to handle. **C**arefully remove the skin and put the eggplant pulp in a strainer to release more bitter juices. **C**oarsely puree or chop the eggplant pulp. Toss with lemon juice to keep it pale in hue.

Warm the oil over low heat in a small sauté pan. Add the garlic and cook a minute or two to remove the bite. Add to the eggplant pulp, stir in the yogurt, herbs, and jalapeños, and then season with salt and pepper. Place in a serving bowl or platter. Sprinkle with chopped walnuts and parsley. Serve with warm pita bread.

☛Note: To drain yogurt, place in a sieve lined with cheesecloth in the refrigerator and let drain for 3 to 4 hours.

Kitchen Conversation

In this savory spread, the bitter flavor of the egg-plant is tempered by the tart and creamy yogurt. The hot accent of the chiles and the addition of the walnuts give it an additional bitter edge. Sometimes the combined bitterness of the eggplant, chiles, and nuts counteracts the tartness of the yogurt. You may be surprised to find that it is not tart enough for flavor balance, and that you will have to add more lemon juice.

If the sour aspects of this dish are too strong for your palate, fold in some additional chopped wal-nuts and up the chiles. Mint will lend some sweet-ness. Dill echoes the tartness, and cilantro will intensify the bitter aspects.

Proper salting should help these bitter, sour, and hot flavors attain balance. Remember, there's the blandness of the bread to contend with, so the puree should be robust in flavor. To test for final taste, dip in some pita and assess the interaction.

Wine Notes

Pairing Pointers: *Acidity is the key to keep up with the bright and tangy spread and the dish's inherent richness.*

Categories: 1A, 2

Specific Recommendations:

1A: *Pinot Grigio—Italy, USA* ▪ *Pinot Blanc—Italy, young French Alsatian*

2: *Albariño—young and fresh—Galicia (Spain)* ▪ *Sauvignon Blanc—light or no oak—New Zealand, Chile* ▪ *Dry Riesling—California, Washington State*

Atascaburras Salt Cod and Potato Puree on Toast with Walnuts

*T*his is a Spanish variation on brandade, *the classic French puree of salt cod and potatoes, but minus the milk and topped with crunchy walnuts. Occasionally pine nuts are pureed and added to the mixture; then it is served in bowls topped with chopped walnuts and chopped hard-boiled egg. But I prefer it as a finger food, spread on toasted bread and sprinkled with the nuts. This specialty of Valencia is a wonderful warm appetizer to serve with crisp white wine or Champagne.* ☛*It is very important while cooking salt cod* not *to boil it or it will toughen. Gradually bring the water up to a bubbling simmer, then reduce the heat and let the fish poach gently in the water.*

Serves 6 to 8 as hors d'oeuvres

1 pound salt cod

1 large or **2 medium baking potatoes,** 8 to 10 ounces

1 tablespoon finely minced garlic

³/₄ cup olive oil

2 teaspoons fresh lemon juice

Pinch freshly ground black pepper

¹/₂ cup coarsely chopped toasted walnuts

¹/₂ cup chopped flat-leaf parsley

12 slices rustic country bread, Italian, French, or sourdough

Soak the salt cod for 24 to 48 hours in cold water, changing the water at least 4 or 5 times. Drain. Place the cod in a large pan with enough water to cover. Slowly bring up to a bubbling simmer, reduce the heat, and simmer until tender, about 10 minutes. Drain and cool a bit. Break up the cod with your fingers, discarding any bones or tough parts.

Bake the potatoes in a 400 degree oven until tender, 45 to 60 minutes. When cool enough to handle, remove the skin from the potatoes. Mash the potatoes with a fork. Warm the olive oil in a small saucepan.

Place the salt cod in a food processor and puree. Add the garlic and gradually beat in the potatoes and olive oil to make a smooth mixture. Do not over-process or the mixture may turn gummy. If it is too stiff, whisk in a little more oil or water. Add lemon juice and pepper to taste. Keep this puree warm over hot water.

Toast the bread. Spread the puree on the bread and sprinkle with walnuts and parsley. Serve at once.

☛Note: Salt cod may also be poached in milk instead of water. This reduces the saltiness.

You may also form the salt cod and potato mixture into walnut-sized balls or little cakes, dip in bread crumbs, and fry until golden. These are called *buñuelos* in Spain. Serve with Ali-Oli Sauce (page 207).

Kitchen Conversation

People are more turned off by the name "salt cod" than by the real thing. The word "salt" as a modifier is anathema. Yet brandade is now more popular than ever. Ah, culinary semantics. In any case, you'll find that guests will devour this appetizer. The creamy mixture of salt cod and potatoes takes on new life with the crunchy, bitter walnut topping, the clean taste of parsley, and the crisp grilled or toasted bread. You may want to increase the garlic or, yes, even the salt, if the potatoes have cut the salt cod edge too much.

Wine Notes

Pairing Pointers: *Salt cod is a peculiar match with wine. Avoid reds, as the salt shatters the wine and the fishiness makes for an unpleasant "metal mouth" effect. High acid is the key.*

Categories: 1A, 2

Specific Recommendations:

1A: *Other Italian—Greco di Tufo, Verdicchio* ■ *Riesling—dry is best—try a halbtrocken from Germany, Austria*

2: *White blends from Provence, Spain* ■ *Sauvignon Blanc—simple and sharp—USA*

Baccalà Mantecato alla Veneziana Cream of Salt Cod

Here is yet another salt cod puree, but this time it is paired, Venetian style, with warm, soft polenta. Please use the long-cooking polenta, not the instant variety whose baby-food consistency is too soft for the rustic cod. (I was shocked on my last visit to Venice to be served instant polenta in some highly reputed and expensive restaurants!)

Serves 6 as a generous appetizer

2 pounds salt cod

Olive oil as needed

2 to 3 cloves garlic, finely minced

2 tablespoons chopped parsley

Salt and freshly ground black pepper

Soak the cod as in the preceding recipe (page 62) and cook it until tender. Flake with your fingers, removing tough parts and bones. Pulse in a food processor and gradually beat in as much oil as needed for a smooth puree. Fold in the garlic and parsley, and season to taste with salt and pepper.

Polenta

1 cup coarse cornmeal for polenta (*not* instant!)

4 cups cold water

Salt and freshly ground black pepper

A little softened unsalted butter

Combine the polenta and cold water in a heavy-bottomed saucepan. Gradually bring up to a boil, stirring often. Simmer over low heat, stirring often, until the polenta is thick and no longer grainy on the tongue. Add salt, pepper, and butter. Hold warm. If it thickens too much, keep adding hot water until you reach a creamy consistency.

To serve, spoon the warm polenta on 6 plates. Place a dollop of salt cod on top, slightly off to one side.

Baccalà con Salsa di Noci   Salt Cod with Walnut Sauce

In case you thought walnuts and salt cod are a Spanish aberration, here is an Italian version of this recipe that covers the whipped salt cod with a sauce of pureed walnuts mixed with chopped parsley and coarse salt.

Prepare the salt cod as in the preceding recipe. Puree 2 cups walnuts in a food processor with a little coarse salt. Be careful not to overprocess and make walnut butter! Add 3 tablespoons parsley and a little virgin olive oil and water for a creamy sauce. Serve over whipped salt cod.

Kitchen Conversation

There's quite a difference between atascaburras *and* baccalà mantecato. *In the* baccalà mantecato, *you play creamy texture upon creamy texture. And contrast sweet, bland, and warm polenta with the room-temperature salty pureed cod. But add the crunch of bitter toasted walnuts or of toasted bread and walnuts, and you reduce the salty quality of the salt cod. You actually may have to add salt! Both the bread and the polenta are neutral foils for the cod, but the different textures and temperatures affect your perception of the cod's saltiness. As another variation, spoon the* baccalà mantecato *over crisp grilled polenta. It's quite tasty but not as sexy a pairing as with the soft and creamy preparation.*

Wine Notes

Pairing Pointers: *While Mom thinks the two salt cod recipes are opposites, and they are from a food standpoint, from a wine point of view they are the same (unless you are preparing salt cod à la Portuguese, with tomatoes, onions, peppers, etc.).*

Categories: 1A, 2

Specific Recommendations:

1A: *Other Italian—Orvieto, Frascati* ■ *Riesling—dry is best— try a halbtrocken from Germany*

2: *Albariño—Spain—or Alvarinho—Portugal, Vinho Verde* ■ *Sauvignon Blanc—USA*

Spicy Fried Chick-peas

*L*ooking for a tasty cocktail snack as an alternative to peanuts or olives? These fried chick-peas are Middle Eastern street food at its best. Salty, spicy, and great with that glass of sparkling wine or a cocktail. ☛You can cook the chick-peas, then deep-fry them and serve hot, à la minute. For longer storage, deep-fry, then bake and store in an airtight container.

Makes 5 cups

2 cups chick-peas, soaked overnight in water

1¹/₂ teaspoons salt

¹/₄ teaspoon freshly ground black pepper

2 tablespoons ground cumin

¹/₄ teaspoon cayenne pepper

¹/₂ teaspoon ground coriander

Peanut oil for frying

Drain the chick-peas and cover with fresh cold water. Bring up to a boil, reduce heat, and simmer for about an hour until tender. To prevent the chick-peas from remaining hard, don't add salt in the beginning of cooking. Add the salt during the last 15 minutes of cooking. Drain. You will now have 5 cups of cooked chick-peas.

Combine all of the spices in a bowl or, better yet, a shaker. Heat the peanut oil in a skillet to the depth of 3 inches. When the oil reaches 375 degrees, deep-fry the chick-peas in batches until golden. Remove with a slotted spoon or skimmer and put in a bowl. Toss with spices. Serve hot.

Or if you want to keep them on hand as a "bar nut," deep-fry until golden, then bake in a 300 degree oven for 40 to 50 minutes until crunchy. Toss with spices. These will keep for at least a week.

Kitchen Conversation

Pass the martinis.

Wine Notes

Pairing Pointers: *Peanuts with an attitude. I love crunchy, salty food with sparkling wine or high-acid, sharp whites. Or a martini.*

Category: 1A

Specific Recommendations:

1A: *Brut Champagne—light and toasty* ■ *Pinot Grigio* ■ *Rosé/blends—young and lively, possibly sweet, even white Zinfandel*

SAVORY
PASTRIES

SAVORY PASTRIES

Briouat Bil Kefta *Moroccan Meat- or
  Potato-Filled Filo Pastries,* **7 1**

Moroccan-Inspired Shrimp Bastilla, **7 4**

Turkish-Inspired Grilled Eggplant Sandwich
  with Spicy Red Pepper and Walnut
  Puree, **7 7**

Onion and Anchovy Coca, **8 0**

Persian-Inspired Chicken Salad Sandwich, **8 2**

Briouat Bil Kefta Moroccan Meat- or Potato-Filled Filo Pastries

These North African pastries usually are made with a paper-thin semolina dough called malsouqua *(Tunisia)* or ouarka *(Morocco)*. As these pastries are time-consuming and a bit tricky to make, we'll use filo dough here. ☛Briouats are similar to Tunisian briks or small Greek and Turkish borek-type pastries. Layers of paper-thin pastry are wrapped around a filling, rolled up into cylinders or folded into triangles or rectangles. They are usually deep-fried or baked, and can be filled with a savory potato mixture, ground meat, or merguez sausage.

Makes 8 large or 16 small briouats

Meat Filling

2 tablespoons olive oil

1 onion, chopped fine

1 teaspoon ground cumin

1 teaspoon paprika

1 teaspoon cinnamon

$^1/_2$ teaspoon cayenne pepper

3 tablespoons parsley, finely chopped

2 tablespoons fresh coriander, finely chopped

8 ounces ground beef or **lamb**

Salt and freshly ground black pepper

3 eggs, lightly beaten

Warm the olive oil in a large sauté pan. Cook the onion over moderate heat for about 7 minutes, then add the herbs and spices. Cook for 2 minutes longer, then add the meat and cook quickly until the meat loses color. Pour the eggs over the meat, stir well, and cook for 3 to 4 minutes, stirring constantly. Adjust the seasoning with salt and pepper. Remove from the heat and cool.

continued

Potato Filling

2 medium potatoes, peeled and cubed

2 tablespoons olive oil

1 onion, finely chopped

3 cloves garlic, finely minced

1 teaspoon salt

¹/₂ teaspoon freshly ground black pepper

4 tablespoons chopped parsley

3 tablespoons chopped mint or **fresh coriander**

1 egg, lightly beaten

1 to 2 hard-boiled eggs, coarsely chopped

Clarified melted butter

8 full sheets filo dough

Cook the potatoes in salted water until they are soft. Drain well and mash. Set aside. Heat oil in a small sauté pan and cook the onion over moderate heat for 7 minutes. Add the garlic, salt and pepper, and cook for 2 minutes. Stir in the herbs. Add the onion mixture to the potatoes, season to taste with salt and pepper. Add the raw egg to bind the mixture and stir in the chopped hard-boiled egg.

To make the briouats, cut the filo dough into strips 5 inches wide and about 12 inches long. Brush with melted butter. Put 1 heaping tablespoon filling on the bottom or along one side, roll, tuck in sides, and continue rolling to seal. Brush with water and egg wash to seal. Or place 1 tablespoon of filling on the buttered filo on one end and fold the filo into triangles.

To bake, preheat the oven to 375 degrees and bake until golden, about 20 minutes. To deep-fry, heat the oil to 375 degrees and deep-fry until golden, about 5 minutes. Drain on paper towels. Serve at once.

To assemble briouats ahead of time, place on baker's parchment-lined baking sheets, cover loosely with parchment or a foil tent (but don't press the foil on the pastries or they will tear when you remove the foil), and refrigerate until needed. They'll keep for a few days.

Kitchen Conversation

Taste each batch of filling and even if you think they are tasty as is, increase the spices! You need to escalate the intensity of flavors, as the filo-dough wrapping will mask some of the seasonings. Salt enough too. For the meat filling you want the sweetness of cinnamon and paprika to be tempered by the tartness of the cumin and not overpowered by heat, or by the sharpness of bitter garlic and fresh coriander. In the mild potato filling you are looking for bright notes of mint and sweet onion, with sufficient assertive salt and black pepper.

Wine Notes

Pairing Pointers: *The choice of wine here is predicated on your choice of filling. The crackling texture of the baked crust creates a need for good acidity and opens up the possibility of sparkling wine; it would be especially nice with the potato filling. The meat briouat would be best with a rosé or red wine. Here the wine's intensity is dependent upon the level of spiciness.*

Categories: 1A, 4, 5

Specific Recommendations:

1A: *Potato—Brut Champagne—crisp, dry, fresh* ■ *Meat— Rosé/blend—dry, spicy—Southern France, Spain*

4: *Potato—Pinot Noir—light, fruity style from anywhere* ■ *Meat—Carignan/blends from Southern France, North Africa*

5: *Potato—Rosé Champagne—spicy, vigorous—USA okay too* ■ *Meat—Zinfandel—medium body, peppery*

Moroccan-Inspired Shrimp Bastilla

Bastilla is a large, flaky pastry usually made with pigeon or chicken. A sweet and savory dish, the poultry is mixed with spicy eggs and layered with almonds and cinnamon, and then topped with cinnamon and powdered sugar. However, in leafing through some of my Moroccan cookbooks, I found a fish bastilla, one made with shrimp, one with shrimp and mushrooms, and even one with beef and spinach. These are obviously contemporary interpretations of this classic pastry. ☛The idea of a shrimp bastilla intrigued me. Anything with shrimp is a hit with guests. So I fooled around with different versions, eliminating the one held together with béchamel, and added the savory egg mixture from the traditional pigeon and almond pie to hold the chopped cooked shrimp in place. It was a hit. When you make this, save the shells after cleaning the shrimp, as they make a wonderful stock to flavor the filling.

Serves 8 as dinner, or 12 to 14 as appetizers

1¹/₂ pounds shrimp (any size), shelled and deveined, shells reserved

2 cups each white wine and water

2 tablespoons olive oil

1 chopped onion

1 bay leaf

2 lemon slices

6 coriander seeds

2 cilantro sprigs

1 dried hot pepper pod

Bastilla Filling

3 tablespoons unsalted butter

1¹/₂ cups chopped onions

1 tablespoon finely minced garlic

1 tablespoon ground ginger

2 teaspoons ground cumin

¹/₂ teaspoon cayenne pepper

¹/₂ teaspoon saffron

Grated zest of 1 large lemon, about 1 tablespoon

4 tablespoons chopped cilantro

4 tablespoons chopped mint

2 tablespoons chopped parsley

1 cup shrimp stock

2 tablespoons fresh lemon juice

6 eggs, lightly beaten

Salt and freshly ground black pepper

8 tablespoons melted clarified butter

20 sheets filo dough or **about 1 package**

Bring the water and wine up to a simmer in a medium saucepan and poach the shrimp for about 5 minutes, or until they are tender and cooked through but not tough. Be careful not to overcook the shrimp; they should still be a bit springy to the touch, as they are going to cook again. Set the shrimp aside in the refrigerator and reserve the poaching liquids.

In a large saucepan, warm the olive oil and sauté the shrimp shells over moderate heat for about 5 minutes, stirring often. Add the poaching liquids and onion, bay leaf, lemon slices, coriander, cilantro sprigs, and hot pepper pod, and simmer for about an hour. Strain and reduce somewhat. You will need only 1 cup of shrimp stock for this recipe, but the rest can be frozen.

For the filling, melt the butter in a large sauté pan over moderate heat. Add the onions and cook them for about 10 minutes, or until translucent and sweet. Add the garlic and spices, and cook for 5 minutes longer. Add the lemon zest, the chopped herbs, and shrimp stock, and simmer until most of the liquid has been absorbed. Reduce the heat and add the lemon juice and beaten eggs, and cook, stirring constantly, until soft curds are formed and the eggs have attained the texture of very soft scrambled eggs. Season with salt and pepper. Remove from the heat and place in a bowl. If there seems to be a lot of excess moisture, place in a strainer and let the liquids drain away. Cool this mixture. Adjust the salt and seasoning when cool.

Chop the shrimp into nice bite-sized chunks. Sprinkle lightly with salt.

Melt the clarified butter and keep it liquid.

Lightly brush a 15-inch pizza pan with the butter. Working with 1 sheet at a time, brush 10 sheets of filo dough with melted butter, and arrange them in an overlapping circular pattern like a pinwheel, letting the edges overhang the side of the pan (butter the overhang too).

Spoon half of the egg mixture on the filo, into a circle about 12 inches in diameter. Top with the chopped shrimp, then the rest of the eggs. Fold the overhanging filo over the top and brush with butter.

Now, again working with 1 filo sheet at a time, brush with butter, pinwheel fashion, and continue with 10 filo layers. Tuck the overhanging edges under the pie. At this point you may cover the pie loosely with a foil tent and refrigerate. Don't let the foil rest on the pie or the filo will tear when you remove it.

Preheat the oven to 350 degrees. Bake the pie until pale gold in color, about 20 minutes. Carefully tilt the pan to drain the excess butter. Place a second pizza pan over the pie and invert the pie onto the second pan to brown the other side. (This step is not essential if the pie seems to be browning nicely on both sides.) Bake until golden brown, about another 20 minutes. Invert the pie again.

Let the pie cool just a bit, then cut into wedges.

Kitchen Conversation

The flavors in this bastilla are quite complex. There is the sweetness of shrimp and onions, the bitter edge to the spices, the tartness of lemon, all tempered by the rich buttery sweetness of crunchy filo. Here are some key points to note along the way. As in the briouats (page 71), all flavors will be muted by the filo. Be sure to reduce the shrimp stock so that it is intensely fragrant, as its power will be muted by the spiced onions and eggs. After the egg mixture is cooked, taste for enough lemon zest and lemon juice; they add a fresh and light dimension to the pie. And check the eggs for salt too. Salt will bring up the spices and herbs. Also, salting the shrimp lightly just before you add them to the pie will bring up their taste.

Serve this savory pie with watercress and orange salad if desired. Or with radish, orange, and watercress salad, to add a refreshing contrast to the richness of the bastilla.

Wine Notes

Pairing Pointers: *We must consider the sweetness of the shrimp, onions, and herbs. The lemon's tartness will be accentuated by the wine. And let's not overlook the crisp texture of the filo. Whites and rosés, dry and off-dry, are my preferences.*

Categories: 1A, 1B, 2

Specific Recommendations:

1A: *Chenin Blanc—floral, zesty—Loire or USA*

1B: *Riesling —lightly sweet, high acid—Germany, Washington State*

2: *Chardonnay—not too oaky, ripe fruit—USA, Australia*

Turkish-Inspired Grilled Eggplant Sandwich with Spicy Red Pepper and Walnut Puree

We're all looking for vegetarian sandwich options, because we're not always in the mood for meat, poultry, or seafood. Eggplant has a particularly meaty character, so you feel as if you are eating something substantial. These eggplant sandwiches also are good to take along for a picnic. If the sandwiches are going to be out of the refrigerator for any period of time, eliminate the mayonnaise in the sandwich spread and just use yogurt or only red pepper puree. ☛While they don't really serve this sandwich in Turkey, it is a compilation of many favorite Turkish tastes: smoky grilled eggplant, spicy red pepper walnut paste so like the "Muhammara"-Inspired Sauce (page 190), tart yogurt, fragrant mint, and their beloved flatbread. All of the components of these sandwiches can be made ahead of time.

Makes 6 sandwiches

Turkish Red Pepper Walnut Sauce

2 large red bell peppers

1 tablespoon finely minced garlic

2 to 3 finely minced jalapeños or to taste

1 tablespoon ground cumin

¹/₄ cup extra virgin olive oil

2 tablespoons fresh lemon juice

1 tablespoon pomegranate syrup

²/₃ cup toasted walnuts, chopped medium fine

Salt and freshly ground black pepper

Roast the peppers in the broiler, over a grill or on a gas flame, turning often, until charred all over. Put in a covered plastic container to steam for about 10 to 15 minutes. Peel, seed, and cut up coarsely. Put the peppers, garlic, jalapeños, cumin, olive oil, lemon juice, and pomegranate syrup in the container of a food processor and pulse until blended. Pulse in walnuts at the end and do not overprocess. The mixture should be chunky and spicy. Season with salt and pepper.

☛Note: After assembling the sandwiches you may have some red pepper puree left over. Enjoy it as a dip with pita. It keeps for about a week in the refrigerator. Or thin it with a little olive oil and spoon over cooked fish. See page 182.

continued

Eggplant

$1/3$ cup olive oil

1 tablespoon finely minced garlic

1 tablespoon toasted ground cumin

2 tablespoons fresh lemon juice

Salt and freshly ground black pepper

1 large or **2 medium eggplants,** peeled and cut into 12 1-inch slices (if baking, cut in $1/2$-inch slices and use 4 slices per sandwich, 2 on each side)

Preheat the broiler or make a charcoal fire. **W**hisk together the olive oil, garlic, cumin, and lemon juice in a shallow bowl. Dip the eggplant slices in this seasoned oil, sprinkle with salt and pepper, and broil or grill until tender, about 2 minutes on each side. Don't let the eggplant get too charred. Set the eggplant slices in a drainer tray. Taste and adjust salt. You could also bake the eggplant in a 400 degree oven until tender, turning once. It will take about 20 minutes.

Sandwich

$1/3$ cup mayonnaise

$1/3$ cup nonfat yogurt

1 teaspoon grated lemon zest

3 tablespoons finely chopped mint

Salt and freshly ground black pepper

6 large pita bread rounds

24 mint leaves

2 bunches watercress, coarse stems removed

Eggplant slices

Turkish Red Pepper Walnut Sauce

In a small bowl, combine the mayonnaise, yogurt, lemon zest, and chopped mint. Add salt and pepper. Cut the pita bread in half. Spread 2 tablespoons of mayonnaise mixture inside each pita on the bottom of the pocket. Place 2 mint leaves and a small sprig of watercress on the mayonnaise. Layer in an eggplant slice atop the cress and mint, top it with a generous layer of red pepper walnut sauce.

Kitchen Conversation

You'll want to be able to taste the eggplant under the spicy, walnut-tinged red pepper sauce, so don't cut the eggplant too thin. Taste the sauce. Does it need salt? A bit more pomegranate for that sweet-sour undertone to pick up the sweet smokiness of the peppers? Do you feel the heat of the peppers? If not, add more. Remember that bread and eggplant are bland. The mayonnaise-yogurt mixture helps keep the sandwich a little moister, but could be eliminated if you want to cut back on fat. Or just use yogurt; it picks up the mint and lightens the total taste of the sandwich.

Wine Notes

Pairing Pointers: *The driving tastes are bitter (eggplant, walnuts, peppers, watercress) and sharp (yogurt and lemon). Also the sweet and sour of pomegranate. A little tannin can play well if you choose red. If not, opt for a sharper, earthier white. The less bitterness, the more flexible the wine selection can be.*

Categories: 2, 5

Specific Recommendations:

2: *Garganega—a zippy Soave or similar wine from Italy* ■
Sauvignon Blanc—crisp, austere, and unoaked

5: *Zinfandel or Merlot—a little tannin and bright fruit*

Onion and Anchovy Coca

*C*oca *is the Catalan word for what we call "pizza." Cocas are very popular as tapas, those fabulous bar snacks served in Spanish tabernas. Toppings are quite varied. For this coca I have chosen sweet caramelized onions, seasoned with thyme and anchovies. It's a savory way to start a meal and tastes great with a glass of sherry, the classic tapas accompaniment.*

Serves 8 to 10

Sponge

1 tablespoon yeast

$1/4$ cup warm water

$1/2$ cup unbleached all-purpose flour

Dough

$3/4$ cup water

2 tablespoons olive oil

3 cups unbleached all-purpose flour

$1^1/2$ teaspoons salt

2 tablespoons olive oil

A little flour for kneading

Cornmeal for dusting the pan

You can assemble the dough by hand and knead it by hand. You can use the electric mixer with a dough hook. Or the dough can be made in the food processor, but it will need some hand kneading after it is assembled. This recipe makes one large oval, about 11 inches by 17 inches, or two 9-inch rounds. I prefer to use the sponge method, as it gives the yeast a head start and makes for a lighter crust.

In a mixing bowl, dissolve the yeast in the warm water. Add the flour and mix to combine. Let the sponge sit, covered, for about 30 minutes. Add the rest of the ingredients and mix on low speed with a dough hook for about 10 minutes, or until the dough leaves the bowl cleanly. Transfer the dough to a bowl, cover with plastic wrap, and allow the dough to rise for an hour. Punch it down on a lightly floured board. Shape into one large ball or two, and place on a floured baking sheet. Cover the dough and allow it to rest in the refrigerator for 30 minutes.

3 tablespoons olive oil

7 cups yellow onions, sliced $^1/_4$ inch thick

2 tablespoons chopped fresh thyme

Salt and freshly ground black pepper

6 salt-packed anchovies, rinsed and filleted

$^1/_4$ cup toasted pine nuts

Heat the olive oil in a large sauté pan. Add the onions and cook over moderate heat, stirring often, until the onions are golden and reduced in volume by almost half. This could take 30 minutes. Add the thyme and cook for 10 minutes longer. Season with salt and pepper. Cool the filling.

To assemble and bake the coca, preheat the oven to 475 degrees. On a floured board or baker's peel, or a cornmeal-dusted baking sheet, stretch the dough into an oval or two rounds and spread with the onions. (Note: If you are using a pizza stone, heat it in the oven for at least 30 minutes before making the pizza.)

Spread the caramelized onions on the coca dough. Top with the anchovy fillets (you should have 12 halves that you can cut in half again to make 24 slivers). Sprinkle with the toasted pine nuts. Bake the coca for 12 to 15 minutes. Serve warm, cut into wedges.

Kitchen Conversation

This is a game of sweet and salt, two of America's favorite tastes. The sweetness of the onions and pine nuts is counterbalanced by the salt of the anchovies. Without them this pie would be boring and on one note. The thyme adds a subtle, musky fragrance, but it is a minor theme. You might want to play with other herbs, such as oregano, marjoram, or mint, and see how they affect the equation.

Wine Notes

Pairing Pointers: *This is a two-note song, sweet and salt. High acidity is needed to cut the salt. While I would normally suggest that we reference the sweetness in the onions with a similar wine, it would clash with the anchovies. Clean, bright, and flavorful whites are best.*

Categories: 1A, 2

Specific Recommendations:

1A: *Other Italian, Verdicchio, Frascati* ■ *Muscadet—the younger the better*

2: *Sauvignon Blanc—fragrant and a little grassy* ■ *Viura, Verdejo*

Persian-Inspired Chicken Salad Sandwich

T his has turned out to be a most requested chicken sandwich. Maybe it's the appeal of the more filling—less bread ratio, as pita is thinner than conventional sandwich bread. Maybe it's the walnuts, maybe it's the herbs. Or the kick of feta cheese. I've taken my inspiration from crossing two Persian recipes. A classic refreshing pita sandwich of feta cheese and leafy herbs is combined with grilled chicken that has been marinated in spices used for Persian jujeh kabab (chicken brochettes). Walnuts added to the yogurt-enhanced mayonnaise create crunch and complexity. I've served this mixture tucked in mini-pitas for cocktail parties, and have seen 500 vanish in 50 minutes! You'll probably enjoy similar success.

Serves 4, or makes 8 hors d'oeuvre portions

Chicken

1/2 small onion

2 tablespoons fresh lemon juice

1 teaspoon paprika

2 teaspoons dried oregano

1 teaspoon finely minced garlic

1/4 cup olive oil

Salt and freshly ground black pepper

2 whole chicken breasts, each weighing about a pound, skinned, boned, and cut in half (4 half breasts)

Lemon Dill Mayonnaise

1 teaspoon grated lemon zest

1 tablespoon fresh lemon juice

2 tablespoons chopped fresh dill

1/2 cup mayonnaise

1/2 cup thick yogurt

Salt and freshly ground black pepper

Sandwich

1/3 cup coarsely chopped toasted walnuts

4 pita bread rounds or **8 mini-pitas**

8 slices feta cheese, about 1/8 inch thick, approximately 3-inch squares

16 large mint leaves

16 large basil leaves

16 sprigs watercress, stems removed

Grind the onion, lemon juice, spices, herbs and garlic in the food processor or blender. Remove the mixture to a nonaluminum bowl or container. Stir in the olive oil and season with salt and pepper. Toss the chicken in this mixture and marinate in the refrigerator overnight.

Preheat the broiler. Broil the chicken breasts about 3 minutes on each side and, when cool enough to handle, cut into 1/2-inch dice. Meanwhile, assemble the lemon dill mayonnaise by combining all of the ingredients in a bowl.

Fold the chicken and walnuts into the lemon dill mayonnaise. Adjust the final seasoning. Cut the pita bread in half and open the pockets. Place the feta cheese, herbs, and watercress in the pita. Then spoon in the chicken salad mixture.

Kitchen Conversation

Believe it or not, the crucial ingredients in this sandwich are the feta, which adds salt, and the sweet mint and basil. They accentuate all the other flavors: the bitter tones of walnuts and watercress, and the tartness of yogurt, and the lemony marinade on the chicken.

Wine Notes

Pairing Pointers: The sharp, clean taste of the greens (watercress, mint, and basil) and the tartness of the feta and yogurt make this a natural white wine dish. Because of the body of the chicken you can select a slightly richer wine. Match to the tart notes. No oak, please.

Categories: 2, 3A, 4

Specific Recommendations:

2: *Sparkling wine—Champagne or not—steely and young* ■ *Chardonnay—light, lean, and unoaked—European*

3A: *Pinot Gris—a sharper style from Oregon or California* ■ *Sauvignon Blanc—rich and tart—New Zealand, Loire Valley, USA*

4: *Merlot—a simpler, herbaceous wine—South America, France* ■ *Pinot Noir—minty, light tannin—USA, Australia*

SOUPS

SOUPS

BASIC STOCKS

Soups

There's something about soup that makes the cooks in the kitchen fight over who gets to prepare it. Perhaps it's because there are few pitfalls and lots of satisfaction in making soup. Techniques are uncomplicated and flavors are relatively easy to balance. With one big batch, as with making stews, you can feed a number of people happily, and, as with stew, you don't have to worry about last-minute preparation. There's none of the trial and error that comes from the pressures of à-la-minute cooking. Soup is unpretentious and satisfying. It represents home and hearth. If you are a novice cook, making soup is a great way to begin your adventure in the kitchen. For soup lovers there is no better way to start a meal or create a one-dish meal than with a hearty soup.

The basis of most good soups is a flavorful broth. However, in the Mediterranean many soups are made with water. A few are enriched with scraps or bones. Meat is a precious and costly commodity; it is not generally used for stock unless it is the remains of another dish. Many cooks add the ubiquitous bouillon cube to lend a meat flavor to soups and stews. Fresh vegetables are used in abundance, and not just as a garnish. Vegetable broths are lighter in flavor and keep the taste of the vegetables clean, bright, and in the foreground, not masked by meaty undertones. Chicken or poultry broths are middle ground in taste; they harmonize subtly and well with other ingredients and don't overpower the taste of the vegetables. Meat broths are deeper in tone, and vegetables usually take a background position. Fish broths, as briefly simmered and delicate as they may be, still will dominate most vegetables with the pervasive perfume of the sea.

Most of the soups in this chapter are of the hearty meal-in-a-bowl variety. Some are based on dried beans, some are enriched by bread. The vegetable purees are based on vegetables, not filler. Carrot soup is all carrots. Green tomato soup is green tomatoes.

Soup reheats very well, so make it in large batches. If you do make a large batch, taste it each time upon reheating, as the flavors or seasonings may have died a bit. Vary the garnishes, changing the herbs, adding bits of fish or shellfish, chicken or meat. A dollop of yogurt, a swirl of pesto or egg and lemon can enliven soup and make it seem new the next time around.

Vecchia Roma's Escarole Soup

*O*n my last visit to Rome I went out for dinner with a group of chefs to a very popular restaurant called Vecchia Roma. We hit it on a slow night, off season, when every dish was sparkling. This is my interpretation of the soup we loved and devoured that night. It is hot, garlicky, and restorative.

Serves 4 to 6

4 to 5 cups strong chicken broth

8 cups washed and chopped escarole

3 tablespoons olive oil

2 cups diced onions

2 tablespoons minced garlic

1¹⁄₂ to 2 teaspoons hot pepper flakes

Salt and freshly ground black pepper to taste

Toasted or grilled bread croutons

If your chicken broth is light, reduce it over high heat until it has robust flavor. Set aside.

Steam the escarole in the water clinging to the leaves. When wilted, drain well and chop very fine.

Warm the olive oil in a saucepan over moderate heat. Cook the onions until tender and translucent, about 10 minutes. Add the garlic and some of the hot pepper flakes, and cook for 5 minutes. Add the broth and chopped escarole, and bring up to a boil. Simmer for 5 minutes. Adjust the seasonings. Add more hot pepper if desired. Serve at once with toasted or grilled bread croutons.

Kitchen Conversation

Rich broth, bitter greens, and a small but subtle amount of heat are what we are looking for. We want heat that doesn't overpower but remains on the tongue as a mild buzz. It's all right if the first sip is not hot, as the heat is cumulative. You want to feel it, but you also want to be able to eat the whole bowl of soup and not have to stop for breath after the fourth spoonful. So add the hot pepper flakes gradually. You can always add more, but you can't take them out. If you've gone too far, add more stock and more croutons!

Wine Notes

Pairing Pointers: *Broth-based soups almost always make for difficult wine matches. Here the bitter, pungent, and green elements of the escarole are your best bet. Some alcohol to grab the stock is essential. A lighter red, a dry rosé, or a medium-rich white offer three distinctively different options.*

Categories: 2, 4

Specific Recommendations:

2: *Rosé blends—earthy with spicy fruit—France, Spain, Italy*

4: *Merlot—soft tannin, leafy flavor—Italy, France, USA*

Havuc Corbasi Turkish Carrot Soup

*C*arrot soups can be starchy and overly filling or too pallid to make an impression. This version is wonderfully delicate, light, and creamy, and it is unusual because it doesn't have the added sweetness and depth of cooked onions found in most other recipes. Here everything depends on the carrots and the quality of the stock.

Serves 6

4 tablespoons unsalted butter

1 pound sweet carrots, peeled and sliced or chopped

4 cups water or **stock**

1 teaspoon chopped fresh dill

Salt, pepper, and sugar to taste

1 tablespoon flour

¹/₂ cup milk

2 egg yolks, beaten

Garnish: 3 tablespoons finely chopped toasted walnuts and 3 tablespoons chopped dill or **3 tablespoons chopped mint and 3 tablespoons almonds**

Melt 2 tablespoons of the butter in a saucepan and sauté the carrots over moderate heat until they are well coated with butter. Add 2 cups of the water or stock and the dill, and simmer until the carrots are very soft, 25 to 30 minutes. Puree the carrots in a blender or processor. Return to the saucepan with the remaining stock or water and bring up to a simmer. Taste and add salt, pepper, and sugar as needed.

Meanwhile, melt the remaining butter in a small saucepan and stir in the flour off the heat. Whisk in the milk and stir until smooth. Return to the heat and simmer until the mixture thickens. Remove from the heat and add a bit of the milk mixture to the beaten egg yolks to temper them. Stir the yolks back into the milk mixture. Add some of the hot soup, a bit at a time, to the egg and milk mixture. Then add egg and milk mixture to the hot carrot soup. Whisk well, but do not boil the soup at this point or it will curdle. Adjust the seasoning. Serve at once, topped with chopped toasted walnuts and a bit more dill.

Kitchen Conversation

So, how were your carrots? If they were naturally sweet, garnish the soup with chopped toasted walnuts and a little chopped fresh dill. It will help balance the sweetness. If the carrots were starchy and flat, it's all right to help Mother Nature and add a little sugar to the soup until the carrots taste like springtime. However, don't go overboard and lose the carrot flavor. To add additional sweetness without jeopardizing the carrot taste, use mint and almonds or grated orange zest as your garnish, as they will accent the sweetness without overpowering the carrots.

Wine Notes

Pairing Pointers: *There are two issues here. First, you want to cut the richness of the soup and second, you want to pick up on the inherent sweetness of the preparation. The thicker the soup, the richer the body of wine. A delicate wine will be lost.*

Categories: 1B, 2

Specific Recommendations:

1B: *Rosé/ blends—refreshing snap of sweetness—USA, France ▪ Gewürztraminer—richer, off-dry with ample spice*

2: *Chardonnay—ripe fruit, textured—Australia, Southwest France, USA ▪ Chenin Blanc—fresh, tropical—France, California*

Panada alla Salvia Bread, Onion, and Sage Soup

*P*anada takes its name from pane, *which means bread in Italian. In this soup the bread is a crucial ingredient, not merely a few tiny croutons sprinkled on top as a garnish. Some versions of panada soak the bread in liquid, then whisk it into the broth to make a thick puree. Others bake the layers of bread in the broth for a thickened cakey soup you carve out with a spoon. What is important is that you use good bread, preferably a rustic country loaf that is a bit stale, so that its flavor is more pronounced and because it absorbs more liquid. If you must use fresh bread, toast it in the oven or in the toaster to crisp it and concentrate its flavor. One of my favorite panadas is made with lots of caramelized onions and slightly musky sage. You may choose to layer the soup with slices of bread or toss in lots of cubed croutons, which are easier to spoon up at the table.*

Serves 6

4 tablespoons unsalted butter

6 large onions, sliced thin

1 tablespoon chopped fresh sage

2 tablespoons flour (optional)

5 cups water or **stock**

Salt and freshly ground black pepper

4 thick slices country bread, toasted and cut into 1-inch cubes, about 1 cup per person, or **8 thinner slices stale** or **slightly toasted bread,** as wide as the soup bowl

1/2 cup grated Parmesan or **fontina cheese**

A few sage leaves for garnish

Melt the butter in a large sauté pan and cook the onions, slowly, slowly, over low heat, turning often until they caramelize. This process could take 45 minutes. You want the onions to turn golden but not brown. And you want them to be very sweet. At this point, you may stir in the chopped sage and flour, if using, and cook for 5 minutes. Add the water or stock, cover the pan, and simmer the soup for 30 minutes. Season with salt and pepper.

To serve, put a layer of cubed bread in each bowl. Top with the hot soup and grated cheese. Or layer bread, grated cheese, then soup, bread, cheese, and soup again. Garnish with sage leaves.

Kitchen Conversation

Are the onions really sweet? Can you taste the sage? If not, add a few more chopped sage leaves as garnish at serving time. Does the soup seem bland? Perhaps you need more cheese to add a salty quality.

As a variation, for an earthy bottom tone, you may add 2 cups of sautéed mushrooms to the well-cooked onions. Or 2 cups of diced seeded tomatoes for a sweet-tart accent. Cook for 10 minutes longer until the flavors mingle. Remember that poultry or meat stock makes for a richer, deeper-flavored soup than just water. You could also try making this with chicken. For a nice Renaissance touch, add a pinch of cinnamon when cooking the onions.

For the ultimate panada, see my version of the classic Venetian Sopa Coada (page 232), where cooked pigeon and pigeon broth are layered with the cooked onions, carrots, and celery, the bread and Parmesan cheese, then baked.

Wine Notes

Pairing Pointers: As bread is somewhat of a blank canvas, the wine choices here are dependent on the sage and onions. If the sage is strong, go with a gutsier herbal white. If the onions are sweet, ripe, rich fruit in your wine is essential. If both are the case, find the middle ground! A light red would be daring. As always, some alcohol is needed to grasp the broth.

Categories: 2, 4

Specific Recommendations:

2: *Sauvignon Blanc—herbal and mineral—France, New Zealand* ■ *Chardonnay—more austere, citrusy—France, Italy*

4: *Pinotage—earthy, peppery with forward fruit—South Africa*

Potato, Leek, and Mushroom Soup, Avgolemono

*T*his soup is of Sephardic origin. We serve it at Passover as an alternative to the ubiquitous matzoh ball soup. However, there's no reason to wait for a holiday, as potatoes, leeks, and mushrooms are readily available all year long. The avgolemono thickener that we associate with Greek cuisine is used in many Sephardic dishes as well.

Serves 6 to 8

4 tablespoons olive oil

6 large leeks, cut in half, mostly the white parts, sliced thin, well washed, **about 10 cups**

1 pound mushrooms, sliced thin

4 potatoes, peeled and diced, **about 6 cups**

1 quart Basic Chicken Stock (page 115) or **vegetable stock to cover**

¹/₃ cup chopped dill

Salt and freshly ground black pepper

2 eggs

2 to 3 tablespoons fresh lemon juice

Chopped parsley (optional)

Heat the olive oil in a wide 2-quart saucepan and sauté the leeks over moderate heat, salting once and stirring often until the leeks are tender and have lost most of their sour, rooty quality, 20 to 25 minutes. Add the mushrooms and sauté for 3 to 5 minutes. Then add the potatoes and stock, and bring up to a boil. Reduce the heat and simmer for about 20 minutes. Add half the dill and season with salt and pepper. (You may prepare the soup up to this point and refrigerate. Bring back up to a boil, then reduce to a simmer. It is supposed to be chunky and a bit brothy. If it thickens while sitting, add more stock.) **T**aste the soup. If it is slightly sour, be prepared to cut back on lemon when making the avgolemono mixture, and omit the rest of the dill. Beat the eggs and lemon juice until frothy. Gradually beat a little hot soup into the avgolemono mixture, then return it to the soup. Remove from the heat, add the rest of the dill, if needed, or parsley, if using, and serve at once.

Kitchen Conversation

Watch out that the lemon and dill don't throw the soup out of balance. Before adding the avgolemono mixture, taste the soup and see if the potatoes and mushrooms have softened the sour, rooty quality of the leeks. Sometimes lemons are sweet; sometimes they are really sour. If you want more tartness, you can always add a bit more lemon at the end, but it's hard to get the sour out after you've put it in. Conversely, if you've gone too far and the soup is too tart, use lots of chopped, clean-tasting fresh parsley as a garnish instead of adding the rest of the dill, which has a sour undertone. Be sure to temper the egg mixture with a little hot soup so it doesn't curdle. Once the eggs have been added you cannot reheat the soup.

Wine Notes

Pairing Pointers: *The avgolemono in the soup demands something more austere in nature and the addition of mushrooms mandates some earthy character. Best to stay with white here, and consider lighter reds and rich, dry rosés.*

Categories: 2, 3A, 4

Specific Recommendations:

2: *Rosé/ blends—peasanty, earthy, flavorful—Spain, Italy, France*

3A: *Sauvignon Blanc—rich, olivey, bright—USA, New Zealand*

4: *Sangiovese—moderately rich, tannic—Central Italy*

Leek and Potato Soup with Almonds and Mint

The inspiration for this soup was the same Sephardic recipe for the leek and potato soup on page 94, but minus the earthy mushrooms and the tart avgolemono. Instead, I've taken the soup in the opposite direction and added a classic Spanish accent—sweet almonds. This is a creamy puree rather than a chunky soup. ☞You have two options to play with the almond flavor. You can puree the leek and potato soup, add cream, and top with mint and toasted almonds as a garnish. Or you can bring the cream and the almonds up to a boil, steep, letting the almonds in the cream intensify the almond flavor, and then add this mixture to the soup, reserving just a few almonds as garnish.

Serves 6 to 8

¹/₄ cup unsalted butter

8 large leeks, cut in half, mostly the white parts, sliced ¹/₄ inch thick, well washed

4 potatoes, peeled and diced, **about 6 cups**

1 quart Basic Chicken Stock (page 115)

¹/₂ cup toasted almonds plus a few for garnish

1 cup cream

Freshly grated nutmeg

Salt and freshly ground black pepper

¹/₄ cup chopped fresh mint

Melt the butter in a large saucepan. Add the leeks and sauté over moderate heat, stirring often, until the leeks are tender, about 15 minutes. Add the potatoes and stock, and bring up to a boil. Reduce the heat and simmer until the potatoes are soft. Meanwhile, combine most of the almonds with the cream and bring up to a boil in a small saucepan. Remove from the heat and let rest for 1 hour.

Puree the potato and leek soup along with the almond cream. Adjust the seasoning with salt, pepper, and a pinch of nutmeg. Sprinkle with mint and serve.

Or puree the potato leek soup, add the cream, and sprinkle the soup with almonds and mint.

Kitchen Conversation

The crucial ingredients to counteract the inherent sourness of the leeks are the sweet almonds and cream, and finally the nutmeg, which adds a very important note of sweetness. Using the almonds as a garnish rather than adding them to the cream keeps their toastiness and adds a nice surface sweetness but it is not as deep as when steeped in cream. The mint is an additional sweet accent that gives an illusion of lightness to the rich soup.

Wine Notes

Pairing Pointers: Here we have real texture and a counterbalance of green/tartness from the leeks. While the almonds and mint are nice accents, don't focus your wine match on them unless you really play them up to the point where they take over. Fortified wines are fun too.

Categories: 3A, 3B

Specific Recommendations:

3A: *Semillon/ blends—thick, flavorful, fresh—Australia, Pacific Northwest ■ Pinot Gris—spicy, aromatic, textured—France, Oregon*

3B: *Madeira—medium rich—Verdelho, lighter Boal*

Sopa de Boletos Spanish Wild Mushroom Soup with Prosciutto, Tomatoes, and Thyme

This is based on a recipe for sautéed mushrooms that were so tasty I couldn't resist adding stock and making a savory mushroom soup. If you can find wild mushrooms, or want to splurge on portobellos, the soup will be much more robust-tasting. If all you can find are those plain old white cultivated mushrooms, to add intensity, soak a small handful of dried porcini in hot water for about an hour, strain the cooking liquid into a bowl, rinse the porcini, then chop and add them and their strained liquid to the soup. For a big taste use meat stock, chicken for midrange taste, and vegetable stock for a milder broth but a more mushroomy effect. Prosciutto is more readily available than Spanish Serrano ham and adds a salty dimension, so be careful when seasoning the soup.

Serves 8

4 tablespoons olive oil

2 large onions, chopped

1/2 teaspoon cinnamon

2 cloves garlic, minced (optional)

1 1/2 cups diced tomatoes

1 1/2 pounds mushrooms, preferably brown, sliced if large and quartered if small

2 teaspoons chopped fresh thyme

4 ounces diced prosciutto

4 to 5 cups vegetable, meat, or **Basic Chicken Stock** (page 115), depending upon juiciness of mushrooms

1/2 cup dry sherry

Salt and freshly ground black pepper

1/4 cup chopped parsley or **parsley and thyme**

Toasted bread croutons (optional)

Toasted almonds (optional)

Heat the olive oil in a large saucepan. Add the onions and a dash of salt, and sauté the onions over moderate heat for 5 to 8 minutes. Add the cinnamon, garlic, if using, and tomatoes, and cook over moderate heat, stirring often for 5 minutes longer. Add the mushrooms, thyme, and prosciutto, and sauté for 10 minutes, stirring often until the mush- rooms give off some juices. Add about 4 cups of stock and bring the soup up to a boil. Reduce the heat, simmer for 20 minutes. Add the sherry, salt and pepper, and serve at once. You may ladle this soup over croutons or top simply with chopped pars- ley, or toasted chopped almonds, or both.

Kitchen Conversation

Watch out for the salt. Prosciutto and sherry both add a salty quality. That bit of cinnamon in the onions will soften the salt factor and accent the sweetness of the onions as they mingle with the earthy mushrooms. The slight acidity of the tomatoes will also help contain the salt. To balance the flavors of the soup, choose either sweet toasted almonds or mild bread croutons and herbs.

Wine Notes

Pairing Pointers: The personality of mushrooms usually dominates a dish, and when they are the focal point, well, you get the idea. Dusty red wines, ethnic in nature, are the best bet, as they will mirror the personality of this soup. Watch out for the salt; it can amplify the tannins, so choose a medium-bodied, soft red.

Categories: 4, 5

Specific Recommendations:

4: *Various Spanish—rustic, flavor-packed—Navarra, Valdepeñas*
   ▪ *Various Italian—ditto!—Montepulciano d'Abruzzo, Torgiano*

5: *Pinot Noir—spicy, earthy with medium tannin—USA, France*
   ▪ *Merlot—not too big, greener in flavor—Italy, France*

Lentil and Chestnut Soup

This is one of my favorite winter soups. It comes from the Abruzzo region in Italy, where the winters can be quite severe. Most legume-based soups are hearty, but this one is made elegant by the luxury touch of chestnuts. Their rich sweetness enlivens the starchy lentils and takes this soup to another dimension. Haute bean cuisine.

Serves 4

¹/₂ pound lentils

2 tablespoons pancetta fat or **olive oil**

1 onion, diced

¹/₄ teaspoon cinnamon (optional)

1 bay leaf

1 teaspoon chopped fresh thyme

4 cups water or **vegetable, meat,** or **poultry stock**

2 tablespoons tomato paste

16 cooked chestnuts, coarsely crumbled

Salt and freshly ground black pepper

Fried bread croutons (optional) for garnish

3 tablespoons chopped parsley

1 tablespoon chopped fresh thyme

Soak the lentils in water to cover for a few hours or overnight. Melt the pancetta fat and cook the onion over moderate heat until tender, about 8 minutes, adding salt and a little cinnamon if desired. The cinnamon will play up the sweetness of the onion, pancetta, and chestnuts. Add the lentils, bay leaf, thyme, and water or stock, and bring up to a boil.

Reduce the heat and simmer until the lentils are tender but not falling apart. Add the tomato paste and chestnuts, and simmer for 5 minutes. Season to taste with salt and pepper. Garnish with fried bread croutons, if desired, and chopped parsley and thyme.

Kitchen Conversation

Usually one enlivens a lentil soup with lemon zest or juice, or even chopped raw onion for contrast. In this soup you take another route altogether by adding tender sweet chestnuts to play off the lentils. As a variation you might sauté a few diced carrots along with the onions to play up the sweetness even more. The tomato paste and additional chopped thyme or marjoram will help keep the soup in balance so that it does not become too sweet. Remember to salt again at serving time, as the lentils will absorb the seasoning, and salt helps the chestnuts taste sweeter.

Wine Notes

Pairing Pointers: The tomatoes echo the need for acidity, already in demand because of the starchier nature of both the chestnuts and lentils. The addition of fresh herbs gives a more complex palate to work with, winewise. This soup presents you with a great opportunity to select a wine that you are in the mood to drink, as it doesn't demand center stage.

Category: 5

Specific Recommendations:

5: *Nebbiolo—honest, generous—Italy (Nebbiolo d'Alba, Gattinara)* ■ *Pinot Noir—spicy, moderately complex— France, USA* ■ *Various Portuguese—ethnic, wholesome— Alentejo, Bairrada, Dão*

Cooking Onions

When raw, most onions are sharp and bitter; when they are undercooked, they taste sour and gassy. Not all onions must be cooked to a caramelized sweetness (see page 81), but only until they are softened and have lost that unpleasant gassy taste. To soften the bite of raw onions that are to be used in salads or as a condiment (see Pork Souvlaki, page 266), sprinkle them with salt, let rest for 10 minutes, then rinse. Or marinate them in a little vinaigrette if they are to be used in a salad.

Bezelye Corbasi Turkish Split Pea Soup with Mint and Paprika

T he Turks love all manner of legume-based soups. This hearty pea soup is brightened by the addition of a little chopped spinach, and it is often accompanied by a bowl of yogurt. Both spinach and yogurt are tart, which helps cut the starchiness of the peas.

Serves 4 to 6

8 ounces split peas

2 tablespoons butter

1 onion, thinly sliced

1 carrot, peeled and thinly sliced

1 bay leaf

5 to 6 cups Basic Chicken Stock (page 115) or **water**

3 teaspoons paprika

1/2 pound spinach, well washed and finely chopped

Milk for thinning

1 teaspoon salt

1/2 teaspoon pepper

3 tablespoons chopped mint for garnish

Cover the split peas with cold water. Soak for a few hours or overnight. Drain.

Melt the butter in a saucepan over moderate heat. Cook the onion until soft and translucent, about 10 minutes. Add the split peas, carrot, bay leaf, and stock or water to cover, and bring up to a boil. Simmer, covered, until the peas are very soft. If the mixture seems dry, add more stock or water as needed. Remove the bay leaf. Add the chopped spinach and 2 teaspoons of the paprika, and simmer until the spinach wilts. Puree the soup in the blender or processor. Add the milk, water, or stock to thin. Season with salt and pepper. Serve hot, sprinkle with chopped mint and remaining paprika.

Kitchen Conversation

If the peas are still starchy and the soup seems flat, add a bit of lemon juice. Did you put in enough salt? The soup will absorb salt as it sits and the seasoning will need to be adjusted at serving time. Also, as the soup sits, it will thicken, and you will have to add stock or water so that it doesn't look like glue. Note how the spinach adds a tart undertone and how the mint and paprika add sweetness for an interesting interplay of flavors.

Wine Notes

Pairing Pointers: *All beans and legumes need wines of substance, hence I usually opt for reds. Gamay (specifically Cru Beaujolais) is excellent. Lighter and excitingly simple red wines are my preference. If you go white, choose one that's ample and outgoing, with herbal accents to commingle with the paprika and mint.*

Categories: 2, 5

Specific Recommendations:

2: *Verdejo—zesty, citrusy, and rich—Spain (Rueda)* ▪
       Sauvignon Blanc—aggressive, muscular—France, New Zealand

5: *Gamay—spicy, exuberant, and mineral—France* ▪
       Tempranillo—coarse, flavorful—Spain (Rioja)

Potaje de Garbanzos y Espinacas
Spanish Chick-pea and Spinach Soup

T his hearty soup is quite versatile in that you can serve it as it is or add cooked salt cod, shellfish, or diced ham for an even more filling one-dish meal. The soup is enriched by a picada, a mixture of fried bread and garlic, and is fairly thick. However, if you want it soupier, thin it with broth or water.

Serves 6 to 8

2 cups chick-peas, soaked overnight in cold water

4 cloves garlic plus 2 for the picada

1 medium onion

1 bay leaf

Salt

1 pound spinach

3 tablespoons olive oil

2 slices bread, crusts removed

10 whole almonds (optional)

Pinch saffron filaments, chopped coarsely

Water or **vegetable stock** if needed

Freshly ground black pepper

1/2 pound cooked salt cod, broken up into bite-sized pieces (see page 62) (optional)

1/2 pound cooked shrimp, diced (optional)

1/2 to 1 cup diced cooked ham (optional)

Chopped hard-boiled eggs (optional) for garnish

Drain the chick-peas and cover with fresh cold water. Bring up to a boil. Simmer for 2 minutes. Cover and let sit 1 hour. Drain and cover with fresh cold water. Add 4 cloves of garlic, the onion and the bay leaf, and bring up to a boil. Reduce the heat and simmer for about 45 minutes, or until tender. Add 2 teaspoons salt after 30 minutes of cooking. When the chick-peas are done, remove the onion and garlic and set aside. Discard the bay leaf. Do not drain the chick-peas.

Remove the stems from the spinach and wash well. Drain. Steam for 3 to 4 minutes in the water clinging to the leaves. Chop the cooked spinach coarsely. Set aside.

To make the picada, heat the olive oil in a small sauté pan. Fry the bread, garlic cloves, and almonds, if desired, until golden. Puree in a blender or processor along with the saffron. Add the reserved cooked onion and garlic cloves, 1 cup of chick-pea liquid, and puree until smooth. Add this to the cooked chick-peas along with the wilted spinach. Stir well and bring up to a simmer. If the mixture is too thick, thin with water or vegetable stock. Season to taste with salt and lots of freshly ground black pepper. Add the cod, shrimp, or diced ham, if desired, and garnish with optional chopped eggs.

Kitchen Conversation

The tart spinach adds a nice contrast to the bland chick-peas. All is in the seasoning. If using ham, hold back on the salt, as ham will provide saltiness, as will cooked salt cod. Shrimp and almonds will provide sweetness.

In Portugal this soup is called sopa de grao com espinafres. *The Portuguese do not use picada for thickening; rather, after cooking, half the chick-peas are pureed and the others are left whole. The soup is garnished with chopped fresh coriander for a bitter accent.*

Wine Notes

Pairing Pointers: *This is one of those "meal in a bowl/rib-stickingly rich" soups. I prefer reds with it, although it's certainly a candidate for a richer white. Acid is the key to cut some of the thickness, while the chick-peas demand a wine of body and substance. Keep the salt in the dish in check, although the bigger the seasoning, the more fun you can have with the wine.*

Categories: 3A, 5

Specific Recommendations:

3A: *Grenache Rosé—ample, balanced, and spicy—USA, France* ■ *Sauvignon Blanc—olivy, green, and pungent—France, USA*

5: *Pinot Noir —young and earthy—USA, France* ■ *Zinfandel—moderate, peppery with softer tannins—California*

Roman Lentil Soup with Fish and Hot Pepper

I *first tasted a version of this soup in a Roman seafood restaurant called Il Pellicano. I had never had fish with lentils in a soup, although I have eaten it served with lentils or white beans as an accompaniment. I was intrigued by the combination. This lentil soup takes a turn toward heat. Instead of a meat stock the lentils are cooked in fish stock, and the bite of the hot pepper and sea-scented fish enliven the soup in a very complex way and make it appear lighter than usual. I prefer to use green lentils, as their taste is deeper, but you may use brown. If you don't presoak the lentils, you'll probably need more than 5 cups of stock to achieve a soupy consistency.*

Serves 6

3 tablespoons olive oil

2 onions, chopped

2 stalks celery, chopped

2 cloves garlic, minced

1 teaspoon hot pepper flakes

1 cup diced tomatoes

1 1/2 cups green (or brown) lentils, soaked in water overnight

5 cups Basic Fish Stock (page 114) or **part fish stock and part water** as needed

Salt

Lots of freshly ground black pepper

Pieces of cooked fish (halibut, cod, flounder) or **shellfish,** about 1/4 cup per person

2 cups chopped bitter greens (page 298) (optional)

1/4 cup chopped flat-leaf parsley

Grilled bread croutons

Heat the olive oil in a saucepan. Add the onions and celery, and cook for about 8 minutes until soft. Add the garlic and hot pepper flakes, and cook for 2 minutes. Add the tomatoes, lentils, and fish stock, and bring up to a boil. Reduce heat and simmer, covered, until the lentils are tender, about 30 minutes.

(You could stop now and reheat the soup base at serving time.) Add the cooked fish and greens, if using, and simmer 10 minutes. Adjust the seasoning and serve at once, sprinkled with ample chopped parsley and croutons.

Kitchen Conversation

This is a most interesting challenge in balancing heat elements. You want both the back-of-the-throat heat of hot pepper and the bite of black pepper on the tongue. The tomatoes add acidity to liven the lentils and keep the heat in check, if you feel you've gone too far. But remember that as the soup sits, the salt and heat will mellow as the starchy lentils drink them up. If you've made the soup ahead of time, add the fish and optional greens upon reheating. If you've gone overboard with heat, add grilled bread croutons to the soup at serving time.

If you don't have fish stock on hand, you can use water and clam broth, but the soup won't be quite the same. It will be good, however, and you might be tempted to add steamed clams to this soup instead of fish!

☞ *Note: As a change of pace, try pureeing the soup to experience how it changes: The pureed soup seems sweeter, the tomato flavor more pronounced, and the fish stock diminishes in flavor. You may need to increase the salt and hot pepper as the pureed lentils absorb more seasoning.*

Wine Notes

Pairing Pointers: We could choose two distinctively different wines here. First, a zippy, fresh white or rosé to bring out the sweetness of the fish and cut the heat; or second, a medium-bodied, light-tannin red because the nature of this soup can stand up to it. Both are intriguing options with room to play. The lentils really add texture, thus emphasizing the possibility of going red.

Categories: 1A, 5

Specific Recommendations:

1A: *Muscadet —a "yellow highlighter" of a wine—France* ■ *Pinot Blanc—fresh, floral, lemony—Italy, California*

5: *Carignan/blends—medium in body/tannin, big on flavor— France* ■ *Napa Gamay —exuberant, fresh, flavorful— California*

White Bean Soup with Shellfish and Pesto

*W*hether it's called habas con almejas *or* guazzetto di cozze, *whether you accent it* en espagnol *with mint or* in italiano *with basil, a classic white bean soup augmented with steamed shellfish and their juices makes an interesting, rich first course. The blandness and creaminess of the beans are piqued by the saltiness of the sea and the slight acidity of the tomatoes. If you are feeling extravagant (or semiextravagant and want to stretch two lobsters to feed four), you could make this soup with lobster. However, clams and mussels are so much more affordable and easier to prepare. If you increase the amount of shellfish, this can become a meal in a bowl. Serve with grilled bread croutons.*

Serves 4

1 cup white beans	**1 tablespoon finely minced garlic**
1 onion	**2 cups diced, peeled, seeded tomatoes**
1 bay leaf	**1 cup white wine,** or as needed
2 cloves garlic	**2 pounds mussels** or **clams,** well scrubbed (allow about 8 mussels or 12 clams per person)
2 tablespoons olive oil	**Basic Fish Stock** (page 114) or **water** as needed
2 cups chopped onions	**Basil Pesto**
Pinch hot pepper (optional)	

Cover the white beans with 4 cups cold water and bring up to a boil. Simmer for 2 minutes. Cover and let sit for an hour. Drain and put in a saucepan with cold water to cover by about 2 inches. Add the whole onion, garlic, and bay leaf, and bring up to a boil. Reduce the heat, add salt, and simmer until the beans are tender but not falling apart. Remove the onion, garlic, and bay leaf, and set the beans aside with their liquids.

Heat the olive oil in a saucepan and add the chopped onions. Cook over moderate heat for 10 minutes until tender; add the garlic and a pinch of hot pepper, if you like, and cook a minute longer. Add the tomatoes and the white beans and their liquids, and simmer for 2 minutes. Set aside.

Put the shellfish in a pan with an inch or two of white wine. Bring to a boil, cover the pan, and steam until the shellfish open. Remove the shellfish to a bowl. Strain the pan juices and add to the soup pot. Remove the clams or mussels from the shells and discard the shells and mussel beards. Heat the beans and add the shellfish. Adjust the seasoning. Thin with stock or water if needed. Serve with a dollop of pesto.

Basil Pesto

4 cups basil leaves, tightly packed

4 teaspoons finely minced garlic

4 tablespoons toasted pine nuts

1 teaspoon salt

$^1/_2$ teaspoon freshly ground black pepper

$1^1/_2$ cups pure olive oil

Put the basil, garlic, and pine nuts in the processor. Pulse to combine. Add the salt, pepper, and gradually add olive oil until you have a green rough puree. (If using this on pasta, add Parmesan cheese.)

Kitchen Conversation

Please remember that clams are salty but mussels are sweet. They will affect how you season the beans. The wine and tomatoes in the soup brighten the blandness of the beans and add a slightly sour element. The cheeseless pesto adds an herbaceous sweetness that brightens the beans and adds depth to the high notes of tomato and wine. Besides the lentil and fish soup (page 106) there is another variation on this combination of seafood and beans. If you cut back on the broth and increase the beans you have a Portuguese seafood stew, Feijoada de Mariscos *(page 210).*

Wine Notes

Pairing Pointers: *A better showcase for a medium-bodied and moderately pungent white wine hasn't come my way yet! The beans add a creamy richness, the shellfish a salty-sweet character, and the pesto a lovely green backdrop. Go to town here. Just keep the oak in check: A little is okay, too much will dominate.*

Category: 2B

Specific Recommendations:

2B: *Chardonnay—steely, gravelly, and lightly oaked—France, Spain* ■ *Sauvignon Blanc—rich, herbal/aromatic—USA (California, Washington State)* ■ *Cortese—youthful, lean, and assertive—Italy*

Greek-Inspired Mussel Soup

*A*nother brothy soup that gets better the more bread croutons you add. The sweet mussels blend well with the anise-scented ouzo, and the subtle bite of garlic is absorbed by the toasted bread. You need a good fish stock for this soup.

Serves 4

2 tablespoons olive oil

3 cups chopped onions

2 cloves garlic, finely minced

Pinch hot pepper flakes (optional)

2 pounds mussels, well scrubbed and debearded, 2 cups after shelling

3^1/$_2$ cups Basic Fish Stock (page 114)

^{1}/$_4$ cup ouzo

Salt and freshly ground black pepper

3^1/$_2$-inch slices Italian bread, grilled or toasted, crusts removed

^{1}/$_4$ cup chopped dill or parsley

Warm the olive oil in a large, deep sauté pan or saucepan. Cook the onions over moderate heat until tender, sweet, and translucent, about 15 minutes. Add the garlic and hot pepper flakes, if desired, and cook for 2 minutes. Add the mussels and 1 cup of the fish stock, and cover the pan. Steam over high heat until the mussels open. Remove the mussels from the pan with a slotted spoon. Remove the mussels from the shells and take off any beards that may have remained.

Add the remaining fish stock and the ouzo to the mussel liquids and bring to a boil. Simmer for 3 minutes and then adjust seasoning. Add the mussels back to the hot broth to warm through for a minute or two. Season with salt and freshly ground black pepper.

Cube the grilled bread and place in 6 soup bowls. Ladle the mussel soup over the bread cubes and sprinkle the soup with chopped herbs.

☛Note: 1^1/$_2$ cups diced chopped tomatoes may be added along with the fish stock.

Kitchen Conversation

This soup is primarily sweet unless you have been more than generous with that pinch of heat, or if the garlic was particularly pungent. If you have added tomatoes, you'll find that they cut the sweetness with their natural acidity. A pleasant soup, tasting of the sea with an anise undertone. The chopped herbs give it a clean freshness.

Wine Notes

Pairing Pointers: *I find mussels to be both easy and difficult to match. Easy in that one can go in so many directions: white, rosé, sparkling, or even red. However, if the shellfish is fishy, beware of red because it will taste like a tin can or excessive oak. With this variation, I prefer dry rosé and light to medium-bodied white wines.*

Categories: 1A, 2

Specific Recommendations:

1A: *Riesling—dry, zesty, sharp—Austria, Germany* ■ *Prosecco—simple and scented—Italy*

2: *Rosé/blends—lively, spicy, moderately rich—France, Spain, Italy* ■ *White/blends—earthy, spritzy—Italy (Verdicchio), Spain (Penedès)*

Yesil Domates Corbasi Turkish Cold Green Tomato Soup

The name was so intriguing I couldn't wait to taste this soup from the Aegean region of Turkey. It was amazing. The texture was rich and creamy, as if yogurt or cream had been beaten into it. The chef assured me that it was just pureed tomatoes, stock, and not much else. As green tomatoes are high in pectin, they emulsify in the blender. Sort of a tart green gazpacho with no tomato sweetness. I had no actual recipe, so this soup is the result of testing and tasting. P.S. It needs the yogurt!

Serves 6

3 pounds green tomatoes, skinned, seeded, and chopped

2 cups Basic Chicken Stock (page 114)

4 tablespoons yogurt

Salt and freshly ground black pepper

Fresh lemon juice to taste

1/2 cup thinly sliced sweet red bell pepper, soup-spoon length

1/4 cup chopped fresh dill

Crumbled feta or **grated tulumi cheese** (optional)

Coarsely chop the tomatoes. Heat the tomatoes in the chicken stock, covered, for 6 minutes. Puree in a blender or food processor with the yogurt. Season with salt and pepper. Chill the soup. Taste and add lemon juice if needed. Garnish with slivers of sweet red pepper, chopped dill, and crumbled cheese if desired.

☛Note: To remove skin on tomatoes, cut a cross on the bottom of each tomato, dip in boiling water for a minute, then peel off skin. If it doesn't come off easily use a knife to peel.

Kitchen Conversation

This is a tricky soup, not because it is difficult to prepare but because everything is riding on the flavor of the tomatoes. They are naturally tart, but the soup may need an added jolt of acidity to taste "right." Yogurt may not be enough, so balance this with a bit of lemon juice if needed.

Crumbled salty feta may also help the flavor balance. Conversely, if the soup is too sharp, add a little milk, which is sweeter than yogurt. The slivers of red pepper lend relief and color.

Wine Notes

Pairing Pointers: *Simple, tart, and unoaked are the three key words here. The nature of the tomatoes and dill demands a wine that virtually mirrors their distinct tart green personality. I recommend working in a narrow wine-palate range here. Sparkling wines of a more austere nature are not a bad choice.*

Category: 1A

Specific Recommendations:

1A: *Brut Champagne sparkling—clean, bright (Chardonnay based)—USA* ■ *Arneis—young, vivid, and aromatic—Italy* ■ *Müller-Thurgau—flinty, austere—Austria, Germany, Oregon*

Basic Stocks
Basic Fish Stock

You can't buy fish stock in a can. So why not make some and keep it in the freezer? Most fish stews and many sauces will profit from your efforts. Really, it's better than bottled clam juice mixed with chicken stock any day.

Makes about 3 quarts

6 to 8 pounds fish frames (bones, heads, tails, with gills removed) (use snapper, rockfish, halibut, sea bass, but no strong-flavored fish)

Water to cover, about 2 quarts

3 cups white wine

3 to 4 medium onions, chopped

5 stalks celery, chopped

1 large bay leaf

4 strips lemon zest

10 black peppercorns

4 whole coriander seeds

3 whole allspice

5 sprigs parsley

2 sprigs thyme

1 red pepper pod (optional)

Wash the fish bones well.

Bring the water, wine, all of the vegetables, spices, and herbs up to a boil in a large stockpot.

Add the clean fish frames and bring all back up to a boil. Reduce the heat to a simmer. Skim often. Simmer for only 20 minutes.

Strain through a colander lined with wet cheesecloth.

Chill in an ice bath, uncovered, until cold. You may freeze the stock, of course.

Basic Chicken Stock

*I*n case you want to make your own stock instead of using canned chicken broth, here is a simple recipe. And I applaud your efforts!

Makes about 4 quarts light stock

6 pounds chicken pieces (necks, backs, carcasses, thighs)

Water to cover

2 medium onions, coarsely chopped

2 small carrots, coarsely chopped

1 large stalk celery, chopped

3 sprigs parsley

6 peppercorns

2 sprigs thyme

1 small bay leaf

2 leeks, greens only, chopped (optional)

2 garlic cloves (optional)

Wash the chicken parts, then put them in a large stockpot, and cover them with cold water. Bring up to a boil. Lower the heat. Skim the scum off the top of the pot. Simmer for an hour, then add the vegetables, herbs, spices, and optional leek greens and garlic, and simmer slowly for 4 to 5 hours. Remove the solids with a slotted spoon or Chinese skimmer. Pour the stock through a cheesecloth-lined strainer. Chill the stock in an ice bath. (Do not cover until it is completely cold.) Degrease. This is a basic light chicken stock. You should have about 4 quarts. To increase the stock's flavor, put it in a pot, bring it up to a boil, and cook at a low boil, skimming if needed, until the stock is reduced by half. Chill again.

☛Note: You see that there is no salt in this recipe. That is because if you salt it and later reduce the stock it will become really salty. Salt the stock only at serving time.

Duck Stock

While you can use chicken stock for the duck recipes, duck stock makes for a richer sauce. If duck is one of your favorite birds and you prepare it often, then this stock should be an integral part of your pantry. It keeps well in the freezer for many months.

Makes about 2 quarts

Carcasses, necks, wings and feet of 2 ducks

2 small onions, chopped

4 carrots, chopped

1 to 2 leeks, chopped

2 cloves garlic, smashed with a cleaver

8 black peppercorns, bruised

8 sprigs parsley

2 sprigs thyme

1/2 bay leaf

Water to cover

Preheat the oven to 450 degrees.

Break up the duck carcasses and place all the bones in a roasting pan. Brown in the oven for about 20 minutes. Add the bones to a stockpot and cover with water. Bring up to a boil and skim. Reduce the heat to a simmer. Drain most of the fat from the roasting pan and brown the vegetables either in the oven or on top of the stove until the vegetables are also browned but not scorched. This will take about 30 minutes in the oven, and maybe a little less time on top of the stove.

Add the vegetables to the stockpot, deglaze the roasting pan with water, and scrape up all of the brown bits and add them to the stockpot. Add the spices and herbs, and simmer for 6 hours. Strain the stock. (If you like, reduce the stock by half for greater strength.) Chill well in an ice bath, uncovered. Degrease. Refrigerate or freeze.

Lamb Stock

Most home cooks look at us in slight bewilderment when we tell them to add lamb stock to a dish. But this is the reason our lamb stews taste so good. If you love lamb stew or want a rich jus for leg of lamb, you'll be happy to have this stock in your freezer. You may reduce it for greater flavor intensity.

Makes about 5 quarts

6 pounds meaty lamb shanks

2 medium onions, chopped

3 carrots, chopped

1 stalk celery, chopped

6 sprigs parsley

2 sprigs thyme

3 cloves garlic, smashed

2 small bay leaves

2 cloves

10 black peppercorns

3 tomatoes, sliced

Water to cover

Preheat the oven to 450 degrees.

Place the shanks in a large roasting pan and brown them in the oven for about an hour and a half. Add the bones and meat to the stockpot and cover with water. Bring up to a boil, skim, and reduce to a simmer. Skim often for the first half hour.

Drain most of the fat from the roasting pan. Then add the vegetables (except the tomatoes) and cook them until they are caramelized, in the oven or on top of the stove. Add the vegetables to the stockpot. Deglaze the pan with water. Add the herbs, spices, and tomatoes, and continue to simmer for at least 8 hours. Strain through a cheesecloth-lined colander. Chill well in an ice bath, uncovered. Degrease. Reduce, if desired. Refrigerate or freeze.

PASTA
RICE & GRAINS

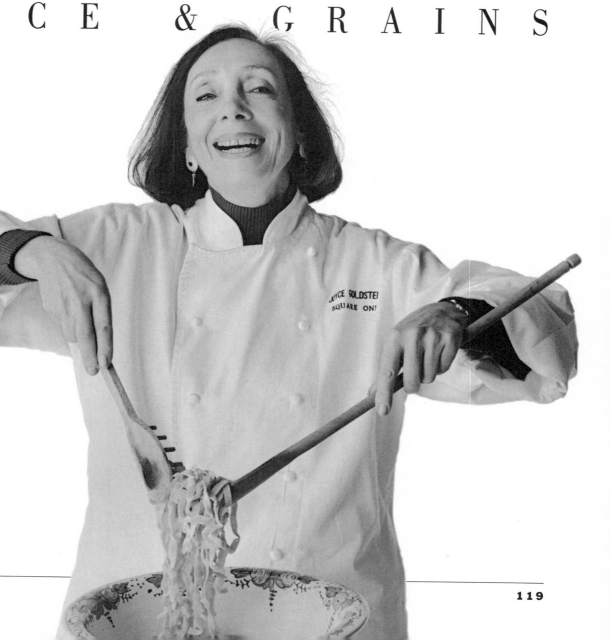

PASTA, RICE & GRAINS

Grains form the basis of the Mediterranean diet and are usually the center of the plate. Whether they come in the form of pasta, rice, wheat, or polenta, grains are not only economical and filling but truly satisfying. If you are on a budget or trying to cut back on cholesterol, a little meat or poultry or shellfish can go a long way if added judiciously to a grain dish. One really doesn't need to eat a 16-ounce piece of meat or an 8-ounce piece of fish to feel happy and nourished. Ask anyone who has fallen in love with pasta, risotto, or pilaf. In fact, these are the recipes you will find yourself cooking over and over again. They are simple, fast, and have become the true comfort food of the nineties.

There is a certain irony in the concept of simplicity in cooking. The "simplest" dishes usually are the hardest to achieve. They are dependent upon using the finest-quality raw materials and real finesse in execution. As a chef I find finesse hard to teach or explain. It is refinement of execution. Finesse is the result of paying attention to the most minute details. Nowhere does this quality of execution stand out more clearly than in making salads and cooking pasta. Making salads and pasta is equally simple and complex at the same time. Artless and artful.

If the noodles are homemade, the dough might be overworked or too soft. The noodles can be tender, tough, or as silken as a baby's skin. They can be cooked perfectly or just under or over. The pasta may absorb too much sauce or resist its cling. There can be too much sauce, or too little. Because pasta is starchy and bland, the seasoning of the sauce is crucial. What may taste perfectly balanced in the saucepan can be annihilated by a mass of carbohydrates. That's why food in Italian restaurants can be good one day and poor the next.

To achieve pasta nirvana, much attention to detail needs to be paid. Then you'll understand why after Americans visit Italy, they come back babbling about a simple little fresh pasta with peas, butter, and cheese. But what noodles! What peas! What butter! What cheese! They all were the best quality and were cooked perfectly. Not a complicated recipe but one that required finesse. Artless and artful. The same holds true with cooking rice and grains. Soggy rice, its grains limp and sticky or so overcooked that they turn to mush in your mouth, does not make a pilaf or risotto to remember. Texture is as crucial as taste. Here are my favorite pasta dishes, risotti, and risotto pancakes; rice pilafs, barley, and wheat; two gnocchi recipes; and one scrumptious polenta.

Orecchiette with Sausage, White Beans, Tomatoes, and Fennel

Fennel seed–scented sausage, accented by sweet fresh fennel, combines with white beans and tomato sauce for a very filling and flavorful pasta. I have chosen orecchiette for this dish, but any shell-shaped pasta will cradle the beans.

Serves 4

1 pound orecchiette or **medium shells**

1 pound fennel sausage, removed from casings

4 tablespoons olive oil

4 cups onions, diced (cooks down to 1½ cups)

1 cup fennel, diced

1 cup cooked white beans (page 208)

2 cups diced plum tomatoes

½ cup chopped mint or **basil**

Bring a large pot of salted water to a boil.

Form the sausage into tiny balls and brown them in a large sauté pan over high heat in 2 tablespoons of the olive oil. Set aside. Drop the orecchiette in the water. Stir once.

Add the remaining oil to the pan and cook the onions over moderate heat until the onions are tender and translucent. Add the fennel and cook for 3 minutes longer. Add the white beans, tomatoes, sausage, and mint or basil and heat through. Cook the orecchiette al dente and drain. Toss with the sausage sauce. Serve at once.

Kitchen Conversation

This is a satisfying meal in a bowl: The beans and sausage are robust and filling, and the tomatoes are just a vehicle to move them around. Be sure to salt the beans and the pasta water or this dish could be too bland. And don't overcook the fresh fennel. It should still have some crunch. Long cooking diminishes fennel's anise flavor. Either mint or basil is sweetly aromatic. Just pick the herb you're in the mood for. If you want to add a bit of garlic, go ahead, but do it after you taste the sausage, as it may be sufficiently garlicky.

Wine Notes

Pairing Pointers: Although you need a rib-sticking red to stand up to this hearty pasta, make certain that the tannins are not of the Arnold Schwarzenegger school. You want firm but not astringent tannins.

Categories: 5, 6

Specific Recommendations:

5: Nebbiolo —medium full, packed with fruit, medium tannin ■
Zinfandel—brambly, supple, and fairly rich—USA

6: Sangiovese —richer style à la Chianti Riserva, Brunello ■
Various Portuguese—rustic and earthy—Dão, Douro

Pasta con Polpette alla Leccese
Pasta with Little Meatballs from Lecce

*M*any years ago spaghetti and meatballs reigned supreme in the average Italian-American home and restaurant. Then this satisfying dish fell into disfavor. Perhaps this resulted from the misguided conception that it should be a one-pound meatball nesting in the middle of a pile of red-sauced noodles, or from the avid campaign launched by Italo-authenticists who insisted that this dish was a purely American invention. The fact is, the pasta and meatballs didn't come from out of nowhere; it was part of a real Italian tradition that, alas, had gone awry due to the American obsession with big meat portions. In Apulia pasta with tiny meatballs, polpette, *is a classic. The meatballs are flavored with salty pecorino cheese and are tossed in a mild tomato sauce with additional pecorino.*

Serves 4

Meatballs

1/2 pound ground pork or **veal** or **a combination of the two**

2 slices stale bread, soaked in water and crumbled

1 clove garlic, finely minced

3 tablespoons chopped parsley

3 tablespoons grated pecorino cheese

Salt and freshly ground black pepper as needed

3 tablespoons olive oil

1 onion, chopped

1/2 cup white wine

2 cups tomato sauce

4 large basil leaves, chopped

1 pound dry pasta, such as orecchiette, penne, rigatoni, or shells

1/2 cup grated pecorino cheese

In a bowl combine the ground meats with the next five ingredients and gently form into tiny meatballs the size of a hazelnut, not a walnut. Brown them over high heat in olive oil in a large sauté pan. Set aside. To the oil remaining in the pan add the chopped onion and cook over moderate heat for 8 minutes. Add the white wine along with the tomato sauce and the basil, and simmer over low heat for 20 minutes. Add the meatballs to the sauce and simmer for 10 minutes longer.

Cook the pasta until al dente. Toss with the sauce and lots of pecorino cheese. Serve at once. Please make sure everyone gets at least 5 meatballs.

Kitchen Conversation

Quite a difference from the old days! These meatballs are light in texture (especially if you don't overhandle them) and mild in flavor; the pork is sweeter than the veal. In fact, the meatballs appear, dare we say it?, delicate, and they mingle well with the pasta. The sauce is not a swimming pool for noodles but a light coating. The acid of the wine and tomatoes and the salt of the cheese are equally matched in intensity. Basil adds a subtle counterpoint of sweetness.

Wine Notes

Pairing Pointers: *Tomato-based sauces will usually dominate the personality of whatever they are served with, and this dish, despite the meatballs, is no exception. Tomatoes demand acidity, and with the addition of meat, one should select a wine with some substance and light tannin. If the basil is a major player, look to pick up on the leafy notes.*

Category: 5

Specific Recommendations:

5: *Sangiovese—the classic match, straightforward, balanced—Italy* ■ *Pinot Noir—exuberant and spicy—Italy, France, USA* ■ *Cabernet Franc—sharp, structured, and herbal scented—France, USA*

Spaghetti "al Testaccio" with Pancetta, Pepper, and Peas

Testaccio is a Roman neighborhood that used to be filled with slaughterhouses. Not surprisingly, in this quartiere most of the restaurants specialize in grilled and roast meats, innards, and hearty stews. This pasta, sometimes called spaghetti alla gricia, is a precursor to the classic spaghetti carbonara but minus the eggs. It is usually made with guanciale, pig's cheek, but as we cannot get this cut of cured meat, pancetta is our best choice. Although they are not traditional to alla gricia, I have added the peas because the balance of meat, pepper, and peas pleases me and reminds me of Rome in the spring.

Serves 4

1 pound spaghetti or **bucatini**

6 tablespoons olive oil

¹/₂ pound pancetta, about ¹/₄ inch thick, cut in ¹/₄-inch strips

1 cup peas, blanched, but cooked long enough to taste sweet

4 to 6 teaspoons freshly ground black pepper

8 tablespoons grated pecorino cheese

Drop the pasta in boiling salted water.

Warm the olive oil in a medium sauté pan over moderate heat. Cook the pancetta, stirring often, until tender but not at all crispy. Add the peas and pepper.

Cook the pasta al dente and drain. Toss with the pancetta and peas. Remove from the heat and add the pecorino cheese. Serve at once.

Kitchen Conversation

Don't be afraid of pepper. It is the needed counterpoint to the salty pecorino and the sweetness of the peas and pancetta. There is not much "sauce" to this pasta, but the ingredients will cling and mingle with the noodles quite well. You might want to try this with penne or rigatoni just to see what happens with a slightly heftier pasta. Between the pancetta and the pecorino, no salt is needed for this dish.

Wine Notes

Pairing Pointers: *The combination of salt (pancetta and pecorino) and fat (pancetta) creates a need for sharpness (acidity). Select a fruity or soft red. Be leery of reds with tannin as they will only accentuate the salt and make for an unpleasant commingling. Here, too, I like whites of a more autumnal nature.*

Categories: 2, 5

Specific Recommendations:

2: *Vernaccia—nutty, mature, and minerally* ■ *Rosé/blends— peppery, floral, and a tad bitter—France, Italy*

5: *Dolcetto—youthful, honest, and crisp—Italy, California* ■ *Merlot—soft, fragrant, and free of bitter tannin—Italy, France*

Garlic

Just because a dish is Italian or a pasta doesn't mean it must have garlic as an ingredient. Garlic is a powerful taste component and introducing it at random may upset the balance of flavors in a dish. For example, in Spaghetti "al Testaccio" garlic would ruin the delicate balance between the bitter black pepper, the salty cheese, and the sweet pancetta. It would tip the scale to bitter and ruin the harmony of a delicate trio.

To mitigate the bitterness of garlic, cook it in water, broth, or milk until it is meltingly tender. Or cover it with olive oil and simmer gently or bake until soft.

There are times when the bite of raw garlic actually gives bottom to a dish that seems to be floating on too many high notes. But be careful. It can add a note of heat that will revisit you for the rest of the day.

Tagliarini with Smooshed Broccoli, Toasted Pine Nuts, and Pecorino

*T*his pasta is so simple and satisfying that you will become addicted to it. I ate it in Rome and tried to reproduce it using our broccoli, but I couldn't get the same results in taste or color. In Rome they use an ancient variety of broccoli called romanesco *that is light green in hue, and whose head is shaped like a cluster of pointy florets. Broccoli* romanesco *is being cultivated in California, but is not yet widely available. To achieve the right color and taste, I have combined broccoflower, a cross between cauliflower and broccoli, and regular dark green broccoli. The color of the puree is a lovely pale green. If you can't get or make fresh tagliarini, use a narrow fettuccine. However, the texture of a fresh noodle is important for balance. Calling the broccoli "smooshed" rather than pureed has made this dish quite endearing to our guests. It could become one of your favorites too.*

Serves 4

1 head broccoflower (a cross between cauliflower and broccoli), 2 cups florets

1 head broccoli, 2 cups florets

1 cup Basic Chicken Stock (page 115) or **vegetable stock**

3 tablespoons olive oil

Salt and freshly ground black pepper

1 pound fresh tagliarini or **fresh fettuccine**

1/2 cup toasted pine nuts

Cook the broccoflower florets in a large pot of salted water until very soft. Drain and reserve some of the cooking liquid. Pulse in a processor until almost pureed, using the cooking liquids if needed. Set aside.

Cook the broccoli florets in salted water until very soft. Remove them with a slotted spoon and transfer to a blender or processor and process until a puree forms. Add enough cooking liquids as needed for smoothness and thinness. Combine the two purees. Warm them over low heat in a large sauté pan with the stock and olive oil. Season with salt and pepper. Cook the pasta until tender. Toss with the broccoli sauce. Top each portion with toasted pine nuts, a grinding of black pepper, and grated pecorino cheese.

Kitchen Conversation

If I'd told you that pureed broccoli made a great pasta sauce, you'd have scoffed and said it was baby food. But it's pretty delicious, isn't it? The pine nuts add sweetness and the pecorino adds salt to make the "smooshed" broccoli sing with round flavor.

Wine Notes

Pairing Pointers: *A favorite of my daughter Elena, although she prefers it with current vintage water! This white wine–leaning dish has several pungent elements—lightly bitter broccoli and salty cheese—that scream for a more austere selection. While one wants personality, don't overdo it; the charm of this dish is in its simplicity.*

Category: 2

Specific Recommendations:

2: *Chardonnay—dry, unoaked, and steely—France, Italy* ■ *Cortese—an archetypal example—clean, flinty, and floral—Italy* ■ *Rosé/blends—fresh, balanced, and earthy—France, Spain*

Ciceri e Tria (Pasta e Ceci) Fresh Pasta with Chick-peas from Apulia

*M*ost of us think of pasta e ceci *(a variation on* pasta e fagioli*) as the ultimate peasant dish. It is a meal served in a bowl—not a pasta, not a soup, but something in between. In Apulia the combination of pasta and chick-peas is given a rather novel twist. The cooked chick-peas are pureed, tossed with fresh noodles, and then the pasta is topped with some of the noodles that have been fried until crisp. The creamy-crunchy combination is quite appealing. However, the flavor may seem a little bland, a stoic comfort food. So, my variation on this theme is to add hot pepper, garlic, and wilted arugula. This gives the dish hot and bitter components. For additional texture, don't puree all of the chick-peas. Why not leave some to bob around in the savory mix?*

Serves 4

1¹/₂ cups chick-peas

1 large onion, diced

2 cloves garlic, chopped

2 carrots, peeled and chopped

3 stalks celery, chopped

1 bay leaf

Salt and freshly ground black pepper

Extra virgin olive oil

²/₃ cup olive oil or as needed

1 tablespoon finely minced garlic

2 teaspoons hot pepper flakes

1 pound fresh tagliarini

6 cups arugula, chopped coarsely

¹/₄ cup grated pecorino cheese

Soak the chick-peas in cold water overnight in the refrigerator. Drain and rinse. Put the chick-peas in a medium saucepan and cover with 5 cups cold water. Bring up to a boil. Simmer for 2 minutes. Let rest for 1 hour. Drain and cover with fresh cold water. Add the diced onion, garlic, carrots, celery, and bay leaf, and bring up to a boil. Reduce the heat and simmer, covered, until the chick-peas are very tender, about 1 to 1¹/₂ hours. Add salt to taste during the last 30 minutes of simmering. Remove the bay leaf and set 1 cup of the chick-peas aside. Toss with a bit of extra virgin olive oil. Puree the rest of the chick-peas with their liquids. The mixture should be quite soupy. Season with salt and pepper and a splash of extra virgin olive oil.

If you've made this ahead of time, add water and oil to thin the sauce and adjust the salt before tossing with the pasta.

Warm 2 tablespoons of the olive oil in a large sauté pan. Add the garlic and hot pepper flakes, and cook over low heat for a few minutes. Toss in the arugula and wilt it quickly in the oil. Return the reserved whole chick-peas to the pan along with the chick-pea puree. Bring up to a simmer. Season to taste with salt and pepper. If it seems too thick, add a bit of water or stock.

Heat $1/2$ cup pure olive oil in another pan and fry about 4 ounces of the fresh tagliarini noodles, which have been cut into shorter lengths, until they become crunchy and golden brown. Drain and set aside.

Bring a large pot of salted water to a boil and quickly cook the fresh pasta until tender. Toss with the sauce, distribute in 4 bowls, and sprinkle with the fried noodles, which have been broken up into smaller pieces. Sprinkle with grated pecorino cheese. Serve at once.

Variation: Some Pugliese versions of this dish cook the noodles directly in the chick-pea puree. Others brown the noodles along with the garlic and hot pepper flakes, then add them to the puree. In yet another variation, for additional texture, you could sauté some chopped onion and celery, about 1 cup of each, before cooking the garlic and hot pepper.

Kitchen Conversation

The mixture of just plain chick-pea puree and fresh noodles is comfort food at its best, but the combination lacks punch and certainly would be a hard sell to those of us for whom this is not mother's milk. Although it's not traditional, I like the mouthfeel of some whole chick-peas mixed with the crunchy noodles. And the hot pepper, garlic, and greens add a bitterness that spikes the blandness of chick-pea soup and noodles. In case you were wondering why use fresh tagliarini, I've tried this with dry pasta and the sauce falls off. You need the porous fresh noodle for the sauce to cling. Fettuccine are too wide; combined with the chick-pea sauce, they make for a dish that is too heavy. The pecorino is crucial; it adds the saltiness that puts the whole dish into balance.

Wine Notes

Pairing Pointers: *Thick and textured, this "pasta" is the ultimate blank canvas. Whether you add arugula or any other green, it, along with a touch of heat from the capsicum, will lead the way. Ample tartness to counterbalance the richness and cut the acid is critical.*

Categories: 1A, 5

Specific Recommendations:

1A: *Arneis or Tocai—zesty, unoaked, and spritzy—Italy* ■ *Pinot Blanc—ditto in personality—Italy, France, USA*

5: *Barbera—bright, raw, and jammed with fruit—USA, Italy* ■ *Tempranillo—minimal oak, tart fruit, and soft tannin—Spain*

Pasta with Shrimp, White Beans, Greens, and Bread Crumbs

*T*his delicious dish can be made with shells, penne, or orecchiette, any shape of pasta that will trap the white beans and the sauce. The shrimp and white beans can be prepared well ahead, refrigerated, and brought to room temperature at cooking time. The toasted bread crumbs can be prepared a day or two before and kept in an airtight container.

Serves 4

1/2 cup white beans

Salt

5 tablespoons olive oil

White wine or water just to cover the shrimp

1/2 to 2/3 pound medium shrimp, shelled and deveined

1 pound pasta (shells, penne, orecchiette)

3 tablespoons finely minced garlic

8 cups escarole or **arugula,** cut into 1/2-inch strips

2 teaspoons grated lemon zest, kept moist in a little lemon juice

2 cups drained, diced canned plum tomatoes (optional)

1 cup Toasted Bread Crumbs (page 133)

Salt and freshly ground black pepper to taste

It is preferable to omit overnight soaking of the beans in order to de-gas them. Cover the beans with cold water, bring up to a boil, boil for 2 minutes, let rest covered for an hour, drain, and then cook in fresh water until tender but not soft, 45 to 60 minutes. Add 2 teaspoons salt during the last 15 minutes of cooking time. Drain the cooked beans and transfer to a bowl. Toss with 1 tablespoon of the olive oil and set aside.

Bring the white wine or water up to a simmer in a wide sauté pan. Add the shrimp and cook until pink, 3 to 4 minutes. Remove with a slotted spoon and reserve the cooking liquids. Refrigerate the shrimp if you are not using them within a half hour.

Bring a large pot of water up to a boil. Add salt and drop in the pasta. Stir well.

While the pasta is cooking, warm the remaining olive oil in a large sauté pan over low heat. Add the garlic and cook for 2 minutes. Add the greens and a few tablespoons of the shrimp cooking liquids, raise the heat to moderately high, and stir until the greens are wilted. Toss in the shrimp, white beans, lemon zest, and tomatoes if using. Add half the bread crumbs and warm through. Season with salt and pepper to taste. Transfer to a warm, deep serving bowl. Drain the pasta when it is al dente and toss with the prawns and greens. Top with the remaining bread crumbs. Serve at once.

Toasted Bread Crumbs

2 cups fresh Italian or **French bread,** cut in cubes, crusts removed

1 teaspoon salt

1 teaspoon freshly ground black pepper

$1/2$ cup olive oil

Preheat the oven to 350 degrees. Pulse the bread cubes in a food processor to make coarse crumbs. Spread on a baking sheet. Stir salt and pepper into the oil and drizzle over the bread crumbs. Bake, stirring occasionally, until golden and crispy but not hard, 15 to 20 minutes.

Kitchen Conversation

In the Mediterranean, bread is sacred. Nary a piece goes to waste. Therefore, it should come as no surprise that bread crumbs are used to thicken soups and, in this case, added to pasta for crunch. The sweet shrimp pair well with the mildly bitter greens, the toasty bread crumbs, and creamy mild beans. A key ingredient is the lemon zest, which adds a bright note and cuts through the starchy beans. Remember to salt enough. Most foods from the sea need salt to taste their best. Taste the tomatoes if you decide to use them. If they are tart, cut back on lemon. And see if they need a pinch of sugar to round out their flavor. Instead of shrimp, you can make this with scallops or tuna. For a vegetarian variation, omit seafood altogether and increase the garlic and tomatoes. Grated lemon zest is an important accent in either case, but especially with the shrimp or tuna. And if you've used fish or seafood, no cheese, please.

Wine Notes

Pairing Pointers: *Select a wine that will bring out the sweetness of the shrimp and the pleasant, bitter edge of the greens, while cutting the creaminess of the beans and providing a playful foil to the bread crumbs. I prefer whites and light rosés with this pasta.*

Category: 1A

Specific Recommendations:

1A: *Other Italian—so many possibilities—Verdicchio, Frascati, etc.* ▪ *Rosé/blends—light, balanced, and dry—USA, Italy, France* ▪ *Prosecco and Italian sparkling—a wonderful match, very fresh*

Pasta con Cozze o Vongole e Rughetta Pasta with Mussels or Clams and Arugula

*T*his pasta is part of a long Italian tradition of pairing shellfish and bitter greens. Often this style is called inzimino. The combination works. The sweet mussels or salty clams and the bitter greens are held in charming balance by the blandness of the pasta and beans.

Serves 4

1 pound arugula or **¹/₂ recipe Braised Bitter Greens** (page 298)

1 cup dry white wine or **water**

4 pounds mussels, scrubbed and debearded, or **4 pounds large clams,** scrubbed

1 pound dry pasta, such as orecchiette, maccheroncini, or shells

3 tablespoons extra virgin olive oil

2 tablespoons finely minced garlic

Hot pepper flakes to taste

1 cup cooked white beans or **chick-peas** (optional)

Salt and freshly ground black pepper

Trim the stems off the arugula, coarsely chop, wash well, and drain. Bring 1 cup white wine or water to a boil in a wide saucepan. Add the mussels or large clams, cover the pan, and steam until the shellfish open. Remove the shellfish from the shells. Pour the cooking liquids through a cheesecloth-lined strainer into a bowl. Reserve.

Bring a large pot of salted water to a boil. Drop in the pasta.

In a wide sauté pan, heat the olive oil and warm the garlic over moderate heat for a few minutes. Add the hot pepper flakes, if desired, and coarsely chopped arugula (or the cooked greens) and stir until wilted. Add the reserved shellfish, their juices, and optional beans, and warm through. Season with salt and pepper to taste. Toss with the pasta and serve at once.

Kitchen Conversation

Taking the shellfish out of their shells makes the pasta easier to eat, and there is less mess to deal with at the table, no need for an extra bowl for shells, lemon finger bowls, extra napkins, etc. However, should you find those elegant, tiny clams called vongole, *steam them in their shells, strain the pan juices to remove grit, and add the clams in the shell to the arugula. They look so appealing, they may be worth the extra work.*

In this pasta bitter greens and garlic mingle with sweet mussels or salty clams. Arugula has a nuttier, more peppery taste than some other greens. If you find it too intense, cut it with milder Swiss chard. Mild and creamy white beans act as mediators to keep the salt or bitterness at bay.

Should you add hot pepper or extra garlic? No and yes. Too much heat and garlic will upset the elegant balance between the bitter greens and sweet mussels. If you want some subtle heat, use just a pinch. In fact, the heat of black pepper would be preferable to hot pepper flakes. You might want a bit of grated lemon zest for contrast. Using saltier clams means that you can add more heat if you want it, and even more garlic. If the dish is too salty, add a spritz of lemon juice or grated zest. As is consistent with Italian tradition with seafood and fish pastas, no cheese, please.

Wine Notes

Pairing Pointers: *Surprisingly, the choice of shellfish makes no difference. The wine-selection criterion is the same as on page 125, with the need for a slightly "bigger" wine because of the somewhat fuller-flavored nature of the mollusks. Keep in mind that the brinier the shellfish, the more sharpness you'll need to cut it. Most red wines will react in an unpleasant manner, although if you keep the tannins at level zero, you'll hedge your bet.*

Category: 2

Specific Recommendations:

2: *Chardonnay—austere, zippy, and mineral scented—France, Italy* ■ *Sauvignon Blanc—herbal, bright, and exuberant— New Zealand, USA* ■ *Albariño, Alvarinho—crisp, refreshing, and citrusy—Spain, Portugal (richer)*

Linguine with Fried Calamari, Radicchio, and Pine Nuts

*T*he idea for this pasta is derived from a tradition of eating fritto misto al mare, *deep-fried calamari or other shellfish, and cutting the richness of the fritto by accompanying it with a salad of bitter greens or, in this case, red as in radicchio. This recipe continues the theme of bitter greens and sweet seafood, made even sweeter here with pine nuts and balsamic vinegar. If you cannot find calamari you may substitute scallops or shrimp, or mussels out of the shell.*

Serves 4

1 pound linguine

Olive or **peanut oil for frying**

8 tablespoons all-purpose flour

8 tablespoons semolina flour

Salt and freshly ground black pepper

12 ounces small squid (calamari), bodies cut in rings, tentacles left whole if small

6 tablespoons olive oil

12 cups radicchio, cut in thin strips (chiffonade in chef lingo)

1 heaping tablespoon finely minced garlic

6 to 8 tablespoons balsamic vinegar

$^1/_2$ cup toasted pine nuts

4 tablespoons extra virgin olive oil (optional)

Bring a large pot of salted water to a boil and drop in the linguine.

Heat a deep frying pan with oil to the depth of an inch or so.

Combine the flours on a saucer and add salt and pepper. Mix well. When the oil is at 375 degrees, dredge the calamari in seasoned flour mixture. Shake off excess flour. Deep-fry until golden and crispy. Drain on towels. Set aside in a warm place.

Warm olive oil in a large sauté pan. Wilt the radicchio in the oil and sprinkle with salt and pepper.

Add the garlic and balsamic vinegar, and toss well. Return the calamari to the pan. Add the pine nuts. When the linguine are al dente, drain in a colander. Toss the sauce with the linguine. If desired, dress the pasta with a little extra virgin olive oil. Serve at once.

Variation: Fry the calamari very quickly over high heat in $^1/_4$ cup olive oil in a small sauté pan. Remove from the pan with a slotted spoon. Set aside. Drain most of the oil. Add the radicchio to the pan and proceed as above.

Kitchen Conversation

As you may be discovering, the bitterness of the radicchio is a wonderful foil for the richness of the fried calamari. Do you notice how the sharpness of the radicchio is also tempered by the sweet balsamic vinegar and toasty sweet pine nuts? This pasta is an exercise in texture as well as taste. Crunchy fried seafood versus soft greens. The semolina flour adds extra crunch to the flour coating. Be sure you have added enough salt so that all of the flavor components are present.

Why call them calamari instead of squid? Because people seem to prefer this seafood with an Italian identity and order more calamari than squid. Menu linguistics strike again.

Wine Notes

Pairing Pointers: *A yin and yang type of dish. This pasta demands refreshing acidity to cut the deep-fry richness of the calamari, the bitter edge in the radicchio, and the oiliness of the pine nuts. At the same time, a level of "sweetness" is required to pick up on the balsamic vinegar, calamari, and the inherent aromatic quality of the pine nuts.*

Categories: 1B, 2

Specific Recommendations:

1B: *Chenin Blanc—chalky, floral with a snap of sweet—France, USA* ■ *Riesling—mineral, fruity with an edge of sweet—Germany, Austria*

2: *Semillon —waxy, fresh, and a little earthy—USA* ■ *Brut Champagne—toasty, nutty, and effusive—France*

Pilaf: Wheat, Barley, or Rice

Pilaf can be made with wheat, barley, or rice. All have distinctive flavor and texture characteristics. Wheat or barley is nuttier and more assertive in flavor. Rice is milder and more neutral.

Turkish Bulgur Pilaf with Chick-peas

*M*ost of us think of bulgur in its familiar tabbouleh *mode, a grain-based salad served at room temperature. We forget that it makes a great hot pilaf. In Turkey wheat pilaf is served simply, or with pine nuts and currants, or mixed with legumes. Here chick-peas are added to the wheat pilaf.* ☛*This is a fine accompaniment to cooked fish, meat, or poultry. Combine it with a few vegetable dishes for a satisfying meal. I especially love this pilaf with leafy, tart spinach and smoky grilled eggplant or a sweet roasted tomato. To brighten this mild and hearty mixture, serve with a dollop of yogurt on top or with a bowl of Esme (page 322), the Turkish tomato "salsa."*

Serves 6

¹/₂ cup chick-peas (see note)

¹/₃ cup butter or **olive oil**

1 large onion, diced

1 large tomato, peeled, seeded, and cut in ¹/₂-inch cubes

2 teaspoons salt

3 cups water or **broth**

2 cups bulgur wheat, medium to coarse

¹/₂ teaspoon freshly ground black pepper

¹/₄ teaspoon cayenne pepper

Chopped parsley, dill, or **mint**

Soak the chick-peas in 1¹/₂ cups cold water in the refrigerator overnight. Drain and rinse. Cover the chick-peas with 1¹/₂ cups fresh cold water and bring up to a boil. Simmer for 2 minutes. Let rest for 1 hour. Drain and cover with cold water. Bring up to a boil and cook until done, 35 to 45 minutes. (The chick-peas should not be mushy or falling apart, as they will continue to cook in the pilaf.) Set the cooked chick-peas aside.

Melt the butter or heat the oil in a medium saucepan or deep sauté pan, and add the onion. Cook over moderate heat for 10 minutes until tender and sweet, then add the tomato and sauté for 3 minutes longer. Add the cooked chick-peas, salt, water or broth, and bring to a boil. Add the bulgur and stir well. Cover the pan, lower the heat, and simmer for 20 minutes. If there seems to be too much liquid, drain it from the pot. Season the pilaf with black pepper and cayenne. Remove from heat and let sit, covered, for 15 minutes until dry, or dry, uncovered, in a low oven. Sprinkle with chopped herbs.

☛ Note: Lentils can be used instead of chick-peas.

Kitchen Conversation

This is really uncomplicated in flavor. The texture is the star. It is important to cook the onion until it loses its gassy, bitter quality and has sweetened, and that your use of herbs was discreet. This is not a foreground kind of dish, but one that makes a great background or middle ground for the rest of the meal.

Cooking Grains

Grains usually provide background flavor, but because they have so much bulk and presence they must be perfectly seasoned. Salt is usually the key. Toasting grains in butter will help bring up their nutty flavors too. Cracked wheat, barley, and rice profit from a few minutes of sautéing before adding the cooking liquids. If you are using broth instead of water, make sure it is not so intense as to mask the basic flavor of the grains.

Roasted Barley Pilaf

*H*ere is a wonderful alternative to rice or cracked wheat. The hearty texture of the barley makes it fun to eat, filling and satisfying. This is an ideal side dish for Dfina (page 239), cooked fish, meat, or poultry, and makes a fine center of the plate if paired with forthright, assertive vegetables.

Serves 6

5 cups water or **stock**

2 tablespoons olive oil

1 onion, diced

2 cups whole barley

Salt and freshly ground black pepper

2 small sprigs thyme (optional)

A few whole peeled cloves garlic (optional)

Heat the water or stock. Warm the olive oil in a large sauté pan over moderate heat. Add the onion and cook until tender and translucent, about 10 minutes. Add the barley and stir well to coat with oil. Add salt and pepper, hot water or stock, and optional thyme sprigs and garlic cloves. Simmer, uncovered, for 35 to 45 minutes, adding water as needed, or until the barley is tender and well puffed. If the grains seem a bit wet, spread on a baking sheet and dry the pilaf in a low oven for about 10 minutes. Barley pilaf reheats well and can be held warm without any major loss of texture.

Kitchen Conversation

Texture, texture, texture. Most of us are used to barley in soup and rarely eat it as a grain. But now you can see the possibilities.

Middle Eastern Rice and Noodle Pilaf

*T*his noodle and rice pilaf is very common in the Middle East. The fried vermicelli provide a texture contrast to the rice. For yet more palate stimulation, add a few toasted nuts. Serve with kebabs, roast meat, fish, poultry, and other vegetable dishes.

Serves 6

6 tablespoons unsalted butter

1 cup vermicelli, broken into 1-inch pieces

1¹/₂ cups basmati rice, soaked for 1 hour, drained well

3 cups Basic Chicken Stock (page 115) or **water**

2 teaspoons salt

¹/₄ cup toasted nuts (optional)

Pinch cinnamon (optional)

In a heavy saucepan, melt the butter over moderate heat. Add the vermicelli and sauté for a few minutes until lightly browned. Then add the rice and sauté for a few minutes longer. Add the stock or water, salt, and bring up to a boil. Reduce the heat, cover the pan, and simmer over very low heat until all the liquid is absorbed, about 20 minutes. Toasted almonds, pine nuts, or hazelnuts or a sprinkle of cinnamon could be added at the end.

Kitchen Conversation

Another study in texture. Basmati rice is the key ingredient, as it holds its firm texture better than any other rice. And it has a subtle aroma that makes this rice more interesting than most. The vermicelli add texture contrast.

Vegetable Paella

The classic Spanish paella is made with a short-grain rice similar to Italian arborio. (In fact, you can use arborio for this recipe if you can't find Spanish short-grain rice.) I am going to give you two methods for preparing vegetable paella. You can make this like risotto, adding hot stock gradually as you cook the rice; this is a last-minute dish and will take about 25 minutes of your attention at the stove. Or you can make the Vegetable Ragout and add Baked Saffron Rice and heat it through. While this technique is not authentic, it is very convenient for last-minute entertaining. This all-vegetable version of paella is a great nonmeat change of pace dinner.

Serves 4

Vegetable Ragout for Paella

2 tablespoons olive oil

2 large onions, diced

Salt and black pepper

2 green bell peppers or **1 red and 1 green,** diced

2 tablespoons dried oregano

1¹/₂ tablespoons finely minced garlic

2 cups diced tomatoes

4 tablespoons tomato puree

3 cups vegetable stock

1 to 2 tablespoons sherry vinegar (optional)

Salt and freshly ground black pepper

1 cup fresh favas, blanched and peeled, or **1 cup peas,** shelled and blanched

1 cup green beans, cut into 1¹/₂-inch pieces, blanched until almost tender

4 large artichoke hearts, cooked, cut into eighths

6 cups Baked Saffron Rice

To make the vegetable ragout, heat the olive oil in a sauté pan over moderate heat and add the onions. Cook for 5 minutes, then add salt and black pepper, and the peppers, and cook for 5 minutes longer, stirring occasionally. Add the oregano, garlic, tomatoes, and tomato puree, and simmer for 8 minutes.

Season generously with salt and pepper and add the vinegar, if you like. Add the stock, all of the vegetables, and baked saffron rice, and heat through. Adjust the seasoning. Serve at once.

☛Note: In winter use cooked white beans in place of fresh favas.

Baked Saffron Rice

This is a Persian-inspired technique for preparing rice that is easy and works well when you need perfect pilaf-style rice ahead of time. The rice can hold for 2 or 3 hours without becoming gummy or mushy. But you must use basmati rice.

Makes 6 cups

¹/₄ cup white wine or **water**

1 teaspoon saffron filaments, crushed

4 quarts water

2 tablespoons salt

3 cups basmati rice, soaked in cold water for 10 minutes

8 tablespoons melted unsalted butter

Salt and freshly ground black pepper

Preheat the oven to 350 degrees.

To make the saffron infusion: Pour the white wine or water into a small saucepan and bring it up to a simmer. Add the crushed saffron filaments. Let steep for 20 minutes.

Bring the water to a boil with the salt. Drop in the rice and cook it quickly, over medium heat, for about 10 minutes. Test a grain with your teeth. It should be almost completely cooked. Drain the rice immediately and rinse it with warm water.

Butter a shallow baking pan (such as a lasagna pan) with some of the melted butter. Add the saffron infusion, salt, and pepper to the remaining butter. Spoon the rice into the prepared pan and drizzle the saffron butter over the rice. Cover the pan with foil and bake for 25 minutes.

Risotto Version of Vegetable Paella

6 cups vegetable stock

Ingredients for Vegetable Ragout

2 cups short-grain rice

Make the saffron infusion as above.

Bring 6 cups stock to a boil, then reduce the heat to a very low simmer. Heat the olive oil in a large, deep sauté pan and add the onions. Cook over moderate heat for 8 minutes, add salt and pepper, the peppers, oregano, garlic, half the tomatoes, and all the tomato puree, and cook for 3 minutes. Stir in 2 cups short-grain rice and coat well with the onion mixture. Add 1 cup of the stock, stir well, and let the stock absorb. Add another cup of stock and let it absorb. Add the saffron infusion to 1 more cup of the stock, and let it absorb. Finally, add 1 cup stock, the cooked vegetables and remaining tomatoes, and optional vinegar, and cook until the rice is almost al dente. Add the last of the stock as needed for a creamy mixture, adjust the seasoning, and serve at once.

Kitchen Conversation

No matter which technique you use for the rice, it is important to season the vegetables very intensely, as the rice will mute their impact. The vinegar rounds out the flavors. It heightens the sweetness of the peas, beans, and red peppers, cuts the bitterness of the green peppers, and even mellows the tomatoes with its deeper kind of acidity. (As we have discovered from making salads, there are different types of acidity that can add high or low notes to a dish. Tomatoes and lemon are higher or lighter acids, whereas most vinegars are deeper in tone.) Don't forget to adjust the salt and pepper again after adding the rice.

Wine Notes

Pairing Pointers: *This dish is very versatile from a wine standpoint. It's color blind. You could go white, red, or rosé and be happy. My recommendation would be to select a wine of low tannin (if red), a minimal use of oak, with a balanced acidity. A more seasoned paella will require a wine with a bit more oomph.*

Categories: 1A, 4

Specific Recommendations:

1A: *Other Italian—Verdicchio, Orvieto, Frascati, Trebbiano* ■ *Sauvignon Blanc—crisp, light, leafy—Australia, New Zealand*

4: *Various Spanish—obvious ethnic choice—Navarra, Valdepeñas, Rioja* ■ *Merlot—earthy, simple, herbal—Italy, USA*

Spanokorizo Greek Spinach and Rice Pilaf

This traditional rustic Greek pilaf, which combines rice and spinach, can be eaten hot or at room temperature. For a complete meal, top it with fried eggs, or chopped hard-cooked eggs, or a little crumbled feta cheese.

Serves 4

6 tablespoons olive oil

2 onions, chopped

1 clove garlic, minced

1 cup long-grain rice, basmati preferred

8 cups spinach, chopped coarsely and washed well

1/2 cup chopped fresh dill

3 tablespoons chopped fresh mint

2 1/2 cups water

Salt and freshly ground black pepper

3 tablespoons fresh lemon juice

Heat 3 tablespoons of the olive oil in a large sauté pan. Cook the onions over moderate heat for about 10 minutes, or until tender and sweet. Add the garlic and rice and sauté, stirring often, for 3 minutes. Add the spinach, dill, mint, water, and salt and pepper, and bring up to a boil. Reduce the heat and simmer covered, stirring occasionally, until water is absorbed. Remove from the heat and adjust seasoning. Toss with lemon juice mixed with the remaining olive oil.

Kitchen Conversation

The final touch of lemon and olive oil rounds out the flavors and accents the leafy quality of the spinach. Did you remember to taste the onions for sweetness? The mint will accentuate the sweetness and the dill will meld well with the tartness of spinach and lemon.

Midyeli Pilav Turkish Mussel Pilaf

*U*nlike risotto, in a classic pilaf all the liquids are added at once. Here you may use a combination of mussel steaming liquor, augmented by fish stock, chicken stock, or even water. In Turkey mussels are prized, and this pilaf is one of the most elegant ways to serve them. However, you may also make this with shrimp.

Serves 4

1 cup white wine

40 mussels, well scrubbed, debearded as best as possible

1/3 teaspoon saffron filaments, chopped and steeped in mussel liquor

4 tablespoons olive oil

1 large onion, chopped

2 cloves garlic, minced

2 stalks celery, chopped (optional)

3 large tomatoes, peeled, seeded, and chopped

1 1/2 cups long-grain rice, washed and drained, basmati preferred

3 cups hot mussel steaming liquor plus Basic Fish Stock (page 114), **Basic Chicken Stock** (page 115), or **water**

1/2 teaspoon salt

1/2 teaspoon freshly ground black pepper

1/2 cup chopped flat-leaf parsley or **1/3 cup chopped fresh dill**

Put the wine and mussels in a heavy kettle. Cover the pot, and steam the mussels until just opened. Remove the mussels from the shells and trim any beards that may remain. Discard the shells unless you want a few for garnish. Save all mussel liquor and strain through cheesecloth into a bowl. Set 1/4 cup of hot mussel liquor aside and steep the saffron in it.

Warm the olive oil in a large, wide sauté pan over moderate heat. Add the onion and garlic, and cook over low heat until soft, about 8 minutes. Add the celery, if using, and the tomatoes, and cook for 3 minutes longer. Add the rice and stir well. Add the steeped saffron, salt and pepper, and the stock or water. Bring up to a boil, reduce heat, and cover the pan. Simmer until the liquids are absorbed. Return the mussels to the pan, stir once, and cover. Turn off the heat and let the pilaf rest for 10 minutes. Fluff once. Sprinkle with lots of chopped parsley or dill and serve at once.

Kitchen Conversation

Here the sweetness of the mussels plays off the sweet onions and tart, sweet tomatoes. The saffron adds a subtle bitter note but not enough to change the flavor equation, unless you've added too much. (Please use saffron filaments rather than powdered saffron, as the powder can sometimes taste medicinal.)

After you've made this dish, you could make the recipe on page 148 for another approach to mussels and rice. And please try this pilaf with shrimp, as they will add a different kind of sweetness and a very different texture to the mix. Use shrimp stock if you made some from the shells or had some in the freezer from making the shrimp bastilla (page 74).

Wine Notes

Pairing Pointers: *The combination of flavors here really calls for a wine with personality. Saffron is always an intriguing challenge, and from a wine perspective, it's wise to keep it in check. The more saffron, the more difficult the pairing. Despite the shellfish I opt for light reds and rosés. A full-flavored white is okay, but play down the oak.*

Categories: 4, 5, 6

Specific Recommendations:

4: *Rosé Champagne, sparkling wine—keep it young*

5: *Pinot Noir—spicy, bright, fragrant—France, Oregon* ■
Tempranillo—unoaked, fresh, round—Spain

6: *Pinotage —rustic, herbaceous, very light in tannin*

Risotto with Mussels, Ouzo, Green Onions, and Hot Pepper

*R*isotto uses a short-grain rice as opposed to the long-grain basmati preferred for pilaf. Unlike a pilaf, in risotto the liquids are added 1 cup at a time until the short-grain rice becomes creamy. Although the addition of feta cheese breaks the Italian rule of no cheese with seafood, this is not a classic risotto but one that combines Italian technique and Greek flavors. The feta adds a wonderful note of salt, which contrasts with the sweetness of the mussels and ouzo and softens the impact of the wine and green onions.

Serves 4

4 dozen mussels, well scrubbed and debearded

1 cup white wine

4 cups Basic Fish Stock (page 114) or **a combination of Basic Chicken Stock** (page 115) **and water**

4 tablespoons olive oil

1¹/₂ cups green onions, chopped

1 teaspoon hot pepper flakes

1¹/₂ cups arborio rice (or carnaroli or vialone)

¹/₂ cup ouzo

1 cup chopped Italian parsley

1 cup crumbled feta cheese (optional)

Steam the mussels open in the wine. Remove the mussels from the shells and pull off any remaining beards. Discard the shells (unless you want a few mussels in the shell as a garnish). Strain the mussel liquor and add to the fish or chicken stock. Bring the stock up to a boil. Reduce the heat and keep at a simmer.

Warm the olive oil in a large sauté pan or wide, shallow saucepan. Add the green onions and cook for 5 minutes. Add the hot pepper flakes and rice, and toss in the oil for 3 minutes. Add the ouzo to the pan and cook until absorbed. Add 1 cup hot stock and cook, stirring occasionally, until the stock is absorbed. Add the remaining stock, 1 cup at a time, stirring occasionally, until the stock is absorbed. Add mussels and heat through. Sprinkle with lots of chopped parsley and top with crumbled feta if desired.

Kitchen Conversation

Taste this with and without the cheese. What do you think? If you choose not to use cheese, remember to increase the salt and pepper. Another time try making this with regular onions instead of green. You will find they are sweeter, less high and grassy in flavor, and less of a contrast to the mussels. This is neither good nor bad, just different. If you use regular onions, you may want to add diced chopped tomatoes for balance. Or do you find the ouzo makes up for the sweetness?

Wine Notes

Pairing Pointers: *A pungent and bold white wine is necessary with this risotto. The feta is critical, because if it's too salty it will wreak havoc on your wine choice. The mussels and ouzo demand a more generous and alcoholic wine. Keep the hot pepper in balance so as not to gut the wine.*

Categories: 2, 3A, or 3B

Specific Recommendations:

2: *Chardonnay—less oaked, moderately complex, steely* ■ *Riesling—rich, light or no oak, powerful style—Australia*

3A: *Gewürztraminer—spicy, floral, ample—France, USA* ■ *Marsanne—packed with fruit, textured, earthy—France*

3B: *If served as an appetizer* ■ *Sherry—fresh, exuberant fino or manzanilla*

Risotto Saltato Risotto Pancakes

*T*he Italians are thrifty cooks and no food goes to waste. What do they do with leftover risotto? Why, make risotto saltato, a rice pancake that jumps (saltare) out of the pan and into the mouth. Usually these are large, flat pancakes, browned on both sides and flipped onto a plate and cut into wedges. I love making small ones, about 3 inches in diameter; they are a perfect foil for a wild mushroom ragout or served with a simple veal chop. ☞While the pancakes can be interlaced with chopped toasted hazelnuts, or stuffed with a bit of fontina cheese that melts inside the pancake, or with chopped sautéed mushrooms or peas, they are really wonderful by themselves. And because we often don't have any risotto left over, here's a fast and easy way to make the pancakes from scratch.

Makes 8 to 10 pancakes

1 1/2 cups water

Salt

1 cup arborio rice

2 eggs

1/3 cup Parmesan cheese

Black pepper

Oil for frying

Optional Fillings

1 cup toasted chopped hazelnuts

1 cup sliced sautéed mushrooms, coarsely chopped (about 2 cups before sautéing), seasoned with thyme or sage

1 cup diced fontina, each 1/2-inch cube dipped in chopped sage

Bring the water to a boil in a medium saucepan. Add the salt and rice, lower the heat, and cover the pan. Simmer until all the water is absorbed. Add the eggs, cheese, and pepper to taste. You probably won't need much salt, as the cheese is fairly salty. Spread this rice mixture on a baking sheet and refrigerate until cool. If using the hazelnuts, stir them in before cooling the rice. Scoop up the rice with a ¼ cup measure and form into flattened pancakes. Do not pack them tightly or they will be as heavy as hockey pucks!

To stuff the pancakes with cheese or mushrooms, place a scant scoop of rice in your hand, make a dent with your finger, cradle the rice pocket in your hand, add the filling, cover the filling with a little more rice, and close the pancake and flatten it gently. Place the completed pancakes on parchment-lined baking sheets until ready to fry. These can be refrigerated for 8 hours, covered with plastic wrap.

To serve, heat peanut or olive oil to film a heavy sauté pan, such as cast iron. Add as many pancakes as you can fit at one time, with room to turn them over. Fry until golden on both sides. Drain on paper towels.

Kitchen Conversation

Form these cakes with a delicate touch. Don't over-handle them or they will become leaden and tough. And don't overfry them and make the outside too hard. You can deep-fry them, but very quickly. Drain well. If you have stuffed them with cheese, be sure to allow enough time in the pan for the cheese to soften and melt. Keep the heat a bit lower so the cooking is a bit slower. If you've added hazelnuts, be careful not to burn them, as they will lose their sweetness and become bitter. Also, if there is a sauce on the plate, don't inundate the pancakes so they become soggy. Keep the sauce or mushroom ragout off to the side, so you can dip bits of crisp pancake in at will and get the best of both worlds.

Potato Gnocchi with Crabmeat, Fennel, and Tomatoes

Many of you may not want to take the time to make gnocchi from scratch. But that's okay. There are acceptable potato gnocchi available commercially. Making gnocchi is fun only when you have the desire and are not in a rush. Or if you have a friend who may want to pitch in and help. It takes about an hour to make enough gnocchi for 4 to 6 people by yourself. So here is a recipe to satisfy cravings for light and delicate homemade gnocchi. ☛*This recipe uses russet potatoes. Bake them for about an hour, and rice them while very warm. Although the egg makes for slightly heavier gnocchi, it does help the dough hold together better.*

Serves 4 to 6

Gnocchi

2 pounds russet potatoes (about 4 large)

1 egg

Salt

Pinch freshly grated nutmeg (optional)

1¹/₂ to 2 cups flour or as needed

Bake the potatoes until they are completely tender. (You may boil them, but baking produces a drier potato that requires less flour.) While still quite warm, cut them in half, scoop out the flesh, and put the potato pulp through a ricer or food mill. Add the egg, salt, nutmeg, if desired, and as much flour as needed to form a soft and smooth dough that holds together well. Knead it on a lightly floured surface until the dough no longer feels sticky to the touch. Dust your hands with flour and then divide the dough into 8 or 10 pieces. Roll these into ropes that are 1/2 inch in diameter. Cut into 1-inch lengths and push them away from you with the tines of a fork to get the traditional grooves. Place on baking sheets lined with baker's parchment and let dry for an hour at room temperature. They may also be refrigerated, but seem to be lightest when they rest at room temperature away from the moistness of the refrigerator.

Bring a large pot of generously salted water to a boil (see note). Cook the gnocchi gently, a few handfuls at a time, until they rise to the top of the pot. Then remove them with a slotted spoon, drain well, and place in a buttered baking dish or bowl. Continue until all are cooked. (If you have a few large pots you can do them all at once.)

Drizzle with melted butter as you drain them, and when all are cooked, toss with the following sauce:

☛Note: Before you form all of the gnocchi, make a few sample gnocchi and test them by cooking them in boiling water to see that the dough holds together and that you have added enough flour and have kneaded the dough sufficiently. There is too much labor involved for you to produce an hour's worth of duds.

Sauce

4 tablespoons unsalted butter

1 small onion, diced, or **4 shallots, minced**

2 small bulbs fennel, quartered, cored, sliced thin, about 1 1/2 cups

2/3 pound crabmeat, picked over (see note)

Tiny pinch hot pepper (optional)

2 cups tomato sauce

1/2 cup chopped parsley or **basil**

Butter as desired

Melt the butter over moderate heat in a medium sauté pan and add the onion or shallots. Cook until tender, stirring occasionally, for about 8 minutes. Add the fennel and sauté for 3 minutes. Add the crab, a pinch of hot pepper, if you like, and the tomato sauce, and warm through. Spoon the sauce over the gnocchi, adding half the parsley and basil as you toss or stir gently. Sprinkle with the remaining herbs. For a really smooth and unctuous sauce, add a bit more butter to the tomatoes at the end of cooking. But no cheese with the crabmeat, please.

Kitchen Conversation

Your gnocchi should be light and hold together well. Some alternate sauces for gnocchi are pesto, thinned with a bit of butter. Or butter and cheese. Or tomato sauce thinned with butter or cream. Then cheese. Given health concerns and diet, I feel guilty saying the richer the better. However, gnocchi don't thrive in austerity. In my experience, when saucing potato gnocchi, less is not more. More rich is better. After you experiment with different sauces, you'll come to your own conclusions. And then we can talk about it! Considering the seafood and tomato sauce tradition for pasta, you might be tempted to omit the fennel. Please don't. The sweetness of the fennel accents the sweetness of the crabmeat and brings something special to the experience. The sweet basil is your call. You might prefer the less obtrusive parsley, especially if you love the crab and fennel combination.

☛Note: Why "pick over" the crabmeat? This is a seafood term that means running your fingers through the crabmeat carefully to get rid of any pieces of shell or cartilage. Picking debris out of your teeth while eating crabmeat sort of spoils the mood.

Wine Notes

Pairing Pointers: *With such richness and sweetness already present, the wine should bend with the dish. Make every effort to select a wine that mirrors the basic taste components, sweet, rich, and delicate. Avoid reds—too much competition.*

Categories: 1B, 3A, 3B

Specific Recommendations:

1B: *Chenin Blanc—tropical, lively, aromatic—France, South Africa* ■ *Champagne—on the drier side—brut plus!*

3A: *Chardonnay —rich, complex, velvety—USA, Australia, France* ■ *Viognier—fragrant, fresh, ample—USA, France*

3B: *If served as an appetizer* ■ *Sherry—medium-rich amontillado style* ■ *Madeira—drier style of Bual or rich Verdelho*

Pumpkin Gnocchi

Using pumpkin squash (zucca *in Italian*) *in pasta and gnocchi is part of a long tradition in Northern Italian cuisine, especially in the Veneto and Lombardia, reaching an epiphany in Mantua, where pumpkin squash is combined with* amaretti *and* mostarda di frutta *for a sumptuous ravioli filling or formed into delicate gnocchi.* ☛*You probably can't buy these gnocchi unless you are in Northern Italy, where they are standard fare, or are fortunate to live near a very adventurous pasta shop. However, once you have tasted them, you will want to make them at home, as they are so seductively delicious. The procedure is the same as for the potato gnocchi, but with a sweeter result. These are best sauced simply with melted butter, sage, and Parmesan cheese, or with butter, sage, hazelnuts, and a little Parmesan.*

Serves 6

---

1 large piece pumpkin squash (not including seeds) or **about 1¹/₂ pounds butternut squash,** enough to give you about 3 cups pulp

1 egg (optional)

Salt and freshly ground black pepper

¹/₂ teaspoon freshly grated nutmeg or to taste

1¹/₂ cups flour or as needed

8 tablespoons unsalted butter

24 sage leaves

12 tablespoons grated Parmesan cheese

¹/₂ cup chopped toasted hazelnuts (optional)

continued

Preheat the oven to 400 degrees. Bake the squash until tender, 45 minutes to an hour. Remove the seeds and peel off the skin. Put the squash pulp through a ricer while still quite warm. Leave this mixture in a strainer to drain for half an hour, then warm the puree slightly in a dry sauté pan to rid it of any excess moisture. Add the egg, if desired, the salt, pepper, and nutmeg, and just enough flour to form a dough that holds together. Knead until the dough is no longer sticky, adding a bit more flour as needed. Repeat the process as for potato gnocchi. Remember to boil a few test gnocchi to make sure they hold together.

To serve, cook the gnocchi in batches in copious amounts of boiling salted water until they rise to the top of the pot. Remove with a slotted spoon, drain well, and put in a buttered baking dish or bowl.

Warm the butter, add the sage leaves (and hazelnuts if using), and spoon over gnocchi. Add the Parmesan and mix gently. Serve at once.

Pumpkin, Squash, Yams, and Sweet Potatoes

The traditional pumpkin type of squash found in European and North African markets is shaped like one of our pumpkins, but its skin is dark green and quite bumpy. Because it is allowed to grow quite large, it is often sold by the piece. The flesh is dark red orange and very sweet. The typical pumpkin found at our markets is smooth skinned, usually orange (or occasionally white) on the outside; the flesh is lighter in color and starchier than its European counterpart. Occasionally one can find a Japanese variety of pumpkin-type squash called *kabocha* at the market. Its skin is dark green and it has orange flesh; it comes closest to the European pumpkin squash in shape, taste, and texture. Alas, it is not widely available. But to prepare Mediterranean recipes calling for *zucca* or *potiron,* we have a few options. We can use butternut squash or banana squash, delicata, or even acorn squash. The flesh of the butternut is closest in texture to the European *zucca* or *potiron,* and is often the sweetest. Acorn and delicata tend to be more delicate in texture, and can be watery or fibrous. In recipes where a pumpkin puree is needed, such as pumpkin polenta or Pumpkin Gnocchi (page 155), any of these squash, pumpkins, yams, or even sweet potatoes will work. Yams are sweeter, denser, and less fibrous than sweet potatoes. After baking or boiling the squash, potatoes, or yams, be sure to drain the puree in a cheesecloth-lined strainer for a few hours to get rid of excess moisture. You don't want soggy gnocchi or wet ravioli filling. Moisture is not a big factor in the polenta recipe.

Kitchen Conversation

The sweet squash and sweet hazelnuts need the salt of the Parmesan cheese for balance. Pecorino would be too sour. Sage adds just enough musty herbal quality that the mixture is not cloying and dessertlike.

Wine Notes

Pairing Pointers: *Rich and sweet are the match points here. This dish provides a model stage for big unctuous whites. This can also pair well with off-dry rosés and blush wine, and with the ample style of sparkling wine too. The sage offers an opportunity to choose a European wine that will pick up on that earthier element.*

Categories: 1B, 3A, 3B

Specific Recommendations:

1B: *Sparkling wines—ample fruit, fresh personality—USA* ■ *Rosé/ blends—lively, effusive, but not too sweet—USA*

3A: *Grenache Rosé—generous, spicy, and autumnal—France* ■ *Semillon/blends—textured, rich, and flavorful—Washington State, Australia*

3B: *If served as an appetizer, Sherry—a medium-rich amontillado style* ■ *Madeira—drier style of Bual or rich Verdelho*

Polenta with Butternut Squash, Yams, or Sweet Potatoes

*T*his recipe combines a classic Northern Italian ravioli filling with traditional polenta. You
can serve the mixture soft and creamy or pour it onto a sheet pan, refrigerate it until set,
and then cut it into strips to be sautéed or baked later. Squash or yam polenta also makes a
nice accompaniment for pork or ham or poultry. When paired with greens or other vegetables, it can
be a satisfying meal in itself.

Serves 6 to 8

2¹/₂ pounds butternut squash or **2 pounds yams**
or **sweet potatoes**

¹/₄ cup milk

4 tablespoons softened unsalted butter

1 teaspoon freshly grated nutmeg

Pinch cinnamon (optional)

Salt and freshly ground black pepper

2 cups coarse cornmeal for polenta

7 cups cold water or more if needed

1 cup grated Parmesan cheese (optional)

2 to 3 tablespoons chopped fresh sage

Preheat the oven to 400 degrees. Bake the squash or yams until soft, about 1 hour. If using yams or sweet potatoes, peel and mash them. If using squash, cut it in half, scoop out the seeds, and mash or put through a ricer. Beat in the milk and butter. Season with the nutmeg, a pinch of cinnamon, if desired, and salt and pepper. Set aside.

Combine the polenta and cold water in a large saucepan and, stirring quite often, bring up to a boil. Reduce the heat and simmer over low heat, stirring often, until thickened, about 30 minutes, or until the cornmeal is no longer grainy on your tongue. Add more water if needed until the polenta is cooked.

Whisk in the pureed squash, optional Parmesan, and chopped sage, and mix well to combine. Season again with salt, pepper, and nutmeg. Serve as is or:

Pour the polenta onto a well-buttered baking pan (16×12×1) and refrigerate. When firm, cover well with plastic wrap.

To serve, cut the polenta into desired shapes, such as triangles, rectangles, squares, or strips, with a knife (use a biscuit cutter if you want rounds or for hearts if you are feeling romantic)! Sauté the polenta in butter or oil until golden on both sides or place it in buttered gratin dishes and bake in a 350 degree oven until hot.

Kitchen Conversation

This is a nice alternative to plain polenta. The sweetness of the squash or yams accents the corn taste of the polenta and cuts the starchiness. But don't forget to salt this adequately, as the polenta and pumpkin both need salt to bring out their sweetness. The nutmeg echoes the sweetness. (Freshly grated nutmeg is always more fragrant and intense than preground.) The cheese adds additional salt, if you want it. However, you probably won't if you've paired this polenta with rich duck with a fruit sauce (see Roast Duck with Caramelized Turnips, Pears, and Thyme, page 234, and Roast Duck with Braised Quince, Black Pepper, Marjoram, and Sweet Wine, page 236). However, you might need the grated cheese if you pair this polenta with greens or with a simple broiled chicken in a garlic-and-herb or peppery marinade. Frying the polenta in butter will also heighten its sweetness. It will be less sweet if you bake it or serve it soft just after adding the potatoes to the hot polenta.

FISH

& SHELLFISH

Fish & Shellfish

Just a few years ago, chicken was the biggest seller in restaurants and at the supermarket. People wanting to cut back on fat and red meat flocked to the poultry counters. But the tide seems to be drifting seaward. Today the fastest-growing segment of the menu, other than vegetarian entrees, is fish and shellfish. More people are not only enjoying fish in restaurants, they have discovered how fast and easy it is to cook at home. For many, fish has become the "meat" of the nineties.

While most of the fish recipes in this book require spice rubs or vegetable- or vinaigrette-based sauces, they do occasionally call for fish stock for a sauce. There is really no perfect substitute. You can use a chicken stock (Alain, a chef friend of mine, calls this "chicken juice," which amuses me). Some cookbooks recommend using a mixture of chicken stock and clam broth in place of fish stock. It's a compromise. Most chicken stock is pretty mild unless you've reduced the hell out of it. But it's not the same as fish stock. And this doesn't help the "fishetarians," people who call themselves vegetarians but really eat fish. So I'll leave you to wrestle with this dilemma and will recommend fish stock when I think it's a good idea.

When cooking fish and shellfish, freshness and timing are crucial. Tired, flabby, and off-tasting seafood should *never* enter your home. Overcooked fish is dry, brittle, mushy, and falls apart. Overcooked shellfish is rubbery and unpleasant. A few years back, serving fish cooked rare was fashionable. However, rare fish is somewhat passé and occasionally risky. Cook it to medium in most cases, except for tuna, which seems to be parasite-free. Having a trustworthy fishmonger is essential. You want to know that the fish has been properly stored and well handled, and comes from safe and unpolluted waters.

Since most fish is delicate and subtle in flavor, you must be careful not to overwhelm it with excessive saucing. Consider what sauce will work with your catch of the day. A meaty tuna and stronger-tasting fish like mackerel can take a bigger sauce than can a delicate sole or sea bass.

In this chapter we will be playing with flavor balance, using delicate acids such as lemon, orange, and wine; fragrant spices and the heat of red and black pepper; sauces with bitter olives and with bitter herbs, with sweet tart tomatoes, sweet almonds, and bitter walnuts, with sweet caramelized onions, sweet fennel, and sweet roasted peppers, with sweet mussels and salty clams. The recipes are fast and simple, but the tastes are complex.

Roast Halibut with 40 Cloves of Garlic

*O*kay, I confess. I made this up. There's no such dish as halibut with 40 cloves of garlic in classic French cuisine. But there should be. Halibut served with braised garlic cloves in a rich sauce of fish stock and cream, liberally strewn with fresh herbs, is a seductive dish that deserves to be a classic, somewhere. Like in your home, when you need a fast and easy showstopper. All the prep—the braising of the garlic, the making of the fish stock—is done ahead of time. At this point you have two options. You can poach the halibut in the sauce, or bake it and spoon the sauce over the top. Poaching leaves the fish more moist, but baking is easier if you are cooking for a crowd.

Serves 4

24 to 40 whole peeled garlic cloves

Water or **fish stock**

Sprigs thyme and bay leaf

2 cups Basic Fish Stock (page 114)

1 cup cream

4 5-ounce fillets of halibut or **cod** or **sea bass**

Salt and freshly ground black pepper

1 tablespoon unsalted butter

1 tablespoon each chopped thyme, sage, and rosemary

3 tablespoons chopped parsley

If baking the fish, preheat the oven to 400 degrees. Cover the garlic cloves with water or stock, add a few sprigs of thyme and a bay leaf, and bring up to a boil. Reduce the heat and simmer, covered, until the garlic is tender, about 25 minutes. (You also can simmer the cloves in olive oil to cover; reserve the oil and use it for another dish.)

Combine the fish stock and cream in a medium saucepan and reduce by half over high heat. Set aside.

If baking, place the fish fillets on a baking sheet and sprinkle with salt and pepper. Drizzle with the fish stock. Bake the fish for about 8 to 10 minutes, or until cooked through but still moist. While the fish is baking, bring the reduced fish stock and cream up to a brisk simmer. Swirl in the butter, herbs, and garlic cloves, and simmer for about 5 minutes. Adjust the seasoning with salt and pepper. Remove the fish from the oven and transfer it with a spatula to warmed serving plates. Spoon the sauce over the fish.

If poaching, bring the reduced fish stock and cream up to a simmer in a wide and shallow saucepan, gently slip in the fish fillets, cover the pan, and poach the fish until tender, about 8 minutes. Remove the fish to warmed plates with a slotted spatula. Reduce the sauce a bit, as the fish will have given off some liquid, then add the butter, herbs, and garlic and adjust seasoning. Spoon the sauce over the fish. Serve with roast or steamed potatoes.

Kitchen Conversation

The garlic cloves can be poached in water or chicken stock or, for this recipe, even a mild fish stock. Just make sure the cloves are tender and cooked through. Then they will be very mild. My preference is to poach the fish, as it will remain more moist and delicate. Baking is acceptable if you are really paying attention and don't cook the fish a minute longer than necessary, and only after you have basted it with a little fish stock.

The herbs add a musky accent that plays off the subtle creaminess and the pale garlic perfume. I know that many of us are cutting back on fat, but the cream really rounds out the sauce and, after reducing, it only comes to a few tablespoons per serving.

I am not being a wimp when I suggest simple roast or steamed potatoes. This dish is delicate in flavor and an assertive vegetable will wipe it out of your taste memory. Try peas. Maybe green beans. Maybe even beets. This just isn't the time to experiment with eggplant or bitter greens.

Wine Notes

Pairing Pointers: *Halibut is a relatively neutral fish, so the garlic and herbs are what one is matching. Rich, compelling white wines and medium-body restrained reds are smart choices. Slow-cooked garlic provides a sense of sweetness, so don't be bashful in highlighting wine of ample fruit.*

Categories: 3A, 4

Specific Recommendations:

3A: *Chardonnay—complex and concentrated—France, California, Australia* ■ *Pinot Gris—rich and honeyed—France, Oregon*

4: *Gamay—clean, fresh, and grapy—France* ■ *Merlot—pretty and soft—Italy, USA, France*

Grilled Fish in Turkish Marinade
of Yogurt, Coriander, Cardamom, and Lemon

A *s the Turks, Greeks, and Indians know, yogurt makes a great marinade for fish or chicken. It tenderizes as it seasons, and provides a tart balance for the sweet spices. This is an ideal dish for a busy day when you have a great desire for flavor but little time to cook.*

Serves 6

1 cup nonfat or low-fat yogurt

1 tablespoon ground coriander

$1/2$ teaspoon ground cardamom

1 teaspoon freshly ground black pepper

3 tablespoons fresh lemon juice

1 teaspoon salt

6 5- to 6-ounce fillets of a firm whitefish, such as cod, halibut, flounder, sea bass, or swordfish

2 tablespoons chopped dill (optional) for garnish

Combine all of the ingredients and marinate the fish fillets for 3 to 6 hours.

Preheat the broiler or make a charcoal fire. Wipe off excess marinade, brush the fish lightly with oil, and sprinkle with salt and pepper.

Broil or grill for about 4 minutes per side.

Garnish with chopped dill, if desired, and serve with a lemon wedge.

You may also cook the fish on a lightly oiled baking sheet in a 400 degree oven for about 12 minutes, or until it tests done.

Kitchen Conversation

We can afford to be a bit assertive with the accompaniments here because the grill/broiler adds another level of flavor called "char." So don't hesitate to serve that spunky walnut-sauced eggplant (page 308) or an aggressive carrot dish (page 306). Pilaf and spinach are middle-of-the-road and will probably delight everyone.

Wine Notes

Pairing Pointers: *This dish appears bold, but remember that brief marinades offer accent rather than take over the dish. The lemon, cardamom, and coriander provide a lovely backdrop. If you grill over wood, you pick up the more bitter elements of the wine.*

Categories: 1A, 1B

Specific Recommendations:

1A: *Sparkling wine—citrusy and lively, no oak—USA* ■ *Alvarinho or Albariño—zippy and tart—Portugal, Spain*

1B: *Riesling—fragrant, ripe, and penetrating—Germany, Pacific Northwest* ■ *Gewürztraminer—spicy, floral, and off-dry—USA*

Poaching Fish

Poaching is a wonderful way to prepare fish if you want to keep it moist and tender. This technique is especially good for fish that is lean and low in oils. Never let the poaching liquid boil. Bring it up to a slight simmer, slip the fish in the simmering liquid, cover the pan, and check after 8 to 10 minutes per inch of thickness for fillets. Boiling will toughen fish, even softened salt cod.

Tonno all'Abruzzese
Seared Tuna with Rosemary, Garlic, and Hot Pepper

Here's a spin on the bitter, hot, and sour theme. Traditionally angler (monkfish), a meaty and slightly chewy fish, is used for this spicy sauté from the Abruzzo region of Italy. Having now tried this with angler, swordfish, cod, and tuna, I think the rich, meaty quality of the tuna is a better foil for the sauce than any of the milder fish.

Serves 4

4 thick slices of tuna, preferably ahi or bigeye, each about 5 to 6 ounces, or **1¹/₂ pounds angler,** cut on the diagonal into 1-inch slices

Salt and freshly ground black pepper

¹/₄ cup olive oil

1 tablespoon hot pepper flakes or more to taste

2 tablespoons chopped fresh rosemary

1 tablespoon finely minced garlic

1 cup dry white wine

1 cup Basic Fish Stock (page 114)

Sprinkle the fish fillets with salt and pepper. Heat the olive oil in a heavy sauté pan over medium-high heat. Sear the tuna slices quickly on both sides and set aside to keep warm. Reduce the heat and add the hot pepper flakes, rosemary, garlic, wine, and stock. Cook over high heat until the liquids are reduced by half, about 5 minutes. Season with salt and pepper. Reduce the heat and return the fish to the pan for a minute or two to coat with the sauce. Serve at once.

Kitchen Conversation

I love this dish. It's so bold in flavor, it surprises people who think fish is bland, safe, and for sissies. Please don't overcook the tuna, as it will lose some of its meaty character. Treating it like rare to medium-rare steak is the key. (If you like well-done steak our conversation ceases here.) Any leafy green—spinach, Swiss chard, even broccoli—is a wonderful accompaniment. The heat and acidity and the bitterness of the rosemary from the sauce don't scare them either.

Wine Notes

Pairing Pointers: *Working with tuna is like working with meat. The texture, when cooked rare, is buttery and almost like filet of beef. This preparation demands a white or red wine with a strong personality, as the ingredients could easily overpower a less assertive wine.*

Categories: 2, 4

Specific Recommendations:

2: *Sauvignon Blanc—herbal and pungent—France, New Zealand* ■ *Verdejo—earthy, grassy, and young—Spain*

4: *Pinot Noir—simple and focused—France, California* ■ *Corvina—modest, fresh, and spicy—Italy*

Tuna Portuguese with Paprika, Garlic, Chiles, Coriander, and Green Onions

We are still playing with the theme of hot and sour with this tuna recipe. This dish sounds as if it should be from Latin America, but it's Portuguese. The African hot peppers, known as piri piri *(see page 321), can be replaced with easier-to-find jalapeños. Fresh coriander, also called cilantro or "Chinese parsley," is an herb that is prevalent in Portuguese cuisine as well. As this marinade is quite intense, rub it on the fish no more than 2 hours before cooking.*

Serves 4

3 tablespoons sweet paprika

2 tablespoons finely minced garlic

3 to 4 finely minced chiles, depending upon preferred heat

1 cup finely chopped fresh coriander (use half for garnish)

1 cup finely chopped green onions (use half for garnish)

1 tablespoon freshly ground black pepper

¹/₄ cup fresh lemon juice

¹/₂ cup olive oil

4 tuna fillets, about 5 ounces each

Salt

Combine the paprika, garlic, chiles, half the coriander and half the green onions, and black pepper in a bowl. Stir in lemon juice and olive oil. Rub this paste on the tuna fillets and marinate in the refrigerator for about 2 hours.

Preheat the broiler or make a charcoal fire. Sprinkle the fish with salt and broil for 3 minutes on each side for medium rare. Serve topped with remaining chopped herbs and green onions.

Kitchen Conversation

Why tuna? Because it has a meaty taste. Back to the steak allusion. One of the "fishy" fishes, like mackerel, would do well here too. Because of the bitter, hot, and sour aspects of the marinade, I like to serve this with tomato-flavored rice pilaf and sautéed greens. It also stays within the ethnicity. But you could serve this with a rice-and-legume combination, like rice and lentils. Or with a white bean stew. Or with no starch at all, just greens. And maybe a little piri piri sauce (page 321) for the bold of palate.

Wine Notes

Pairing Pointers: *This preparation needs a refreshing rosé or medium-full and abundantly fruity reds. If you use an oilier fish for this, play down the tannins and oak. Pungency with some restraint is the key. The chiles, green onions, and coriander all pair well with an herbaceous wine.*

Categories: 1A, 5

Specific Recommendations:

1A: *Rosé/ blends—spicy, bold, young—France, Spain* ■
Arneis—lemony, concentrated, fresh—Italy

5: *Sangiovese —earthy, leafy, clean—Italy, Argentina* ■
Cabernet/blends—soft, olivey, free of tannin—Chile, Pacific Northwest

Grilled Fish in a Spanish Marinade

Here is an aromatic spice rub for fish that doesn't have the heat of chiles, but gives you the option of heat on the side: You can offer a bowl of Hazelnut Romesco Sauce as an accompaniment.

Serves 4

4 fillets of a firm and meaty whitefish, such as northern halibut, flounder, or cod, each about 5 ounces

3 cloves garlic, minced

1¹/₂ tablespoons ground cumin

3 tablespoons paprika

4 tablespoons fresh lemon juice

4 tablespoons olive oil

Salt and freshly ground black pepper

Hazelnut Romesco Sauce (page 316)

Place the fish fillets in a shallow nonaluminum dish. Combine the garlic, cumin, and paprika with the lemon juice and olive oil, and rub this paste on the fish. Cover and refrigerate for 2 to 4 hours.

Preheat the broiler or make a charcoal fire. Sprinkle the fish with salt and pepper, and broil or grill for 3 minutes on each side, or until the fish tests done.

Kitchen Conversation

This classic Spanish spice rub is in a style called adobado. The sweet paprika and garlic mixture usually is rubbed on mild-tasting chicken and pork. So why not fish? They are all relatively neutral canvases. The cumin and lemon add a tart note, but that's probably not tart enough. Serve with a lemon wedge, as you'll find more acid is needed to bring up the flavor of the fish. You could accompany this with just potatoes and a sweet or mild vegetable. Here's an opportunity to make romesco sauce and turn this fish dish into a party.

Wine Notes

Pairing Pointers: *This dish calls for tartness and a little "green" as a backdrop. The cumin needs to be cut by acidity, as it's clearly dominant from a wine standpoint. The garlic and paprika require an earthy wine.*

Categories: 2, 4

Specific Recommendations:

2: *Sauvignon Blanc—steely, grassy, and bright—Italy, France* ■ *White/blends—earthy, olivey—Spain, Portugal*

4: *Various Spanish—simple, understated, and rustic—Somotano* ■ *Barbera—sharp, ample with soft tannin—Italy*

Greek-Inspired Ouzo, Fennel, and Orange-Marinated Fish

*O*uzo, raki, and Pernod are anise-flavored liquors that contribute to a fragrant marinade for fish. Ground toasted fennel seeds heighten the licoricy perfume. For the citrus base, orange juice or, better yet, blood orange juice is excellent, as it adds acidity and sweetness and a hint of color. The herbs of choice are fresh thyme and mint.

Serves 4

$^1/_4$ cup olive oil

1$^1/_2$ tablespoons finely minced garlic

1 teaspoon ground toasted fennel seeds

2 teaspoons chopped fresh thyme

3 tablespoons chopped fresh mint

Grated zest of 1 orange

4 tablespoons fresh orange juice

2 tablespoons fresh lemon juice

$^1/_3$ cup ouzo or **Pernod** or **raki**

4 5- to 6-ounce fillets of fish, such as salmon, snapper, cod, or sea bass

Salt and freshly ground black pepper

Warm the olive oil in a small sauté pan over low heat. Add the garlic and cook for a minute or two to remove the bite. Remove from the heat and add the fennel seed, thyme, mint, zest, juices, ouzo, salt and pepper. When cool, pour this marinade over the fish fillets and marinate for 3 to 4 hours in the refrigerator.

Preheat the broiler or make a charcoal fire. Brush the fish lightly with oil and sprinkle with salt and pepper. Broil for about 3 to 4 minutes per side. Or you may bake the marinated fillets for 8 to 10 minutes in a 450 degree oven. Spoon any excess marinade over the fish after baking or grilling.

Kitchen Conversation

How'd you do with this one? Did the sweetness of the orange balance the bittersweet anise flavor of ouzo and fennel? The lemon helps balance the bitter and the sweet; perhaps you might need a bit more lemon to accent both. Please be sure to add enough salt so that you can taste the spices and the herbs, the orange and the anise. Serve this with a simple rice pilaf and green beans and sautéed fennel. Or try asparagus or spinach, which both do well with orange accents. If you want to play with the Greco-Mediterranean theme, roast potatoes garnished with crumbled feta cheese, olives, and grilled onions, and a pan ragout of greens, fennel, and artichokes avgolemono (page 294) will get you there.

Wine Notes

Pairing Pointers: *Prominent tastes come from the marinade. Pick up on the citrus notes (sweet and tart), the ouzo (bitter and tart), and the fennel (sweet and earthy). While this could work with light reds, I prefer white wines. If you decide on a red, keep the citrus to a whisper and up the anise of ouzo and fennel.*

Categories: 1A, 2, 3A

Specific Recommendations:

1A: *Chenin Blanc—firm, orange scented—South Africa, France* ■
Pinot Grigio—crisp, citrusy, assertive—Italy, Oregon

2: *Chardonnay—lean, flinty, refreshing—USA, France* ■
Gewürztraminer—floral, sweet spiced—France, Germany

3A: *Viognier—big, full, and rich with moderate alcohol— France, USA*

The Echo Effect

This means repeating a theme in a dish. For example, if fennel seed is a seasoning in a sausage or marinade, using fresh fennel as a vegetable accompaniment or as part of the dish would be playing with the echo effect. Or ouzo or Pernod, then using fresh fennel. All of these play with the theme of anise but in different parts of a recipe.

Roast Fish with Sicilian Sweet-and-Sour Onions

Many years ago, I stood on a terraced hillside in the ancient Sicilian town of Ragusa Ibla, looking at the spectacular view. All along the rock walls were trays of tomatoes and tomato paste, spread out to dry in the hot sun. Although sun-dried tomatoes appear to be trendy in America, they are part of a strong Italian tradition of keeping tomatoes in the repertoire of the cuisine when fresh, ripe tomatoes are out of season. ☞Sun-dried tomatoes are available dry or packed in oil. The dry ones need to be reconstituted in a little water or they will be too chewy. However, soaking them can leach out a lot of the flavor. (If you use oil-packed sun-dried tomatoes, you do not have to soak them.) With the dry tomatoes, soak a third in hot water to get a full-flavored tomato liquid to add to the onion mixture, then add the rest of the tomatoes without soaking. They will soften enough if you prepare the onion mixture a few hours ahead of time. Combining the tomatoes with currants is an Arabic touch, also part of the Sicilian tradition.

Serves 4

¹/₄ cup olive oil

3 yellow onions, sliced ¹/₄ inch thick (4 to 5 cups)

2 tablespoons red wine vinegar or to taste

1 tablespoon honey or **to taste**

¹/₃ cup sun-dried tomatoes, preferably oil packed, cut in thin slivers

3 tablespoons currants, plumped in hot water, drained and liquids saved

6 tablespoons chopped fresh mint

4 5- to 6-ounce fillets of cod, snapper, flounder, halibut, or **sea bass**

Salt and freshly ground black pepper to taste

Preheat the oven to 450 degrees.

Heat the olive oil in a large sauté pan. Add the onions, sprinkle lightly with salt, and cook over moderate heat until very tender, 15 to 20 minutes, stirring occasionally. Do not let them brown. Add the vinegar and honey, and cook for 5 minutes. Add the sun-dried tomatoes, currants, and 4 tablespoons of the mint. Cook for a few minutes longer. Taste for seasoning. You may not need any additional salt if the tomatoes have been salted, but you will need pepper. Adjust the sweet-and-sour ratio. If you'd like it sweeter, add some of the currant soaking liquids. Check again for salt.

Sprinkle the fish fillets with salt and pepper, and place in a lightly oiled baking dish. Cover with the onions. Bake for 8 to 10 minutes, or until the fish tests done (poke with a knife and take a peek). You may need to cook this a little longer if the onions were cool when you put them on top of the fish. Remove the fish to serving plates and top with the remaining chopped mint.

Kitchen Conversation

Our palates seem to like counterpoint and contrast, so sweet and sour is an appealing taste combination. By cooking onions until they are sweet, and adding elements that play up the sweetness, you'll find that the key to balance is a tart component such as vinegar. Sweet fragrant mint, salty-sweet sun-dried tomatoes and sweet currants lend complexity to the onions. It's all a question of balance, balance, balance. Can you taste the tomatoes under the sweetness of the onions and currants? If you are short on time, serve this fish with simple roast potatoes, but for a more interesting meal, try the Pugliese Potato Pie (page 290), and watch the tomatoes, onions, and sweetness come alive. For a necessary taste contrast and relief, serve Braised Bitter Greens (page 298), such as a mixture of escarole, chicory, mustard greens, or broccoli rabe.

Wine Notes

Pairing Pointers: *The balance of sweet and tart is what wine is all about. Don't let the vinegar in this scare you. Just make certain that the wine is sharper than the dish. The sweetness of the onions can be mirrored through ripe fruit.*

Categories: 2, 3A, 4

Specific Recommendations:

2: *Garganega—lean, minty, and ripe—Italy*

3A: *Riesling—rich, medium full, and opulent—France, Washington State*

4: *Pinot Noir—dense, attractive, and seemingly sweet—USA*

Roast Fish with Walnuts, Raisins, and Moroccan Spiced Onions

This recipe plays with the theme of sweet and sour, also with an accent on sweet but with the addition of crunch from bitter walnuts. Caramelized onions are a traditional "sauce" in Morocco. They may be strewn over a lamb tagine or over a roast fish. For extra crunch hold a few onions aside to deep-fry. Sprinkle these crisp onions lightly with cinnamon and put them and the toasted walnuts over the fish at serving time.

Serves 4

Sweet Charmoula Spice Paste

1/2 teaspoon freshly ground black pepper

1/2 teaspoon cinnamon

1/2 teaspoon ground ginger

4 5- to 6-ounce fillets of a firm whitefish or **1 whole fish,** about 4 pounds

Salt

4 tablespoons olive oil

6 large onions, sliced 1/4 inch thick

1 teaspoon cinnamon

2 teaspoons ground cumin

1/2 teaspoon ground ginger

1 teaspoon ground cumin

1/4 teaspoon crushed saffron threads, steeped in 1/8 cup water

Olive oil, as needed, about 4 tablespoons

1 tablespoon grated orange zest

Salt and freshly ground black pepper

1 cup brown raisins, soaked in orange juice with a little lime juice

2 to 3 tablespoons honey to taste

1/2 cup toasted walnut halves (or large pieces)

Vinegar or lemon juice if needed for balance (optional)

Combine all of the spices and the saffron infusion in a small bowl. Add enough olive oil to make a spreadable paste.

Lightly salt the fish and rub with the charmoula spice paste. Marinate in the refrigerator for 2 to 3 hours.

Heat the olive oil and sauté all but 1 1/2 cups of the onions until very soft and tender, sprinkling them lightly with salt, 15 to 20 minutes. Add the spices and orange zest, and cook slowly until the onions are caramelized. Season with salt and pepper. Stir in the raisins and their soaking liquids.

Adjust the seasoning, adding the honey, vinegar, or lemon juice for balance. Simmer for 5 minutes to blend flavors.

Fry the remaining 1½ cups onions in oil until crisp and golden brown but not burned. Drain on towels and sprinkle lightly with cinnamon and salt while warm.

Preheat the oven to 450 degrees. Place the fish on an oiled baking pan, cover with the caramelized onions, and bake until the fish is fork tender, or about 10 minutes for fillets and 25 to 30 minutes for whole fish (about 10 minutes per inch of thickness). Sprinkle with crispy fried onions and walnuts.

Kitchen Conversation

You didn't think I would let a Moroccan fish dish go by without some reference to charmoula, did you? (See page 314 for more.) Here we are using a sweet rather than a tart and spicy version of the marinade. It should be subtle; a light massage will do.

It is important to cook the onions until they are very, very sweet and caramelized. Add the sweet spices midway in the cooking process so they don't scorch. For this recipe the raisins are soaked in bitter orange juice until they plump. Bitter orange adds a tart edge and a citrus perfume. As we can't always find bitter Seville-type oranges, I've added a little lime juice to approximate the tang. I love how the raisins pick up the citrus flavor and hold it. Fold in the raisins at the end of cooking so that the orange juice doesn't dissipate. My addition is the crispy fried onions, just carrying the sweet onion theme to its logical extension. The walnuts add bitterness and crunch and provide counterpoint to the sweet flavors. As a variation, you might try almonds to see if you prefer this sweeter nut. Serve this dish simply, with couscous.

Wine Notes

Pairing Pointers: *Although I'm rarely an advocate of finding stunt doubles in wine to mimic the food, here it works! Select a wine with richness, sweet spicing, and a little bitterness (for the walnuts). This dish is a real candidate for Alsatian varietals. Light, spicy reds or rosés can be playful options.*

Categories: 2, 3A, 4

Specific Recommendations:

2: *Rosé/blends—aromatic—France, USA*

3A: *Gewürztraminer—lush, spicy, round—France, Oregon*

4: *Gamay—young, jammy, harmonious—France, British Columbia*

Fish with Olives

We've played with the themes of mild and creamy, hot and sour, and sweet and sour. Now let's follow the olive trail with four fish recipes where olives go from simple accent to main ingredient, from foreground to middle ground. Bitter-salty olives will be partnered with other bitter flavors, and with sweet and with sour. I wish you could taste all of these dishes at one sitting. Please try each of them and let your taste memory do the work. Or take notes.

Roast Sea Bass with Radicchio, Olives, and Rosemary

A blend of bitter radicchio and rosemary and tart green olives could make for a difficult dish, but here they are quite harmonious. These are signature tastes of Roman cooking, combined in one sauce. Potatoes mashed with fragrant olive oil are a perfect foil for this triumvirate of bitter and tart. Try serving this with a braised artichoke, which is bitter in a different way.

Serves 4

4 5- to 6-ounces fillets of sea bass (or another firm whitefish)

Salt and freshly ground black pepper

6 tablespoons pure olive oil

5 cups radicchio, cut in fine strips

32 green cured olives, pitted and sliced

4 teaspoons finely minced fresh rosemary

2 to 2^1/$_2$ cups dry white wine

4 tablespoons extra virgin olive oil

Preheat the oven to 450 degrees. Sprinkle the fish with salt and pepper, and place on a baking sheet. Warm the olive oil in a sauté pan over moderate heat. Add the radicchio and sauté for 2 minutes. Add the olives, rosemary, and wine, and reduce a bit. Add salt and pepper and extra virgin olive oil, and pour mixture over the fish. Bake for 8 to 10 minutes until the fish is tender. You also can cook the fish, covered, in the pan with the sauce.

Kitchen Conversation

At first bite you will be surprised by the intensity of flavors, but then you'll be hooked. Especially if you have paired this with roast or olive-oil mashed potatoes, a comforting and interesting foil for the dominant bitter taste. I like to up the ante and echo the bitterness with another kind of bitterness, the braised artichoke. Did it work for you? Would you prefer a more neutral vegetable? No vegetables? Just the delightful tug-of-war between fish and potatoes? Will the wine guy hate me for such a challenging dish?

Wine Notes

Pairing Pointers: *I love a challenge! The olives and radicchio provide strong, bitter flavors that can work well with a variety of wines. Opt for whites with bright acid and austere structure, or a red with supple tannin and green herbal notes. The sharper the components, the greater degree of tartness needed in the wine.*

Categories: 2, 4

Specific Recommendations:

2: *Vernaccia —dusty, mineral scented, and nutty—Italy* ■ *Chardonnay—flinty, rustic, unoaked—France, Spain* ■ *Sauvignon Blanc—grassy, bright acid—USA, France*

4: *Merlot—leafy, peppery, straightforward—South America, Eastern Europe* ■ *Nebbiolo—balanced, medium intensity, charred—Italy*

Roasting Fish

Roasting is actually the same technique as baking. Although it sounds more elaborate, it's still the same. Very often fish that are to be roasted are better if marinated. (For example, try charmoula, page 314.) The marinade adds moisture as well as flavor. If the fish is lean, it should be basted with additional liquids such as fish or chicken broth or the marinade, or covered by a blanket of cooked vegetables or a savory rich sauce. Anything to hold the moisture in the delicate flesh.

Fish with a Moroccan Sauce of Roasted Peppers, Lemon, Olives, and Fresh Coriander

Fleshy and sweet roasted peppers, tart lemons, and salty olives combine in a lively, refreshing sauce for fish, broiled, steamed, or baked. Here the olives are an accent rather than foreground. If you are not in the mood for the bitter aura of fresh coriander (cilantro), you could use a mixture of sweet parsley and mint.

Serves 6

1 whole lemon, peeled, white pith removed, segmented, and chopped coarsely

2 roasted red peppers, cut in 1/4-inch dice

16 to 20 Moroccan green or **black olives,** pitted and coarsely chopped (about 1/2 cup)

2 tablespoons chopped fresh coriander

2 tablespoons fresh lemon juice

1/2 cup extra virgin olive oil

Salt and freshly ground black pepper to taste

6 5- to 6-ounce fillets of fish, such as tuna, swordfish, halibut, or sea bass

Combine all ingredients except fish in a bowl. Keep at room temperature. Spoon over cooked fish. (You may broil, grill, or bake the fish.)

Kitchen Conversation

This dish is a study in sweet and sour, punctuated by salt. Because the peppers take on a smoky sweetness after roasting, the lemon seems even more tart and the olives appear saltier rather than bitter. To bring the three elements in balance, you may even want to add a little more salt! This is supposed to be a very sprightly sauce to wake up a mild fish, even one stimulated by a little charmoula. However, if it's too intense for your palate, add a bit more fruity olive oil and some tomato puree. Of course, to stay in the ethnic flow, serve this with couscous, but potatoes or rice would work as well. Even the robust barley pilaf (page 140). Grilled eggplant, mild greens, even green beans with almonds—the call is yours.

Wine Notes

Pairing Pointers: *A savory commingling of textures and flavors—yet another challenge in wine selection. Sweet and smoky notes from the peppers, sharpness from the lemon, and salt from the olives. These demand a wine with high acid and, if you want red, pick one with soft tannin.*

Categories: 3A, 5

Specific Recommendations:

3A: *Chardonnay—mouthfilling, rich, citrusy—Australia, New York* ■ *Viognier—generous, perfumed, forward—California*

5: *Syrah/blends—spicy, soft, exploding with fruit—Southern France, Australia* ■ *Various Portuguese—coarse, peppery—Alentejo, Colares*

Fish with a Sauce of Black and Green Olives, Rosemary, Orange, and Garlic

*L*et's go from olives as an accent to olives as the main ingredient. This sauce is a tapenade with a Roman kick of rosemary. Briny olives and bitter rosemary are balanced with orange zest and fragrant olive oil.

Serves 6

$1/4$ cup chopped kalamata olives

$1/4$ cup chopped green picholine olives

2 teaspoons finely minced garlic

1 tablespoon grated orange zest

2 tablespoons chopped fresh rosemary

2 tablespoons fresh lemon juice

2 tablespoons fresh orange juice

$1/2$ to $2/3$ cup extra virgin olive oil

$1/2$ teaspoon freshly ground black pepper

6 5- to 6-ounce fillets of firm fish, such as swordfish, tuna, halibut, snapper, or sea bass

Combine all of the sauce ingredients and leave at room temperature. Spoon over broiled, grilled, baked, or poached fish fillets.

☛Note: For more pungency, you may want to marinate the fish in a paste of finely minced garlic, rosemary, lemon, and olive oil for about an hour before cooking.

Kitchen Conversation

Tapenade, the Provencal olive puree, is traditionally served with many harmonious companions, such as potatoes, green beans, beets, carrots, fennel. If you want to push the taste envelope, try a more bitter vegetable, such as broccoli, cauliflower, or eggplant. But you might need a neutral mediator like a potato to make peace with these assertive flavors.

Wine Notes

Pairing Pointers: The olives and rosemary give this dish a decidedly earthy and herbal character. While a red could work, bold and pungent whites with tart but balanced acidity are most harmonious. This is a classic dish for Sauvignon Blanc. If you want red, Cabernet Franc as part of a Cabernet blend would be your best choice.

Categories: 1A, 2

Specific Recommendations:

1A: *Prosecco and Italian sparkling/non-Champagne/French sparkling ■ Alvarinho—Portugal—Vinho Verde—Spain— pétillant and bright*

2: *Sauvignon Blanc—grassy and herbaceous—South America, USA ■ Vernaccia—mineral, aromatic, and ripe—Italy*

Generic Fish Cooking Instructions for Fish Sauce Recipes

6-ounce skinless fillets of fish

To bake: Preheat the oven to 450 degrees. Sprinkle fish with salt and pepper in an oiled baking dish. Bake for 8 to 10 minutes. Place on serving plates and spoon sauce over the fish.

To broil: Preheat the broiler or make a fire in the grill. Brush the fish lightly with olive oil and sprinkle with salt and pepper. Grill or broil 3 to 4 minutes per side. Place on serving plates and spoon sauce over the fish.

To poach: In a large deep sauté pan with high sides, bring poaching liquid to the depth of 2 to 3 inches (white wine, fish stock, or water) to a boil. Lower heat and reduce to a bare simmer. Poach fish fillets uncovered for 6 to 7 minutes. Carefully lift out of poaching liquid with a slotted spatula. Drain or blot fish dry with a clean cloth towel. Place on serving plates. Spoon sauce on top.

Three Assertive Sauces for Fish

Salsa Sporca

porca means dirty in Italian. Must be those specks of sage, capers, and olives spotting the pristine red tomato sauce. Here is another sauce with olives, but it is more complicated in flavor, with the addition of tart-sweet tomatoes, salty capers, and aromatic herbs. The tomatoes dominate and the olives act as salt. Incidentally, considering its Italian pedigree, this would make a great pasta sauce. You could add tuna, shrimp, or just serve it as is.

Serves 4

1¹/₂ cups tomato sauce

3 tablespoons capers, rinsed and chopped

1 tablespoon chopped fresh sage

2 tablespoons chopped fresh thyme

4 tablespoons chopped green olives

Freshly ground black pepper
(you may not need salt)

Extra virgin olive oil for richness

4 5- to 6-ounce fillets of a firm, meaty fish

Whisk the tomato sauce, capers, herbs, olives, and pepper to combine. Add the olive oil to taste. Warm in a small saucepan and spoon over the cooked fish. Or bake the fish under this sauce.

Kitchen Conversation

This is a tricky balancing act. Lots of intense little flavor bursts popping up in your mouth with each bite. The tomato sauce coats your mouth and adds acidity combined with sweetness. Be sure that the salt of the capers or the residual salt of the bitter olives doesn't get out of hand. If it does, add a teaspoon of sugar for balance, or a bit of citrus. This sauce is assertive! Potatoes and strong-flavored vegetables such as eggplant, broccoli, cauliflower would be the best accompaniments. Maybe zucchini would look nice, but you'll have a hard time finding its flavor because of the competition from the sauce.

Wine Notes

Pairing Pointers: *At first glance, this would appear to be a perfect match for white wines. However, I'd prefer medium-bodied, nontannic reds. Those that are a bit more rustic in nature stand up well to the boldness of the sauce. Keep tannins on the softer side.*

Category: 4

Specific Recommendations:

4: *Corvina—simple, straightforward, ripe—Italy* ■ *Merlot—soft, leafy, smooth—Pacific Northwest, South America, Southern France* ■ *Pinot Noir—earthy, spicy, uncomplicated—France*

Salsa Piccante

L et's see what happens when you change the salsa sporca by removing the bitter olives and adding some heat to the tomato sauce. Piccante means spicy, but don't make this so hot that you can't taste the fish.

Serves 4

2 tablespoons olive oil

1 tablespoon hot pepper flakes

1 tablespoon finely minced garlic

1 tablespoon chopped rosemary

1^1/$_2$ cups tomato sauce

2 tablespoons capers, rinsed and chopped

Salt and freshly ground black pepper to taste

4 5- to 6-ounce fillets of a firm, meaty fish

Warm the oil in a small saucepan over moderate heat. Add the hot pepper flakes and garlic, and cook for 2 minutes. Add the rest of the ingredients. Simmer for 3 minutes. Adjust the seasoning. Spoon over grilled fish or bake the fish with the sauce.

Kitchen Conversation

This sauce is as intense as salsa sporca but in a different way. The hot pepper and garlic combination is a force to be reckoned with. The garlic adds bottom notes. The rosemary is pushed back a bit by the heat, and the tomato seems a little more tame as well. You can play with the counterpoint of these elements until you reach your own sense of flavor balance. Serve with assertive vegetables as with salsa sporca.

Wine Notes

Pairing Pointers: *When you are working with heat, be careful with alcohol and tannin. Select wines similar to those suggested for fish with salsa sporca. A dry and refreshing rosé would also be a nice foil.*

Category: 4

Specific Recommendations:

4: *Gamay—fresh, quaffable—France* ■ *Carignan/blends—light, refreshing—soft red or rosé—Spain, France, North Africa*

Turkish-Syrian "Muhammara"-Inspired Sauce

T his spicy sauce is equally at home in Syria and Turkey. It is served as a condiment for bread, usually in the meze format. But it makes a vibrant sauce for fish. You will find a variation of this sauce with the Turkish-Inspired Grilled Eggplant Sandwich, page 77.

Serves 4

1 tablespoon hot pepper flakes

2 teaspoons ground cumin

1/2 teaspoon ground allspice

1 1/2 cups toasted walnuts

4 tablespoons pomegranate syrup

2 roasted red peppers

1/2 cup extra virgin olive oil

1 cup tomato puree or sauce

Chopped parsley, mint, dill, or fresh coriander

4 5- to 6-ounce fillets of a meaty fish, such as tuna or swordfish

Combine all of the ingredients except the fresh herbs and fish in the container of a food processor. Pulse to combine. The walnut should be somewhat chunky. Thin with more tomato puree and olive oil, enough to make a spoonable mixture to put over grilled or baked fish. Sprinkle with chopped herbs of your choice.

Kitchen Conversation

Not a sauce for sissies. This is a culinary high-wire act. Now you see what happens when you have heat, bitter walnuts, sweet peppers, plus tart-sweet tomatoes and pomegranate. The power struggle between these assertive flavors results in an intensely flavorful sauce that will wipe out a pallid-tasting fish, but will stand up to tuna or another meaty fish. The bitter walnuts push forward, followed by hot and sour. In the background of this flavor riot lies the sweetness of peppers and allspice. Serve with rice or wheat pilaf or potatoes. They calm the palate. If you want vegetables, choose those with big taste such as eggplant, broccoli, or bitter greens. Or maybe no vegetables. Why compete for attention?

Wine Notes

Pairing Pointers: *Choose extremely assertive whites with high acid and ripe flavors, or exuberant reds. Pomegranate always commands center stage and requires bright, sharp wines with juicy sweet fruit. The allspice, cumin, and hot pepper allow for some playful exchange; don't overlook off-dry white wines here.*

Categories: 1A, 2, 4

Specific Recommendations:

1A: *Rosé/blends—spicy, effusive, mild sweetness*

2: *Gewürztraminer—moderately rich, fragrant, sweetly spiced—USA*

4: *Barbera—ripe, brambly, slightly peppery—Italy*

Sea Bass Acqua Pazza

*A*cqua pazza *means crazy water. There are many versions of this Italian recipe; a few are wetter than others. Some poach fish in wine and stock, and serve the vegetables on the side; some poach fish in tomatoes and wine, then add the cooked vegetables to the sauce. I like to bake the fish atop the vegetables, pour a bit of the "crazy water" on top, and spoon the rest on after the fish comes out of the oven. This classic Mediterranean vegetable combination of eggplant, peppers, tomatoes, and zucchini is reminiscent of Provençal* ratatouille *and Catalan* samfaina.

Serves 4

4 5-ounce fillets of sea bass (or halibut or rock cod)

Salt and freshly ground black pepper

6 tablespoons olive oil or as needed

2 cups diced onions

1 cup white wine

$1/2$ cup Basic Fish Stock (page 114)

2 cups diced, peeled, and seeded tomatoes

1 large eggplant, peeled, cut in 1-inch dice

2 zucchini, cut in 1-inch dice

1 green or red bell pepper, cut in 1-inch dice

$1/2$ cup chopped fresh basil

Preheat the oven to 450 degrees.

Sprinkle the fish with salt and pepper, and refrigerate until needed.

Heat $1^1/2$ tablespoons of the olive oil in a large nonstick sauté pan. Cook the onions over moderate heat until soft, about 10 minutes. Add the wine, fish stock, and tomatoes, and simmer for 3 minutes. Season with salt or pepper. Set aside.

Heat 3 tablespoons olive oil in a large nonstick sauté pan and cook the eggplant over moderately high heat until soft, turning often, adding oil as needed. Be sure the eggplant is cooked through and translucent. Opaque areas tell you that those parts are still undercooked and probably bitter. After all the eggplant is cooked, set it aside. Heat the remaining olive oil in a nonstick sauté pan and cook the bell pepper and zucchini over moderate heat until tender, stirring occasionally, about 5 minutes. Add the eggplant to the zucchini and pepper, and stir in the basil. Season with salt and pepper.

Place the fish atop a bed of the eggplant mixture and top with half the tomato sauce. Bake for 8 to 10 minutes until the fish is cooked through. Remove the fish and vegetables to serving plates and spoon the remaining sauce over the fish.

☛Note: Because eggplant is so porous it is a sponge for olive oil. That is why I suggest using a nonstick pan, as you will need much less oil.

Kitchen Conversation

This dish is simply savory. None of the taste elements is so powerful that it needs taming. As the eggplant is cooked through and maybe even a little browned, it mingles happily with the tomatoes and other vegetables. They, in turn, don't overpower the fish. The basil provides a sweet herbal accent, which is so harmonious with the vegetable mixture. Serve this with roast potatoes or with mashed potatoes seasoned with garlic, and a little more basil. For a Greek accent, try the sauce with oregano.

Wine Notes

Pairing Pointers: *This is an uncomplicated and flavorful dish that wants wine to play a supporting role but not be center stage. Reds can work if they are light on tannin. Dry rosés and medium-rich, unoaked whites are lovely accompaniments.*

Categories: 1A, 4

Specific Recommendations:

1A: *Cortese—distinctive, zesty, a bit tart—Italy* ■ *Chardonnnay—light, crisp, unoaked—Northern Italy, France*

4: *Rosé Champagne—medium body, velvety—France* ■ *Pinot Noir—light, simple, autumnal—France, Italy, New Zealand*

Shrimp "Au Poivre" Sautéed Shrimp
with Garlic, Lemon, and Cracked Black Pepper

*M*any of us know and love the French classic steak *au poivre, where a rich cut of meat is coated with cracked black pepper and the pan is deglazed with wine, stock, or cream. Here is another take on the pepper and wine sauce, but using shrimp instead of steak. The shrimp are sweet, the garlic and black pepper hot, and the wine and lemon just sour enough to temper the heat and keep the sweetness of the shrimp in evidence.*

Serves 6

2 pounds shrimp, about 6 large or 8 to 9 medium per person

Salt

2 tablespoons olive oil

1 cup dry white wine

1¼ cups Basic Chicken Stock (page 115) or **Basic Fish Stock** (page 114)

1 tablespoon finely minced garlic

1½ teaspoons grated lemon zest

2 tablespoons fresh lemon juice

2 tablespoons cracked black pepper

1 teaspoon salt

⅓ cup extra virgin olive oil or **butter**

Shell and devein the shrimp.

Sprinkle them lightly with salt. Heat the olive oil in a large sauté pan and sear the shrimp quickly on both sides over high heat. Remove the shrimp from the pan with a slotted spoon and set aside.

Deglaze the pan with the white wine and stock. Then add the garlic, lemon zest, lemon juice, and cracked pepper. Reduce the liquids by half (to about 1¼ cups), return the shrimp to the pan, season them with a bit more salt, and swirl in the extra virgin olive oil or butter to smooth out the sauce.

Kitchen Conversation

Be sure you have salted the shrimp to bring up their sweetness. If you've gone overboard on the lemon or the wine is too tart, you'll be rescued by a swirl of fine olive oil or butter at the end of cooking. That's why it's there—to smooth things over both in taste and texture. To stay consistent with the meaty allusion to steak au poivre, *serve this with fried potatoes and maybe a leafy, tart green like spinach. Incidentally, to get more mileage out of one recipe, try this shrimp sauté as a sauce for pasta.*

Wine Notes

Pairing Pointers: *This is a balancing act. Taste the dish. Is it more tart (lemon) or hot (pepper)? The acidity of the wine should be rather high. If the dish is peppery, select a red with some tannin to soften the bite and allow the other flavors to come through.*

Categories: 1A, 3B, 4

Specific Recommendations:

1A: *Muscadet—clean, steely, zippy—France, California Pinot Blanc*

3B: *Sherry—dry, fresh manzanilla or fino*

4: *Various Spanish—sharp, peppery, vibrant—Penedès, Rias Baixas*

Gambas al Ajillo y Almendras Sautéed Shrimp with Wine, Garlic, Hot Pepper, and Toasted Almonds

G ambas al ajillo is a very popular dish in Spanish tascas or tapas bars. To the classic version of the recipe I've added another element of texture and sweetness, the toasted almonds. You'll see how the sweetness of the shrimp is intensified by the sweetness of the almonds. Don't forget to salt the shrimp appropriately to bring up their sweetness.

Serves 6

2 pounds shrimp

Salt and freshly ground black pepper

¹⁄₄ cup olive oil

1 cup white wine

2 tablespoons minced garlic

1 teaspoon hot pepper flakes or to taste

²⁄₃ cup toasted sliced almonds

Shell and devein the shrimp. Sprinkle with salt and pepper. Heat the olive oil in a large sauté pan and sear the shrimp quickly over high heat. Remove the shrimp from the pan with a slotted spoon. Add the wine and reduce quickly by half. Stir in the garlic and hot pepper flakes, and cook for 1 minute. Return the shrimp to the pan and add the almonds. Cook for 1 minute. Serve at once.

Kitchen Conversation

The balance of this dish is more sweet and hot than sweet, hot, and sour. Look out for the subtle qualities of tartness. Wine alone is milder than wine and lemon. As to pepper, pay attention to how the heat of red pepper differs from the bite of black pepper. You feel red hot pepper in the back of the throat rather than on the tongue as with black pepper. So add it gradually. Red pepper heat is truly cumulative—taste once, taste twice, and taste again. Take care not to overwhelm this dish with heat. You still want to taste the sweet shrimp and sweet, toasty almonds.

Serve with saffron rice and asparagus or peas, green beans or spinach. Or try it as a sauce for pasta, especially if you've made the dish too hot.

Wine Notes

Pairing Pointers: *Wines of some earthiness and rusticity are best with garlic. The hot pepper enforces this characteristic; wines that are refreshing are needed to cut through the heat. The acidity provides a lovely contrast to the oiliness and texture of the nuts. Play the regional trump card!*

Categories: 2, 5

Specific Recommendations:

2: *Verdejo—fresh, citrusy—Spain* ▪ *Brut Champagne—toasty, nutty—France*

5: *Tempranillo —young, lightly oaked, vanilla scented—Spain* ▪ *Cabernet/blends—soft, fragrant, smoky—France, South Africa*

Cozze Gratinati Baked Mussels, Pugliese Style

*I*f you dine in France you'd not be surprised to find a fish or shellfish dish gratinéed under a layer of melted cheese. If you dine in Italy and ask for grated cheese for your seafood pasta, the waiter will look at you in amazement. Cheese with fish? Well, here's a surprise: an Italian recipe that combines shellfish and cheese, a rare occurrence. It is from Apulia, where this taboo is broken. This can be served either as a savory appetizer course or as an unusual light meal, accompanied by a variety of vegetable salads. The sweetness of the tender mussels plays very nicely off the crunch of the crumbs and the saltiness of the cheese.

Serves 6 to 8 as an appetizer or 4 for lunch

4 pounds mussels, well scrubbed and debearded (about 6 per person as an appetizer)

³/₄ cup toasted or **dry bread crumbs**

6 tablespoons grated pecorino cheese

4 cloves garlic, finely minced

6 tablespoons chopped parsley

Freshly ground black pepper

Olive oil as needed

Lemon wedges (optional)

Preheat the oven to 450 degrees or preheat the broiler.

Open the mussels with a knife and save the liquids. Or you may steam them very briefly in a tiny bit of white wine or water until they just crack open. Reserve all the liquids and pour them through a cheesecloth-lined strainer and into a bowl.

Discard the top shells and loosen the mussels in the bottom shells. Carefully pull off any recalcitrant beards that may have remained. Arrange the mussels in the shells in gratin dishes, overlapping them a bit to keep them from tipping over. Drizzle with the strained mussel liquids.

Combine the bread crumbs, pecorino, garlic, and parsley, and sprinkle over the mussels. Then sprinkle with a few grinds of black pepper. Drizzle with the olive oil and bake in a hot oven or place under the broiler until the crumbs are golden. Serve with lemon wedges if desired. This dish probably does not need salt, as the pecorino should provide enough salinity.

Kitchen Conversation

What you are looking for is the texture contrast between crunchy and tender/juicy and the balance between salt and sweet. If this is too salty or if the garlic is too "hot," a good squeeze of lemon will help. Acid is the leveler for excessive heat or salt. Sweet and salt work well with clean, leafy tastes. So if you are serving this dish as a light meal, accompany it with spinach or bitter greens.

Wine Notes

Pairing Pointers: *Clean, refreshing white wines, almost metallic in their austerity, will be best. If you'd love to highlight a noble white wine, such as a French white Burgundy or any other rich Chardonnay, this would be a great opportunity.*

Category: 3

Specific Recommendations:

3: *Chardonnay—complex, textured, earthy—France, California, Australia* ■ *Sauvignon Blanc—scented, full—New Zealand, France* ■ *Marsanne—generous, dusty, assertive—France*

Mythia Me Domates Greek Mussel Stew

I first ate this snappy little mussel stew in Greece. It was paired with a glass of rosé wine. At first I thought, what an odd combination. I've eaten both white wine and red wine fish stews but never rosé. In fact, it was one of the tastiest wine and food pairings I've tried. Not one to leave a good idea alone, I thought, why not steam the mussels in rosé wine to begin with instead of in the more conventional white? (I've given both options so you can play with the taste combinations. The tomatoes, hot pepper, and feta cheese are also optional.) ☛ *In Greece shellfish is usually served as a meze or appetizer. Of course you could eat this as a main course, but it makes an ideal opening for a bigger dinner.*

Serves 6 to 8 as a meze or 4 as a main course (accompanied by lots of grilled bread to sop up the juices)

4 pounds mussels, well scrubbed and debearded

2 cups rosé or **white wine**

¹⁄₄ cup olive oil

1¹⁄₂ cups finely chopped onions

4 to 6 cloves garlic, finely chopped

1 hot chili pepper, finely chopped (optional)

3 cups chopped canned plum tomatoes (optional)

¹⁄₈ teaspoon ground allspice or **cloves**

1 tablespoon dried oregano

1 cup chopped parsley

Salt and lots of freshly ground black pepper

1 cup crumbled feta cheese (optional) for garnish

Put the mussels and wine in a large, wide saucepan, cover, and bring up to a boil. Steam until the mussels just open. This can be a matter of moments, especially if the mussels are small. Do not overcook! Remove the mussels with a slotted spoon and set them aside, covered. Strain the mussel steaming liquids through cheesecloth into a bowl and reserve.

Heat the olive oil in the large saucepan and sauté the onions until translucent, about 8 minutes. Reduce the heat and add the garlic, optional hot pepper and tomatoes, if using, allspice or cloves, oregano, and reserved mussel liquids. Simmer for about 15 minutes, stirring occasionally, until thickened. Season to taste with salt and pepper.

While the sauce is simmering, pick through the mussels and remove any beards you missed in the first cleaning process. Add the mussels in their shells to the sauce, stir well, and warm through. Serve hot or warm. Sprinkle with chopped parsley and garnish with feta cheese if desired.

Kitchen Conversation

Rosé wine is sweeter than most white wines. Balancing this dish depends upon the wine you used for steaming the mussels. Salt will help tame the tartness if the wine is a bit on the sour side. Black pepper or hot pepper will reduce sweetness. If you used tomatoes you are now playing with another element, the tartness or tart sweetness of the tomatoes. If too sweet, the saltiness of the feta will also help cut the sweetness; if too tart, up the heat a bit.

Wine Notes

Pairing Pointers: *Don't be scared off by the use of rosé, but steer clear of off-dry blush wines such as white Zinfandel. Of course whites will work here too.*

Categories: 1A, 2

Specific Recommendations:

1A: *Rosé/blends—light, fresh, tangy—European* ■ *Sparkling wine—earthy, balanced—France, Italy, Spain*

2: *Garganega—modest, lively, citrusy—Italy* ■ *Sauvignon Blanc—bold, grassy, a little coarse—France, USA*

Fish Recipes with Shellfish Sauces

What follows are two fish recipes with shellfish sauces: one with sweet mussels and bittersweet ouzo, the other with salty clams, sweet peas, and sweet mint. The fish is almost a backdrop for these lively shellfish stews, but it does provide a stage for the shellfish light entertainment dancing on the plate.

Fish with a Sauce of Mussels Steamed in Ouzo

*T*his Greek-inspired dish is very simple to prepare, yet delivers a great deal of complex flavor. The ouzo plays off the natural sweetness of the mussels, which in turn accents the sweetness of the fish. Serve topped with lots of chopped parsley (or part dill and parsley) and have plenty of warm bread to sop up the juices.

Serves 4

3 tablespoons olive oil

4 cups diced onions

1½ tablespoons finely minced garlic

⅛ teaspoon ground allspice

4 fillets of northern halibut, cod, flounder, or **sea bass,** about 4 ounces each

Salt and freshly ground black pepper

White wine or **Basic Fish Stock** (page 114)

2 pounds mussels, scrubbed and debearded

1 cup ouzo

¾ cup chopped Italian parsley

Preheat the oven to 450 degrees.

Heat the olive oil in a large, wide sauté pan. Add the onions, sprinkle lightly with salt, and cook over moderate heat for 10 minutes. Add the garlic and allspice, and cook for 2 minutes longer. Keep warm.

Place the fish fillets on a baking sheet. Sprinkle with salt and pepper, and generously drizzle with wine or fish stock. Bake for 8 to 10 minutes, depending upon the thickness of the fillets. While the fish is baking, add the mussels and ouzo to the cooked onions, bring up to a boil, and cover the pan. Steam the mussels until they just open. Remove the fish fillets from the baking sheet and place in warm soup bowls. Add the fish juices to the mussels. Season with black pepper. Spoon the mussels, onions, and all the pan juices over the fish. Top with chopped parsley.

☛Note: If you are a steamed mussel aficionado, you could make this without the fish. Allow 1 pound of mussels per person and double the rest of the ingredients.

Kitchen Conversation

Sweet allspice, combined with sweet onions, bitter-sweet ouzo, and sweet mussels, makes for a dish of complex sweetness but one that is not cloying. Parsley is not just a garnish here. It actually adds a clean, herbal taste that echoes and yet lightens the richness of the ouzo and the mussels, but doesn't fight with them. Rather than serving this in a bowl with toasted bread, try quartered steamed new potatoes as an alternative for sopping up the delicious pan juices. Rice is not a great choice, as it will absorb all the juices, leaving you with insufficient sauce for the fish. If you want to do this as a pan roast, braising the fish instead of baking it, see the recipe on page 204 for instructions.

Wine Notes

Pairing Pointers: Opt for simpler, unoaked white wines. Crisp acidity and leaner styles are most appropriate. If you do garnish with lots of parsley, use that to your advantage and play with a more herbaceous wine. Don't overlook the possibility of a fresh, sparkling wine.

Categories: 1A, 2

Specific Recommendations:

1A: *Muscadet—lively, pétillant, refreshing—France* ■ *Pinot Grigio—fresh, unoaked, inviting—Italy, Oregon*

2: *White/blends—bright, uncomplicated—Europe* ■ *Gewürztraminer—spicy, floral, intriguing—France, USA*

Pan-Roasted Fish with a Sauce of Clams, Peas, Mint, Onions, and Wine

T his Spanish fish dish is best served in a bowl with cut-up roast potatoes, or with grilled bread to sop up those wonderful pan juices. Saffron rice is an alternative, although it will drink up quite a bit of the juices on the plate. However, as this recipe has a good deal more liquid than the previous recipe for fish with mussels, you can afford to lose some sauce.

Serves 4

4 tablespoons olive oil

3 cups diced onions (will cook down to about 1¹⁄₂ cups)

4 teaspoons finely minced garlic

8 tablespoons chopped mint

8 tablespoons chopped parsley

2 cups white wine

2 cups Basic Fish Stock (page 114)

4 5-ounce fillets of mild whitefish

36 to 40 very small or 24 medium clams

1 cup fresh peas, blanched

Salt and freshly ground black pepper

12 to 16 small roast potatoes, quartered (optional)

Heat the olive oil in a sauté pan. Add the onions and cook over moderate heat until translucent, about 10 minutes. Add the garlic and herbs, and cook for 2 minutes. The onions can be prepared ahead of time up to this point. Add the wine and stock to the onions and bring up to a simmer. Add the fish to the onions, cover the pan, and simmer for a few minutes. Add the clams and peas, cover the pan, and simmer until the clams open and the fish is done. If you've used stock, you'll probably have too many pan juices. If so, remove the fish and clams to a platter, cover and keep warm, and reduce the pan juices by half. Season to taste. Spoon the sauce over the fish and serve at once with potatoes if desired.

Variation: You can change the direction of this dish to make it more Italian by cutting the wine and fish stock by half, adding tomatoes to the sauce, and using basil instead of mint. Serve with soft Polenta (page 64).

Kitchen Conversation

This is called a pan roast because the fish is "roasted" in the pan with the sauce rather than grilled or baked and the sauce spooned over. The flavor of the pan juices penetrates the fish rather than resting on the surface. (If you like this technique you might try it with the previous recipe, increasing the liquids by adding fish stock to the ouzo.) The mint and peas add sweetness, which balances the saltiness of the clams and the tart quality of the wine.

Wine Notes

Pairing Pointers: The peas and mint add delightful sweet notes and, if the clams are not overly briny, a crisp but off-dry white wine can enhance this perception of sweetness. If the clams are really salty, steer clear of sugar and select a wine with enough acidity that it will act like a lemon.

Categories: 1B, 2

Specific Recommendations:

1B: *Chenin Blanc—chalky, sharp, tropical—France ■ Riesling—crisp, balanced, mineral—Germany, Pacific Northwest*
2: *Chardonnay—lean, pedigreed, lightly oaked—Italy, USA, France ■ Sauvignon Blanc—minty, herbal, young—New Zealand, California*

Seafood Stews and Soups

Fish and shellfish are not inexpensive so a fish stew is usually served for special occasions. If you are in the mood for a seafood extravaganza but are low in cash, you can make a little fish and shellfish go a long way by stretching a basic fish stew with lots more broth and calling it a soup. Extend it with lots of grilled bread, steamed new potatoes, beans. And maybe a voluptuous sauce like aioli or romesco, which will make you feel rich indeed.

Suquet de Pescado Catalan Fish Stew

*T*he name suquet *comes from the Catalan Spanish word* suc, *which means juice. This dish can be as juicy as you like. In other words, you could serve it as a soup or a stew. The base sauce is thickened with a* picada *of bread, garlic, and almonds, but it is still quite brothy. Garnish with grilled bread croutons, and Ali-Oli Sauce, a garlic mayonnaise. Quartered roast or steamed potatoes and steamed asparagus make tasty (but unconventional) additions to round out this stew and make it more of a meal in a bowl.*

Serves 6

Sofregit (the base)

3 tablespoons olive oil

3 onions, chopped

2 red bell peppers, chopped

3 cloves garlic, minced

3 cups peeled, seeded, and chopped tomatoes (canned plum tomatoes okay)

Salt and freshly ground black pepper

Picada (the thickener)

2 tablespoons olive oil

1 thin slice bread, no crust

1 cup toasted sliced almonds

3 peeled cloves garlic

1^1/$_2$ cups brandy

4 cups Basic Fish Stock (page 114)

2 pounds assorted meaty whitefish, cut in chunks

1 pound new potatoes, roasted or steamed, cut in halves or quarters (optional)

1 pound asparagus, cut in 2-inch lengths after steaming (optional)

Chopped parsley for garnish

6 slices country bread, toasted or grilled and rubbed with garlic, cut into croutons, for garnish

1^1/$_2$ cups Ali-Oli Sauce (garlic mayonnaise)

To make the sofregit, heat the olive oil in a large sauté pan. Add the onions and cook for 8 minutes. Add the peppers and cook for 5 minutes longer. Add the garlic, tomatoes, salt and pepper, and cook until quite thick. This can be done ahead and left at room temperature for a few hours.

To make the picada, heat the olive oil in a sauté pan and fry the bread until golden on both sides. Add the almonds and garlic, and stir for a minute. Put them in a blender or processor and chop to coarse crumbs.

Bring the sofregit up to a simmer in the pan. Add the brandy and fish stock, and bring up to a boil. Add the fish, reduce the heat, cover the pan, and simmer until the fish is almost done, about 5 minutes. Stir in the picada, add the cooked potatoes and asparagus, if using, and warm through.

Season to taste with salt and pepper. Sprinkle with chopped parsley. Serve in soup bowls with garlic croutons and a dollop of ali-oli sauce.

Ali-Oli Sauce (Aioli)

1¹/₂ cups mayonnaise

4 to 6 cloves garlic, ground to a paste with 1 teaspoon coarse salt

Fresh lemon juice to taste

Salt and freshly ground black pepper

Combine all the ingredients in a bowl and season to taste.

Kitchen Conversation

In suquet *the sweetness of red peppers and almonds and the tart-sweet tomatoes are highlighted by the creamy, garlicky, tart ali-oli. (For the echo effect, try* Hazelnut Romesco Sauce, *page 316.) This is really a great soup or pan stew. So why the additions of asparagus and potatoes? Because I've found that many diners feel that they're not getting a "full meal" if there are no accompaniments. Grilled bread may not suffice. In the classic Spanish or Mediterranean mode, this dish would have been preceded by assorted tapas or a large, composed appetizer plate. American diners expect every plate to have a protein, starch, and vegetable when, in fact, these components can balance out over the course of a meal, or even over the course of the day.*

Wine Notes

Pairing Pointers: *The almond and bread provide enough distraction to allow a red wine. A medium-bodied red from a warmer climate (softer tannins, riper fruit) would be my recommendation. You could also straddle the fence and opt for a dry rosé, which gives you red wine flavor and white wine personality.*

Categories: 2, 5

Specific Recommendations:

2: *Rosé/blends—earthy, rustic—Spain, France, Portugal* ■
Albariño or Alvarinho—bright, lemony—Spain, Portugal

5: *Various Spanish—soft, ripe, delicious—Navarra, Penedès* ■
Pinot Noir—medium, spicy, toasty—France

Fabes con Almejas White Bean Stew with Clams

Fabada, or white bean stew, is a specialty of Asturias in Spain. Usually the stew is made with sausages and ham, but this version with clams is especially delicious. I love how the briny, salty clam juices work with the mild and creamy beans. The beans can be cooked the day before and reheated, the clams steamed just before you need them. Garnish with chopped mint and parsley.

Serves 4

1 pound large dried white beans

2 onions, chopped

5 cloves garlic, peeled and crushed

Bay leaf

Salt

4 tablespoons olive oil

2 onions, chopped

4 cloves garlic, minced

A few strands saffron, crushed

1 to 2 teaspoons dried chili pepper flakes

1 tablespoon paprika

²/₃ cup white wine

36 small clams, well scrubbed

¹/₄ cup chopped flat-leaf parsley

¹/₄ cup chopped fresh mint

Freshly ground black pepper

Wash the white beans, transfer them to a large saucepan, and cover the beans with fresh cold water. Bring to a boil and simmer for 2 minutes; let sit for 1 hour. Drain and cover with fresh cold water. Add the onions, garlic, and bay leaf, and bring up to a boil. Reduce the heat, add 2 teaspoons salt, and simmer, covered, until the beans are tender, about 1 hour. (Check them after an hour and monitor cooking progress carefully, as you don't want the beans to be mushy.) You may stop now, remove the beans from the heat, and set them aside for a few hours at room temperature or refrigerate them overnight. Bring the beans back up to a simmer just before you steam the clams. They should not be too brothy.

Heat the olive oil in a wide sauté pan and cook the onions over moderate heat until tender, about 10 minutes. Add the garlic, saffron, chili pepper flakes, and paprika, and cook for 2 minutes longer. Add the white wine and clams, and bring up to a boil. Cover the pan and cook until the clams open, a matter of minutes. Spoon them and their juices over the white bean stew. Heat together for 2 minutes and adjust seasoning. You may want more pepper and, if the clams are not salty, you may need a little salt too. Ladle into soup bowls with the clams on top, sprin-

kle with mint and parsley, and serve at once.

☞Note: You can also make this dish with mussels.

Kitchen Conversation

In fabes con almejas, *the white beans are background and the clams are foreground. As the bland beans are many and the clams are few, the latter should be mighty. Hot pepper, garlic, mint, all contribute to their liveliness, plus their own inherent salty taste. Serve this dish with wilted greens as a full meal. However,* fabes con almejas *would make a fine first course, or tapa, before a light entree. And conversely, you could toss the stew with orecchiette or pasta shells for a very Southern Italian–inspired pasta. You can even add the greens!*

Wine Notes

Pairing Pointers: *This dish requires a wine of richness and power. The bland, thick creaminess of the white beans is a nice texture to enhance while providing some intensity of flavor to match up with the clams (always forward), plus the heat and garlic. While a nuanced Chardonnay may get lost, a concentrated but simpler one would be lovely. Fruity reds are great with this dish.*

Categories: 3A, 5

Specific Recommendations:

3A: *Chardonnay—full bodied, earthy, textured—France, USA* ■ *Marsanne—musty, robust—France*

5: *Sangiovese —tart, leathery, ripe—Italy, California* ■ *Various Portuguese/Spanish—simple, forthcoming, and not tannic*

Feijoada de Mariscos Portuguese White Bean Stew with Shellfish

Many of us associate feijoada *with the classic Brazilian black bean and meat extravaganza served with rice, greens, oranges, and hot sauce.* Feijoada *is also served in Portugal, where it is prepared with white beans and called* feijoada branca. *While most* feijoadas *are cooked with sausage and pork, shellfish* feijoadas *are starting to appear on Portuguese restaurant menus. As you've seen from* Fabes con Almejas *(page 208), this is not such an outlandish notion. This version, however, is a bit more extravagant but well worth the effort and expense. The white bean stew can be made the day before. Serve in soup bowls as is or on a plate with Braised Bitter Greens (page 298). For a piquant accent, pass the piri piri hot sauce (page 321).*

Serves 6

---

1 pound or **2 cups dried white beans**

2 medium onions, chopped

2 cloves garlic, peeled

1 bay leaf

4 tablespoons olive oil

2 large or 3 medium onions, chopped

5 cloves garlic, minced

2 teaspoons hot pepper flakes

5 to 6 tomatoes, peeled, seeded, and chopped

Salt and freshly ground black pepper

3 small lobsters, steamed and cut in sections with the shell on, cracked where needed

2 cups Basic Fish Stock (page 114) or **part stock and part white wine**

24 large shrimp

48 manila clams, about 2¹/₂ pounds

¹/₂ cup chopped cilantro

First make the white bean stew. Cover the beans with 6 cups cold water in a large saucepan. Bring up to a boil. Simmer for 2 minutes. Let rest for 1 hour. Drain and cover with fresh cold water. Bring up to a boil, add the onions, garlic, and bay leaf, and simmer until the beans are cooked but not soft. (Add salt after 30 minutes.) Remove the bay leaf.

In a large saucepan, warm the olive oil. Cook the onions over moderate heat until soft, about 10 minutes. Add the garlic, hot pepper flakes, and tomatoes, and simmer for 5 minutes. Drain the beans and add to the onions and tomatoes. Simmer for 20 minutes. Season with salt and black pepper.

Steam the lobsters in salted water for about 8 minutes. Cool a bit, remove the heads, cut in half lengthwise, clean, and cut into sections, cracking the claws, etc., where needed. Chill until needed.

Heat the bean stew in a very wide, shallow saucepan, adding the fish stock or wine and stock to thin.

Add the lobster sections, shrimp, and clams, and cook, covered, until the clams open and the shrimp are cooked through. Sprinkle with chopped cilantro.

Kitchen Conversation

Where the White Bean Stew with Clams on page 208 is quite a rustic dish (just salt and starch), this one is a Cinderella story. From humble beginnings to a richer life due to the company it keeps: prestigious lobster, elegant shrimp, and those in attendance, the salty, jaunty clams. The sweet, rich shellfish and the mild beans need a little spice to brighten their partnership. That is where the piri piri hot sauce and bitter greens come in, along with flavor bursts of salt from the clams.

Wine Notes

Pairing Pointers: This hearty shellfish stew demands wines of concentration and abundant character. Reds are nice, especially given the presence of the tomatoes, but don't pick wines that are too oaked or too tannic.

Categories: 3A, 4, 5

Specific Recommendations:

3A: *White/blends—richer, earthy examples—Provence, Southwest France*

4: *Carignan/blends—simple, straightforward—France, Spain*

5: *Various Portuguese—spicy, clean—Alentejo, Bucelas, Dão*

POULTRY & MEAT

In the Mediterranean tradition, poultry and meat were foods for festive occasions. They have never dominated the center of the plate as they have in America. However, partly due to greater health awareness, in the past few years meat consumption in our country has dropped. That doesn't mean we are becoming a nation of vegetarians, but we are putting poultry and meat in a different position on the plate—as a smaller portion or as a flavor component in a grain-based dish. Or as something we eat less often. Maybe on festive occasions.

The quality of poultry and meat in the Mediterranean is different from ours. Some recipes just can't be translated and followed slavishly by us. The average leg of lamb in Italy weighs about 1 to 2 pounds, the meat is pale pink and butter-tender. It cooks in minutes as opposed to hours. Pork is sweet, lean, and tender. It doesn't dry out because it cooks so quickly, whereas our new lean pork becomes dry easily.

Rather than sitting confined in a pen, eating formula feed, European chickens range freely for food, which makes them more flavorful and gives their flesh a firmer texture. A true stewing hen takes hours to cook, whereas ours will fall apart if subjected to the same long cooking process. Their birds also taste like chickens. Not like corn or cotton.

What follows are a few recipes for poultry. The first is a savory recipe for a simple sauté of chicken with a Greek-inspired tomato sauce and salty feta cheese. Then comes chicken cooked in three nut-based sauces—one from Italy made with sweet hazelnuts, one from Spain, with sweet almonds, and one from the Balkans made with bitter walnuts. Next follow a few simple marinades for grilled chicken, the first one based on tart yogurt, the next one on fragrant Moroccan spices in olive oil, and the third with tart and sweet pomegranate. There are two duck recipes, one with caramelized bitter turnips and sweet pears, and the other with sweet and tart quince and lemon. And there's a voluptuous recipe for a pigeon and bread pudding from the Veneto.

In this section you'll find a few choice recipes for beef: a Milanese fillet with sweet, rich sauce of cream, cloves, and bay; a Greek-inspired grilled flank steak rubbed with bitter and sweet spices; a Moroccan beef stew scented with sweet spices; and a hearty red wine–braised daube from Provence, perfumed with orange peel.

It should come as no surprise that most of the meat recipes are for lamb, the Mediterranean meat par excellence. Leg of lamb is rubbed with Moroccan bitter-edged mechoui spices and basted with saffron, ginger, and black pepper butter. Or marinated in tart yogurt, scented with sweet spices such as aniseed, cinnamon, and coriander. Or roasted Sicilian style with bitter rosemary, garlic, pepper, and tart lemon zest. Or stuffed with a Turkish savory walnut-laced ground lamb filling, and rubbed with bitter and sweet spices.

There are three succulent lamb stews. One from Spain called *al chilindron* is made with sweet roasted red peppers and a spice mixture of cumin, paprika, and strips of lemon zest. The Roman lamb stew, made *alla cacciatora,* or hunter's style, is assertively flavored with tart wine and vinegar, bitter hot pepper, garlic, and rosemary or oregano, and the salt that comes from anchovy. The last lamb stew is Greek in inspiration, with the classic egg and lemon avgolemono thickening added at the end.

We continue the theme of egg and lemon with a Greek pork and celery stew and a Renaissance recipe for pork loin with a sweet sauce of dried fruits and citrus. Pork is put in a spicy souvlaki marinade and grilled on skewers, or given a pungent mustard rub. We follow the bitter theme with a mustard and black pepper–encrusted veal chop.

Chicken Peloponnese

We have become a nation of chicken eaters. Therefore, we chefs are always trying to find new ways to satisfy cravings for the bird. This simple Greek-inspired chicken dish is a variation on the classic meze garides me feta, or shrimp with feta cheese and tomato. Although I know it's not in the classic Greek tradition, when I am in the mood for comfort food, I like to serve the chicken atop a bed of fresh pasta. When the feta and tomatoes mingle with the noodles, it's deliciously satisfying. For a more classic accompaniment, try orzo or roast potatoes.

Serves 4

4 tablespoons olive oil

1 onion, finely chopped

1 tablespoon finely minced garlic

2 to 3 teaspoons dried oregano

3 cups canned plum tomatoes, pureed coarsely with their juices

1/2 cup ouzo or **white wine** (optional)

Salt and freshly ground black pepper

8 half breasts of chicken, bones and skins removed, pounded to uniform 1/3-inch thickness between sheets of plastic wrap

1 cup crumbled feta cheese

1/4 cup chopped fresh dill or **Italian parsley**

Heat 2 tablespoons of the oil in a medium sauté pan and cook the onion over moderate heat until tender, about 8 minutes. Add the garlic and oregano, and cook 2 minutes. Add the tomatoes and ouzo or wine, if using, and cook for about 10 minutes over low heat until thickened. Season with salt and pepper, and set aside. This sauce can be made ahead of time.

Sprinkle the chicken breasts with salt and pepper. Heat the remaining olive oil in a large sauté pan and sauté chicken until golden on both sides, about 6 minutes. Add the sauce and simmer for 2 minutes. Top with crumbled feta cheese and chopped dill or parsley, and serve at once.

Kitchen Conversation

We are dealing with some challenging flavors here: the acidity of tomatoes, the salty assertiveness of feta cheese, the bitter undertones of garlic and oregano. The key is to play them off each other in just the right proportions. If you used wine, you've accented the tartness of the tomatoes; if you used ouzo, this adds a bittersweet quality of anise and alcohol. If the tomatoes are too tart, add a pinch of sugar. Feta cheese can be mild or quite salty. Dill or parsley will cut back on the saltiness of the cheese. However, all of these assertive tastes are softened if you serve this dish with bland rice, orzo, pasta, or potatoes.

Wine Notes

Pairing Pointers: *Although you may want to try a rosé, this is essentially a white wine preparation. Simple herbal whites play up the salt of the feta and the tart aspect of tomato and feta. The herbs chime right in.*

Categories: 2, 4, 5

Specific Recommendations:

2: *Sauvignon Blanc—medium body, herbal, unoaked* ■
White/blends—European—even retsina

4: *Pinot Noir—clean, herbal style—California, Burgundy* ■
Merlot—lighter style, olive scented—Washington State, South America

5: *Pinot Noir—bigger style, well-integrated oak—France* ■
Cabernet/blends—lighter style, cooler climate—Pacific Northwest

Chicken with Nut Sauces

Three delicious recipes for chicken with nuts follow. The first is Italian and pairs sweet toasted hazelnuts, earthy mushrooms, and cream in a rich and voluptuous sauce. The second is Spanish and adds a classic picada thickening of almonds and garlic to sherry, with just a little cream for a sweet and fragrant sauce. The third, Balkan in inspiration, uses bitter walnuts, spiced onions, and tart lemon for a complex and assertive sauce. These are fun to play around with, depending upon your mood.

Petti di Pollo con Crema di Funghi
Sautéed Chicken with Mushrooms, Hazelnuts, and Cream

T*he last time I was in Rome I revisited a favorite old restaurant, Da Costanza, situated in part of the 2,000-year-old Teatro di Pompeo off the Corso Vittorio. Designers would be hard pressed to come up with a more romantic environment for dining. Alas, I was alone. I decided I needed a really great meal. To begin with, as a* primo *I ordered the classic* carciofi alla romana, *mint and garlic-perfumed artichokes. Then, thinking that wouldn't be too filling, I decided to order a version of this dish. In Rome it is most often prepared with turkey breast (described as "turkey chest" on the menu!) and fresh porcini mushrooms, not an easy find here. You can intensify the flavor of brown crimini mushrooms or portobellos with dried porcini. An infusion of dried porcini liquids will elevate even those little white button mushrooms. I've added the hazelnuts for another dimension of flavor.*

Serves 4

¼ cup dried porcini

8 boneless half breasts of chicken or **4 turkey breast fillets,** each about 8 ounces

1 cup flour

Salt and freshly ground black pepper

4 tablespoons olive oil

4 cups finely chopped mushrooms (crimini, portobellos, etc.)

1 cup Basic Chicken Stock (page 115)

1 cup cream

6 to 8 tablespoons toasted chopped hazelnuts

1 tablespoon chopped thyme (optional)

3 tablespoons chopped parsley (optional)

Rinse the porcini to eliminate most surface dirt, then soak them in a cup of very hot water for about an hour. When the porcini are quite soft, pour the soaking liquids through a cheesecloth-lined strainer into a bowl and set aside. Rinse, squeeze dry, then chop the softened porcini.

Pound the chicken or turkey breasts slightly to a uniform $1/3$-inch thickness between sheets of plastic wrap. Dip the chicken or turkey in flour that has been seasoned with salt and pepper. Warm the olive oil in a large sauté pan over moderate heat. Sauté the chicken or turkey gently 2 to 3 minutes per side, or until almost cooked through. You don't want the meat to develop a crust. It must remain tender. Remove from the pan and keep warm.

Add the mushrooms to the oil in the pan and cook briskly over moderately high heat for 2 to 4 minutes until the mushrooms start to give off some liquid.

Add the stock, $3/4$ cup of the porcini liquids, and the porcini, and simmer for 2 minutes. Add the cream and hazelnuts, simmer until thickened. Return the chicken to the pan. Simmer for 2 minutes longer, or until cooked through. Place the chicken on 4 plates; if the sauce is too thin, reduce it a bit longer, then spoon the sauce over the top. Sprinkle with chopped thyme or parsley if desired.

Kitchen Conversation

Try this once without the hazelnuts and see if you miss them. I think they add to the dish rather than complicate it. In my mind, and in my mouth, the earthy mushrooms and the sweet hazelnuts become one, or the whole is more than the sum of its parts. A slightly acidic vegetable like asparagus or leafy spinach is an ideal accompaniment (although in Rome this dish is served as is; the vegetables come later). As it is so rich, no starch is needed. Rice or potatoes would push it and you over the edge. If you must inhale every drop of sauce, use bread or a spoon. If you find the earthiness a little powerful, try a sweeter vegetable like peas or beans to heighten the sweetness of the hazelnuts. The parsley will add a clean edge. And the thyme accents the earthy qualities of the sauce.

Wine Notes

Pairing Pointers: *This rich and earthy preparation can work with either reds or whites. The need is to cut the richness of the cream, so opt for a wine with reasonably firm acidity. If you select a red, don't bully the dish with too much tannin and extract.*

Categories: 3A, 5

Specific Recommendations:

3A: *Chardonnay—earthy textured with acidity—France, Washington State* ■ *Semillon/blends—not too ripe, fat— USA, Australia*

5: *Sangiovese —a richer-styled Chiantilike wine* ■ *Gamay— Cru Beaujolais or a stand-in like big Dolcetto, soft Nebbiolo*

Spanish-Inspired Chicken with Braised Garlic, Nuts, and Sherry

*T*his is a variation on the Spanish dish *pollo in pepitoria, minus the traditional thickening of mashed hard-boiled egg, but with the addition of braised garlic puree to enrich the picada, the classic Catalan sauce thickener made of nuts and bread. Some versions add a dice of Serrano ham or a pinch of saffron to the sauce. You can make this with chicken pieces, but boneless breasts are faster and seem to be what people are really cooking at home. You may try it either way. Just don't pound the chicken with the bones!*

Serves 4

1 small head of garlic (about 12 cloves), peeled

3 cups Basic Chicken Stock (page 115) (about 1 cup will be needed for garlic)

4 tablespoons olive oil

1 slice bread, crust removed

1 cup slivered almonds

8 chicken breast halves, bones and skins removed, pounded to ⅓ inch between sheets of plastic wrap

Salt and freshly ground black pepper

¾ cup amontillado sherry

2 tablespoons chopped fresh thyme

¼ cup cream (optional)

4 tablespoons chopped fresh parsley for garnish

4 tablespoons toasted slivered almonds

Put the garlic in a small saucepan, cover with the chicken stock, and simmer until tender. Remove the garlic cloves with a slotted spoon and puree them in a blender or food processor, using some of the stock if necessary. Set the puree aside as well as any extra cooking liquids. Do not wash the processor.

Heat half the olive oil in a large sauté pan and sauté the bread until golden. Set aside. Sauté the nuts until golden, stirring occasionally. Puree the bread and almonds in the processor or blender. Set aside.

Sprinkle the chicken with salt and pepper. Heat the remaining olive oil in a large sauté pan over moderate heat. Sauté the chicken breasts until golden on both sides. Remove the chicken from the pan and set aside to keep warm.

Add the sherry, chopped thyme, stock, garlic puree, and the nut mixture, and reduce over high heat. Add the cream if desired.

Return the chicken to the pan to warm through. Season with salt and pepper. Garnish with parsley and a few almonds.

Kitchen Conversation

This dish is sweet and rather rich, so the accompaniments need some bitterness or acidity for balance. Saffron-scented rice might add just the edge you need for contrast. Or omit all grains and serve asparagus or spinach. If you prefer to echo the sweetness of the almonds, sherry, and cream, choose peas or green beans. As a variation, and for a more intense sauce, cook 2 to 3 minced cloves of raw garlic in the oil with the bread, add bread and garlic to nuts, and puree for the picada thickening, omitting the milder cooked garlic puree. This will make the sauce less sweet and add a more bitter undertone.

Wine Notes

Pairing Pointers: The nuts add richness of flavor and richness of texture, much as cream would. The roasted garlic provides sweetness, as does the amontillado. (To make this more savory than sweet, opt for a fino sherry rather than an amontillado in the preparation of this dish.) A flavorful and medium-bodied white might appear to be overkill, but it really works well. Medium-bodied reds, rustic in style, are also nice tablemates.

Categories: 2, 5

Specific Recommendations:

2: *Chardonnay—rich, firm—France, Spain, USA* ■
White/blends—Rhône varietals, regional Spanish

5: *Pinot Noir—medium rich, medium tannin—France, Oregon* ■
Tempranillo blends—regional Spanish reds are hits

Chinese in Walnut Sauce

In Spain they love to use sweet almonds to thicken a sauce. In the Balkan countries and Russia, bitter walnuts are the nuts of choice. Try this recipe, featuring walnuts, spiced onions, and tart lemon, for an interesting variation. Some versions of this dish bake the chicken breasts and spoon the sauce over the top. I like to sauté the chicken breasts and add the walnut sauce to the pan. Try it both ways and see which you prefer. This sauce is also excellent spooned over roast chicken or turkey, and would even work well with fish.

Serves 4

4 whole chicken breasts
or **a 4-pound roasting chicken**

Salt and freshly ground black pepper

1¹/₂ cups ground toasted walnuts

4 cloves garlic, minced fine

1 tablespoon grated lemon zest

¹/₄ teaspoon cayenne

¹/₄ teaspoon cinnamon or **cloves**

2 tablespoons olive oil

2 tablespoons unsalted butter

1 onion, chopped

1 tablespoon flour

1¹/₂ cups Basic Chicken Stock (page 115)

1 to 2 tablespoons fresh lemon juice or **vinegar** to taste

4 tablespoons chopped fresh dill or **fresh coriander**

If you prefer, remove the bones and skin of the chicken breasts, pound them slightly between sheets of plastic wrap. Or leave the bones in and the skin on for baking or frying.

Season the chicken with salt and pepper.

Combine the ground walnuts, garlic, lemon zest, cayenne, and cinnamon with a little salt.

If sautéing the chicken breasts, heat the oil in a large sauté pan over high heat and brown the breasts quickly on all sides. Set aside. Add the butter to the pan, sauté the onion for 8 to 10 minutes over moder-ate heat until softened. Add the flour, stir well, and cook for about 4 minutes to get rid of the raw flour taste. Add the stock, stir well, and bring up to a boil. Reduce the heat, simmer for a few minutes. Stir in the walnut mixture and adjust the seasoning with the lemon juice, salt, and pepper. Add 2 tablespoons of the dill or fresh coriander. Return the chicken to the pan to coat with the sauce and finish cooking.

Please taste again for salt, lemon, and herbiness. Sprinkle with the remaining herbs if you need their accent, and serve at once.

If roasting the chicken breasts, preheat the oven to 350 to 375 degrees. Sprinkle the chicken breasts with salt and pepper, drizzle with a little olive oil and lemon juice, and roast until done, about 35 minutes. Spoon the sauce over the chicken and bake for 5 minutes longer. Sprinkle with the herbs and serve with lemon wedges.

If roasting a whole chicken, preheat the oven to 350 degrees. Cut a lemon into quarters. Rub the chicken with the lemon and put the lemon quarters and 12 peeled garlic cloves in the cavity. Place the chicken on a rack in a roasting pan. Sprinkle the chicken with salt, pepper, and a pinch of cayenne. Baste with a mixture of 5 tablespoons melted butter or olive oil, 4 tablespoons lemon juice, 2 minced cloves garlic, and a good pinch of cayenne or hot pepper flakes. Roast for about 1 hour, or until the juices run clear when the thigh is pierced with a knife. Carve the chicken and serve with the sauce.

Kitchen Conversation

This sauce is a challenge because there's no cream to subdue the bitterness of the walnuts. The hot and sweet spices help a bit, as does the tartness of the lemon, a crucial ingredient for balance. However, because the chicken is so bland, you won't find the bitterness is overpowering. Dill will add a sour component, and fresh coriander will add more bitterness if you like it. As an accompaniment you might want to serve baked polenta for sweetness, and leafy spinach or beets and greens for a sweet-and-sour accent. If you don't want polenta, try a wheat pilaf to echo the nutty quality, and glazed carrots or carrots and beets to add sweetness.

Wine Notes

Pairing Pointers: *The chicken is a neutral canvas. What's interesting here is the interplay of thick texture, the bitterness of the walnuts, and the sweet-hot nuances of the spicing. Reds or whites can do the job.*

Categories: 2, 5

Specific Recommendations:

2: *Brut Champagne or other sparkling wine—rich, toasty* ■ *Semillon—waxy texture, nutty flavors—Pacific Northwest, Australia*

5: *Merlot blends* ■ *Syrah/blendsMediterranean-style reds, lighter*

Marinades for the Grill

Here are three recipes for grilled or broiled chicken, one in a tart, spiced yogurt marinade, the second in a spiced Moroccan herb mixture, and the third in a sweet-and-sour pomegranate marinade. The first produces a very tender bird with a mild tang. The second, a tart, hot, and herbaceous bird. The third produces a bird with a smoky-sweet char to the skin and a tangy undertone. You may serve them as is or with Sour Plum Sauce (page 328) or Quince Preserves (page 370). The yogurt-marinated chicken also takes well to Esme sauce (page 322).

Grilled Chicken in a Middle Eastern Spiced Yogurt Marinade

*M*ost supermarket birds are sorely lacking in flavor. They can benefit from an intense marinade. Here the yogurt acts as a tart flavor component as well as a tenderizer. The spices are Persian, Turkish, and Afghani in inspiration. I prefer to use boneless thighs for this dish, but you could use boneless breasts, whole or cut in chunks, if you are very careful not to overcook them. Small broiler halves would also work well.

Serves 6

4 cloves garlic

1 small onion, chopped

1 tablespoon paprika

1 teaspoon cinnamon

1 teaspoon turmeric

$1/2$ teaspoon ground cardamom

$1/4$ teaspoon cayenne

$1/4$ cup fresh lemon juice

1 cup yogurt

18 boneless chicken thighs or **12 boneless breasts,** cut in large $1^1/_2$-inch cubes

Olive oil as needed

Salt

1 teaspoon freshly ground black pepper

Chopped Italian parsley

Lemon wedges

Puree the garlic, onion, spices, lemon juice, and yogurt in the container of a blender or food processor. Place the chicken in a nonaluminum container and cover with the marinade. Turn well to coat. Cover and refrigerate for 4 hours at least and up to 12 hours.

Preheat the broiler or make a charcoal fire. Thread the chicken on skewers, brush with a little oil, and sprinkle with salt and pepper. Cook for 4 to 5 minutes per side for thighs, 3 to 4 minutes per side for boneless breast cubes. Sprinkle with parsley and serve with lemon wedges.

Kitchen Conversation

The first question is, did you broil or did you grill the chicken? The grill adds a smoky dimension that softens the impact of the spices. The broiler leaves the spices more in the foreground. Sweet cinnamon and cardamom, tart yogurt and lemon, bitter turmeric, onion, and garlic will be brightened by a squeeze of lemon. And don't forget to salt, as salt will heighten the spices. You can serve this with a neutral rice or nutty barley pilaf (page 140). Almost any vegetable would work well, sweet glazed carrots (page 304), tart spinach with a few pine nuts and raisins, grilled eggplant with its subdued smokiness, or sweet grilled red peppers. Whichever direction your vegetable takes—sweet, sour, or bitter—those spices in the marinade will be subtly accented.

Wine Notes

Pairing Pointers: *The use of yogurt in the marinade provides velvety texture to the chicken as well as a tart background flavor. The sweet spices offer an opportunity to show off wines of similar flavor, such as Gewürztraminer, Muscat, etc. Go white/rosé unless you grill; then light reds will work too.*

Categories: 1B, 2, 4

Specific Recommendations:

1B: *Gewürztraminer—spicy, off-dry American examples are best* ■ *Muscat—spritzy Moscato d'Asti, not too sweet*

2: *Gewürztraminer—dry and aromatic—Alsatian* ■ *Rosé blends—floral Mediterranean cuvée, not too alcoholic*

4: *Gamay—perfect dish for Beaujolais* ■ *Carignan/blends— Southern France, California, or Spain*

Moroccan "Passport" Chicken

*N*o, you don't need a passport to eat this. We served it at a fund-raising benefit for 750 guests. The event was called "Passport." Cooking for this many people is a major challenge, especially when the guests are highly sophisticated and experienced diners. You want to capture their attention with big taste, hence the strong spice rub, and to serve that many guests, the dish has to reheat and hold without a major loss of flavor or texture. This was a big hit and is an ideal party dish. ☛The vegetable ragout can be made ahead. The chicken can be grilled or broiled, and the two combined and carefully warmed in a 350 degree oven. The flavors are still strikingly present, not washed out. For aromatic punch and freshness of flavor, sprinkle with chopped mint and cilantro just before serving and accompany with couscous. Just as good for 6 guests as for 750. But much less work.

Serves 6

---

2 tablespoons paprika

2 teaspoons ground ginger

1¹/₂ teaspoons turmeric

¹/₂ teaspoon cayenne

2 teaspoons freshly ground black pepper

1 tablespoon minced garlic

¹/₄ cup fresh lemon juice

¹/₂ cup olive oil

18 boneless chicken thighs (or 12 quail)

¹/₄ cup chopped fresh mint

¹/₄ cup chopped fresh cilantro

Make a paste of the spices, garlic, and lemon juice. Add the olive oil and rub this marinade on the chicken thighs or quail. Cover and refrigerate overnight. Keeping the skin on protects the chicken from toughening while broiling. If you remove it, be very careful while cooking not to ruin the chicken by letting it char and become hard.

To serve, preheat the broiler or make a charcoal fire. Broil or grill the chicken or quail for 5 minutes on each side.

Serve with couscous and place atop a vegetable ragout (page 278) that has been seasoned with slivers of preserved lemon and Moroccan black or green olives. Sprinkle with chopped mint and cilantro.

Kitchen Conversation

Most of the flavor elements in this dish are bitter, sour, and hot. Only the mint adds a note of sweetness, and it is a surface grace note at that. You may even want to heighten the sour with a wedge of lemon. After all, the chicken and couscous are bland. And the vegetables have some sweetness.

Wine Notes

Pairing Pointers: *North African marinades and pastes are often dominated by this bitter and hot mélange of flavors. While an off-dry wine can provide interesting contrast, I recommend the medium-bodied reds, spicy and chockful of fruit.*

Categories: 1A&B, 5

Specific Recommendations:

1A&B: *Chenin Blanc—floral, fruity, and balanced—Vouvray, California* ■ *Rosé/blends—not too sweet—white Zinfandel, Rosé d'Anjou*

5: *Syrah/blends with lots of Grenache—Southern Rhône Valley, Australia* ■ *Pinot Noir—spicy, herbal*

Grilled Chicken in a Pomegranate Marinade

From bitter, sour, and hot we go to sweet, sour, and bitter, with the addition of caramelization that comes from broiling or grilling. This pomegranate-based marinade seems Russian or Persian in its mixture of flavors. However, in Italy, Spain, and the Middle East, pomegranate juice has also been used for marination. The tart-sweet syrup helps the bird to develop a delectable char that crisps the skin. (If you prefer chicken without the skin, be careful not to toughen the flesh by charring it too long; in this case, it might be best to grill or broil until brown, then finish the cooking in a 400 degree oven.)

Serves 6

Marinade

1 medium onion, grated

2 cloves garlic, minced

3/4 cup pomegranate syrup

1/4 cup red wine

Honey (needed for balance if pomegranate is very tart)

2 teaspoons ground coriander

2 teaspoons freshly ground black pepper

1/2 teaspoon ground cloves

Pinch cayenne or to taste

1 teaspoon salt

3 tablespoons chopped cilantro

3 pounds boneless chicken parts, with skin

Combine all marinade ingredients and pour over the boneless chicken thighs or breasts. Marinate overnight, covered, in the refrigerator.

Preheat the broiler or make a charcoal fire.

Thread the chicken on skewers. Broil or grill for 4 to 5 minutes on each side.

Kitchen Conversation

Don't panic if the skin on the chicken turns almost black. It will taste great—caramelized, slightly bitter, and crunchy—while the flesh is infused with mild sweet spices. Serve with Sour Plum Sauce (page 328) and a cracked wheat or barley pilaf topped with chopped cilantro, green onions, and optional toasted walnuts if you didn't add them to the plum sauce. The walnuts' bitterness will be a nice contrast to the sweetness. For an interesting tart note, serve with sautéed spinach with lemon zest or pomegranate seeds, or sautéed spinach topped with yogurt seasoned with a little cinnamon.

Wine Notes

Pairing Pointers: It's a challenge to match wine and pomegranate because of the push-pull of sweet, tart, and bitter. Flavorful reds, exploding with fruit and devoid of discernible oak, are best.

Categories: 4, 5

Specific Recommendations:

4: *Gamay Beaujolais, Napa Gamay* ■ *Dolcetto or Barera— Italy, California*

5: *Pinot Noir—gushing with fruit* ■ *Tempranillo or other Spanish red—crianza styles, unoaked*

Charring

Most people love food cooked on the grill. They are attracted to the primitive caveman notion of cooking over wood, with fire and smoke, and all that it connotes. But what they really love is the charred surface on the food. Charring brings up a sweetness or a bittersweetness and provides a crunchy texture that is especially appealing on food that might ordinarily be considered bland, like chicken or zucchini. Adding sugar to a marinade in the form of honey or pomegranate promotes charring. The meat may darken and look almost black, but it will not taste burned. Just deliciously charred.

Sopa Coada Venetian Pigeon "Soup"

*T*his is a very old Venetian recipe that dates back to either the Middle Ages or the Renaissance. The dialect name coada *comes from the Italian* covare, *which means to brood, hatch, or smoulder. This soup "broods" for at least 3 hours in the oven, until it is ready to hatch.* ☛*Layers of sautéed country bread are topped with boned, braised pigeon, aromatic vegetables, grated Parmesan cheese, then covered with a rich pigeon stock and baked in the oven for many hours. The dish emerges golden, the stock fully absorbed, the bread soft and puddinglike. And the aroma is incredible!* ☛*Although there is some work connected to making this dish, after it is assembled it can be held in the refrigerator, minus the broth. When ready to bake, cover with hot broth, and put in a low oven for about 3 hours until you are ready to serve it. If you like, after scooping it into soup bowls, ladle a little more hot stock over the mixture and pass additional Parmesan.* ☛*Too rich and too thick to be served as a soup course,* sopa coada *is like a pigeon bread pudding and should be served as a main course or a rich first course before a very light second course.*

Serves 6

---

3 squab (pigeons), each weighing about 1 pound

6 tablespoons unsalted butter

2 tablespoons olive oil

1 very large onion, cut in small dice

2 ribs celery, cut in small dice

2 large carrots, peeled, cut in small dice

1 cup white wine

1 1/2 to 2 quarts Basic Chicken Stock (page 115)

Salt and freshly ground black pepper

Pinch cinnamon

1 1/2 pounds country-style bread, crusts removed, sliced 1/2 inch thick

Additional butter for frying bread

1/4 pound grated Parmesan, preferably Parmigiano Reggiano

Cut the squab into quarters and reserve the livers. **M**elt the butter with the oil in a wide saucepan over moderate heat. When the butter and oil are bubbling, add the chopped vegetables and sauté for 10 minutes. Add the pigeon quarters and sauté until golden, turning occasionally. Add the white wine and let it evaporate in the pan. Then add the chicken broth, a little salt and pepper, and a pinch of cinnamon, and cover the pan. Simmer for 30 minutes. Add the livers and simmer for 5 minutes longer.

Remove the pigeons and livers from the pan and carefully pull the meat from the bones. Cut any large pieces into bite size. Cut the livers into small pieces. Set the meat and livers aside. Taste the broth that remains in the pan. If it is not as rich as you would like, strain the broth, reserving the vegetables, and reduce the stock with the bones until quite intense in flavor. You should have $1^{1}/_{2}$ to 2 quarts of stock.

Meanwhile, melt some butter in a large sauté pan and sauté the bread until pale gold on both sides. (Or toast the bread and spread it lightly with butter when warm.)

Preheat the oven to 300 degrees.

Line a 3- to 4-inch-deep casserole or a large cazuela with one third of the bread. Sprinkle with grated Parmesan, then top with half the pigeon and liver pieces, half the aromatic vegetables, then bread, then cheese, then remaining pigeon and aromatic vegetables, then bread. Add pigeon stock to cover. Sprinkle with Parmesan. Cover tightly with foil.

Bake in the oven for $2^{1}/_{2}$ to 3 hours, adding stock as needed. (Push down on the bread with a wooden spoon and if the mixture seems dry, add more stock.)

To serve, cut into wedges or scoop out portions with a large spoon. Place in soup bowls, top with a little hot broth, and grated Parmesan.

Kitchen Conversation

Sweet, voluptuous, intense. This is so rich you will be blown away by the texture before you take time to assess the flavors. The sweet cinnamon and vegetables should be a subtle undertone. The Parmesan's salty quality is mellowed by the broth. The light gaminess of the squab also is subdued by the bread and rich broth.

Wine Notes

Pairing Pointers: *Reds are really best with this sumptuous hearty "soup." As no one specific taste element dominates, this is the perfect opportunity to feature the wine. Complex but not overly bold is the rule of thumb. While you want a wine of character, you don't want to overpower the subtle flavors of this dish. If you prefer, a rich, complex white would suffice nicely.*

Category: 5

Specific Recommendations:

5: *Syrah/blends—rich, peppery but not extracted—France, Australia ■ Pinot Noir—spicy, rich—France, Spain ■ Merlot—ample, complex— France, USA, Italy*

Two Duck Recipes Playing with Sweetness

Here are two duck recipes that play with sweetness, one with a bitter edge added by turnips, the other with the tart sweetness of quinces and lemon. The rich duck takes easily to both. Simple accompaniments are best, as these dishes are intensely flavored. Serve with roast potatoes, cooked in duck fat, or with rice pilaf. Bitter greens or tart leafy spinach are fine foils for fruit sauces.

Roast Duck with Caramelized Turnips, Pears, and Thyme

*B*itter and sweet, turnips and pears, blended with assertive honey, musky thyme, and the richness of duck meat. The ducks can be roasted ahead of time and reheated. Remember that one duck will serve 2 generously, and that one duck will not really feed 4 unless your guests have eaten a very filling first course. Two ducks can feed 5, however, if you cut the duck in eighths, giving everyone some meaty breast and thigh.

Serves 4 or 5

2 ducks, each about 5 pounds

Salt and freshly ground black pepper

4 sprigs thyme

3/4 cup full-flavored honey, such as chestnut, buckwheat, or lavender

2 cups Basic Chicken Stock (page 115) or **Duck Stock** (page 116)

3 teaspoons chopped thyme

2 tablespoons duck fat or **unsalted butter**

4 medium or **8 small turnips**

2 pears, not too ripe

Sugar

3 to 4 tablespoons pear brandy (optional)

Preheat the oven to 500 degrees. Prick the ducks all over with a fork. Place the ducks on racks in shallow roasting pans. Sprinkle the ducks inside and outside with salt and pepper, and place thyme sprigs in the cavities.

Roast for about an hour, basting the birds three times with boiling water during the first half hour to help draw out the fat and crisp the skin.

Meanwhile, combine the honey, stock, and chopped thyme in a small saucepan and bring up to a boil. Reduce the heat and simmer for 15 minutes, or until reduced.

Lower the oven temperature to 400 degrees. Baste the ducks with some of the honey mixture during the last 30 minutes.

When the ducks are cool enough to handle, cut into quarters or eighths.

While the ducks are roasting, peel the turnips and cut into wedges, if small, or large dice, if large. Cook in boiling salted water until crisp-tender, about 4 minutes. Drain and set aside. Peel, core, and dice the pears.

Melt a little duck fat or butter in a large sauté pan. Sauté the turnips and pears over moderate heat, sprinkling them with a little sugar to help them caramelize. Add the brandy, if desired, then add the reduced honey sauce to the pears and turnips, simmer for 5 minutes, and spoon this mixture over or around the duck.

If you have prepared the ducks ahead of time, warm the duck pieces in a 400 degree oven for about 10 minutes. Warm the sauce separately. Spoon the hot sauce over or around the ducks.

Kitchen Conversation

The bitter turnips are tamed by the sweetness of the pears and the honey. The thyme adds a musty, subtle perfume. Serve with sautéed bitter greens to echo the turnips. Roast potatoes or potato pancakes are a nice foil for both the duck sauce and greens. They have a crunchy texture for palate interest, but won't conflict with the main flavor themes.

Wine Notes

Pairing Pointers: *Duck demands bigger wines than chicken. Acid (tartness) is mandated to mitigate richness. We need rich whites and medium to full-bodied reds with ripe fruit to pick up on the caramelized sweetness of turnips and pears.*

Categories: 3A, 5

Specific Recommendations:

3A: *Viognier—young and ripe—France, California* ■ *Semillon/blends—vibrant—Australian*

5: *Syrah/blends—Australian Shiraz/blends* ■ *Zinfandel— medium body, medium tannin, brambly fruit*

Roast Duck with Braised Quince, Black Pepper, Marjoram, and Sweet Wine

I n this Balkan-inspired recipe for duck and quince, usually the duck is wild and the dish is braised. As we don't have ready access to wild ducks, and as most Americans have an aversion to duck that is braised, and obsess on "crispy," we roast the birds separately to crisp the skin and then spoon the sauce over (or around to preserve that yearned-for crispiness) just minutes before serving. ☛A word about quinces. I love them; there is nothing quite like their tart-sweet perfume. But I am a realist. In Brooklyn, where I grew up, I didn't see too many quinces in my supermarket. If you can find quinces, or have a tree, lucky you. If you can locate quince preserves, use apples for the sauce and stir in enough quince preserves for taste. Or just use apples. It won't taste the same, but it will be good.

Serves 4 to 5

1¹/₂ pounds quinces (4 to 5 large) (see notes 1 and 2)

Juice of 1 lemon

3 tablespoons unsalted butter

¹/₂ cup sugar

¹/₂ teaspoon cinnamon

1 teaspoon grated lemon zest

1 cup water or sweet wine or as needed

2 ducks, about 5 pounds each

¹/₄ cup honey

¹/₄ cup fresh lemon juice

1 tablespoon lemon zest

¹/₂ teaspoon cinnamon

1 tablespoon chopped fresh marjoram

1 teaspoon salt

2 teaspoons freshly ground black pepper

¹/₂ cup Duck Stock (page 116)

¹/₂ cup sweet wine (Marsala, port, etc.)

For the sauce

5 ounces pancetta, diced

1 onion, diced

1 tablespoon chopped fresh marjoram

1 teaspoon black pepper

2 teaspoons grated lemon zest

1 cup Duck Stock (page 116) or **Basic Chicken Stock** (page 115), or more as needed

1 cup Marsala, sweet white wine, or **port,** or to taste

Salt and freshly ground black pepper

Peel the quinces, cut in half, and remove the cores and seeds. Cut the quinces into $1/2$-inch slices and keep in a bowl of cold water with the lemon juice to keep them from discoloring.

Remove the quinces from the water and sauté quickly in the butter and sprinkle with the sugar, cinnamon, and lemon zest. Cook, stirring often, for about 15 minutes. Add the water or sweet wine and simmer for 20 to 30 minutes longer.

☞Note 1: You can cook the quinces a day ahead, let them rest at room temperature, and then add them when needed to the sauce. They will redden more after a day's rest.

☞Note 2: If you can't find quinces, use 3 to 4 pippin or Granny Smith apples. Apples will cook more quickly than quinces and do not need to be prepared the day ahead. Sauté them for 5 minutes, then simmer in sweet wine for 5 to 8 minutes longer. You may want to cut down on the sugar or add a bit of pomegranate juice for color.

Preheat the oven to 450 to 500 degrees. Prick the ducks all over with a fork.

Make a paste of the honey, lemon juice, lemon zest, cinnamon, marjoram, salt, and pepper. Rub some of this paste inside and outside the ducks. Place the ducks on racks in roasting pans. Sprinkle outside with salt and pepper. Baste the ducks for the first 30 minutes with boiling water to release all the fat. Reduce oven temperature to 400 degrees. Then combine the remaining spice paste with a little stock or part stock and part sweet wine, and baste 3 to 4 times until the ducks are cooked, about another 30 minutes. Set the ducks aside and, when cool enough to handle, cut them into quarters or eighths.

While the ducks are roasting, make the sauce. Put the pancetta in a sauté pan and cook over moderate heat until the pancetta starts to give off some fat. Add the diced onion and cook over moderate heat until the onions are soft, about 8 minutes. Add the marjoram, pepper, and lemon zest, and cook a few minutes longer. Add 1 cup stock, the quinces, and their juices to the sauce. Simmer the quinces in the sauce until tender, about 30 minutes longer. Add the sweet wine to taste and simmer for 20 minutes. If using apples and optional quince preserves, add at the end when sauce is reduced, and just warm through. Season to taste with salt, and lots of black pepper.

☞Note 3: If you have prepared the ducks ahead of time, warm in a 400 degree oven and warm the sauce separately. Spoon over or around the ducks.

Kitchen Conversation

The quinces are sweet and perfumey and act as a wonderful foil for the bitter black-pepper heat. Pancetta adds salt and sweetness and lemon adds acid for balance. If you used apples, increase the lemon zest and/or add a bit of pomegranate syrup for a more intriguing taste. The tartness cuts through the richness of the duck. Serve with rice, cracked wheat or barley pilaf, and greens or spinach.

Wine Notes

Pairing Pointers: *This duck has the added factor of bitterness supplied by the black pepper, so we'd best stick with reds, especially Syrah.*

Categories: 5, 6

Specific Recommendations:

5: *Pinot Noir—bigger, tannic—France (Côte de Nuits), California* ■ *Sangiovese blends—not overoaked—Tuscany, California*

6: *Syrah/blends—France, USA, Australia*

Dfina Sabbath Beef Stew with Eggs and Chick-peas

*I*n the Orthodox Jewish tradition it is forbidden to light a fire or work on the Sabbath. In order that there be a midday meal on Saturday, housewives put one-pot stews in a very low oven before sundown on Friday and keep them there until lunch the next day. This Egyptian dfina is a typical Sabbath stew. The name comes from the Arabic dfi'ne, which means buried; in this case, the cooking pot was buried in the ashes of a wooden fire. The eggs in their shells are also buried in the stew, much like hamin eggs (eggs cooked for many hours with brown onion skins), with a similar creamy texture. In Morocco the dish may be called a dafina, but it becomes a skhina when sweet potatoes, roasted barley or rice, and sometimes a meat loaf, seasoned with sweet spices, are added to the pot to be cooked along with the meat, chick-peas, potatoes, and eggs. One hour before the meal is to be served, the top of the pot is removed so that the stew may brown.

Serves 6 to 8 (probably a few more with the Moroccan additions)

---

2 tablespoons olive oil

2 large onions, chopped

6 cloves garlic, minced

3 pounds cubed stewing beef or **brisket**

6 potatoes, peeled and cut in half if large

1½ cups chick-peas, soaked overnight, drained, and rinsed

1 teaspoon each ground ginger and allspice

Salt and freshly ground black pepper

6 to 8 eggs, washed

Water or **beef stock**

Heat the oil in a heavy stewpot and cook the onions over moderate heat until pale gold, about 15 to 20 minutes. Add all the other ingredients and water or stock to cover. Bring to a boil and reduce the heat to a simmer. Preheat the oven to 250 degrees. Cover the pot and place in the oven and cook for 8 hours, or until meat and chick-peas are tender. (Or cook at 300 degrees for 4 to 5 hours.)

To serve, remove the eggs from their shells and put them back in the stew. This stew also could be simmered over very low heat on top of the stove.

To turn this into a Moroccan *skhina,* add 12 dates or dried apricots to the stew when adding the liquids and the following:

³/₄ pound ground beef, not too lean

¹/₂ cup bread crumbs

¹/₂ teaspoon ground mace or **grated nutmeg**

Salt and freshly ground black pepper

2 eggs

2 tablespoons olive oil

¹/₄ cup chopped parsley

Mix all ingredients well, form into a long loaf, and wrap in cheesecloth and tie the ends. Place among the cubed meat in the stewpot.

If adding sweet potatoes, peel and cut 1 pound potatoes into large chunks. Rub with a paste of 1 beaten egg, 3 tablespoons sugar, ¹/₂ teaspoon cinnamon, pinch of cloves, and ¹/₂ cup ground almonds. Wrap in cheesecloth and tie. Add to the stewpot.

If adding cracked wheat or barley, wash 2 cups of the grains well and mix with 6 cloves garlic, 1 teaspoon paprika, ¹/₂ teaspoon cayenne, 1 teaspoon cumin, and ¹/₃ cup oil. Tie in cheesecloth and add to the stewpot.

To serve, unwrap meat loaf, sweet potatoes, and barley and serve along with the stew.

Kitchen Conversation

Complicated and comforting at the same time. So many different textures and taste sensations. The textures are as you would expect after such long, slow cooking—uniformly soft. This is no stir-fry! The basic stew of beef, potatoes, and chick-peas gains flavor interest from the sweetness of the onions and allspice, and the undertone of ginger. I like the Moroccan addition of dates or apricots for additional sweetness. I also find that the sweet potatoes, while increasing the starch component considerably, are a good addition. The sweet meat loaf takes some getting used to. Somehow the long cooking with the mace or nutmeg really accentuates the perfume of this spice. The addition of heat in the barley is a welcome touch; it keeps all these sweet aromatics in line. You might want to add a bit of cayenne heat to the stew itself, although that is not part of the tradition.

Wine Notes

Pairing Pointers: Stews and long-cooked meat dishes take on a unique characteristic vis-à-vis wine. As the fat is all cooked away by the stewing process, you are matching wine with the basic flavors and texture of the stew. The strong undercurrent of sweetness is essential here and commands a wine of great ripeness and full body.

Categories: 5, 6

Specific Recommendations:

5: *Carignan/blends—ripe, spicy—France, Spain, North Africa* ■ *Cabernet/blends—fruity, ample, smooth—South America, Australia*

6: *Sangiovese—bigger style, ripe, smoky—Italy* ■ *Zinfandel—honest, straightforward, spicy—California*

Filetto di Manzo alla Panna
Fillet of Beef with Bay, Cloves, and Cream

I was planning a dinner to celebrate the foods of old Milan, before the days of alta moda and nuova cucina, and decided to prepare this nineteenth-century recipe. It called for searing a whole filet and simmering it in cream for 2 hours. But I just couldn't bring myself to do it. It's not that I have trouble cooking meat with dairy. I have braised veal and pork roasts in cream, and they were moist, tender, and delicious. However, these meats are usually served well cooked, and accustomed as I am to rare beef, I balked at the thought of a well-cooked fillet. Especially for what it costs! So here's a way to have my rare beef and the cream sauce too. This is not a diet dish, but for the occasional indulgence it's worth a try. A good time will be had by all!

Serves 4

4 cups cream

2 whole cloves

1 bay leaf

2 tablespoons unsalted butter

1 tablespoon olive oil

2 pounds beef fillet

1 cup beef stock

Bring the cream, cloves, and bay leaf up to a boil in a medium saucepan. Reduce the heat and simmer until reduced by half. Steep for an hour or two to permeate the cream with the scent and taste of cloves and bay. Strain the cream before using.

Cut the fillet into 4 steaks and sprinkle with salt and pepper. Heat the butter and oil in a heavy-bottomed sauté pan and sear the meat on both sides. Cook the beef until rare to medium rare, and remove from the pan and keep warm. Add the beef stock to the pan and reduce by half, then add the cream and reduce a little further. Spoon the sauce over the beef.

In an alternate method, you can sear a whole trimmed fillet in the oil and butter. Transfer to a roasting pan and roast in a 400 degree oven for 20 minutes (or a 350 degree oven for 25 to 30 minutes) for rare. Slice and then spoon the warm sauce over the beef.

Kitchen Conversation

Rich. Rich. Rich. But delicious. The bitter bay leaf is tempered by the sweet cloves and cream. Nineteenth-century Milanese, enamored of French cuisine, would have served this dish with pureed potatoes. Richness was not a negative in those days. However, if that traditional accompaniment throws your fat detector off the chart, serve the beef with roast potatoes. You can play up the sweetness of the cream by serving this with whole roasted onions. If you like, add an element of tartness with sautéed spinach or steamed spears of thick asparagus to keep the dish from being too rich and too sweet.

Wine Notes

Pairing Pointers: *This dish demands a noble and complex red. As fillet is fairly neutral (lean, not much flavor from fat), you are really choosing a wine to match up with the rich sauce. Cream requires a counterbalance, either tannin or acid, preferably both. The cloves offer a sweet note to match with ripe fruit, the bay leaf a bitter element to mirror some tannin.*

Category: 6

Specific Recommendations:

6: *Cabernet/blends—full, deep, complex—France, USA* ■ *Merlot—rich, herbal with some tannin—France, Washington State* ■ *Zinfandel—robust, earthy—California*

Brizoles Greek-Inspired Flank Steak
with Coriander, Nutmeg, and Oregano

Brizoles is a rustic country dish that combines rib steak baked atop a bed of potatoes and tomatoes. The meat is cooked until quite well done, almost falling apart. Since most of us eat steak at home so rarely, it seems a shame (and wildly extravagant) to treat it as if it were pot roast. I like to rub this spicy and fragrant marinade on a lean flank steak, broil it rare, and slice it thinly across the grain. And serve the potatoes and tomatoes on the side.

Serves 6

3 tablespoons finely minced garlic

2 teaspoons kosher salt

2 tablespoons cracked black pepper

3 tablespoons ground coriander

2 tablespoons ground cumin

1/2 teaspoon freshly grated nutmeg

4 tablespoons dried oregano

3 to 4 tablespoons fresh lemon juice or **red wine vinegar**

Olive oil

Salt

2 pounds flank steak

Put the garlic in a mortar and with the pestle grind it to a paste with the kosher salt. Add the spices and herbs and enough lemon juice or vinegar and olive oil to moisten the spice paste. Rub this on the steaks and let them marinate at room temperature for an hour or in the refrigerator for at least 3 hours. **P**reheat the broiler or make a charcoal fire. Brush the steaks with olive oil, sprinkle with salt, and broil or grill until rare, about 4 minutes per side. Slice across the grain.

Kitchen Conversation

We are playing a game of bitter (oregano, cumin, coriander, and garlic) and sweet (nutmeg), tempered by the tart lemon or vinegar. In line with the traditional brizoles recipe, which bakes the steak atop sliced potatoes and tomatoes, why not offer a potato and tomato gratin as an accompaniment? Or little roast potatoes, rubbed with oregano and garlic before baking and paired with a roast tomato. The slight acidity of the tomato will echo the lemon or vinegar, making the steak and potato combination seem less rich.

Wine Notes

Pairing Pointers: *Broiling or grilling can dry out the meat. Since this is a dish without sauce, a juicy, young, fruit-packed red wine will add succulence. The broiling or grilling also adds a bitter note, which is echoed by the oregano and coriander, so a wine with some tannin is okay.*

Categories: 5, 6

Specific Recommendations:

5: *Nebbiolo—medium intensity, truffley, balanced—Italy* ▪
Cabernet Franc—moderately rich and leafy—France, USA

6: *Merlot—plump, olivey, smooth—USA, France* ▪
Syrah/blends—jammy and opulent—California, Australia

Boeuf en Daube Provençal Beef Stew

*J*ust like a Moroccan tagine or Provençal tian, *the name of this dish is taken from the utensil in which it is cooked. A* daubière *is a pot-bellied casserole with a snug-fitting lid that keeps the meat moist while cooking. Some* daubes *are made with lamb, but beef is the classic choice, and any leftover stew meat can be shredded and used as a cannelloni and ravioli filling.* ☛Daube de boeuf *is traditionally cooked with salt pork; a calf's foot, for its gelatinous thickening of the sauce; red wine; tomatoes; and a strip of orange peel. Sometimes olives or mushrooms are added. Like all stews, a daube can be made ahead of time and reheated very carefully over low heat. It's an ideal dish for entertaining and for working folks who live on leftovers.* Daube *is traditionally served with noodles or macaroni.*

Serves 6 to 8

3 pounds stewing beef

Marinade

1 large bouquet garni (a few sprigs of parsley and thyme, 1 small bay leaf)

2 3-inch-long strips orange peel

12 peppercorns

3 whole cloves

4 cloves garlic, crushed

1 quart red wine

3 onions, quartered or sliced thickly

3 tablespoons olive oil

1/2 pound salt pork, cut in lardons (small strips)

1 calf's foot (optional)

2 pounds tomatoes, peeled, seeded, and chopped

1 pound carrots, peeled and cut into 2-inch rounds

1 pound mushrooms, left whole if small, cut in quarters if large, or **1 cup black olives,** pitted (optional)

Chopped thyme and parsley

Salt and pepper

Cut the beef into 2-inch cubes.

Tie the bouquet garni, strips of orange peel, peppercorns, cloves, and garlic in a cheesecloth bag. Place the beef cubes in a deep nonaluminum container and cover with the red wine, onions, olive oil, and cheesecloth bag. Mix well, cover, and refrigerate for 24 hours.

Put the salt pork in a pot of cold water, bring up to a boil, and simmer for 10 minutes. Drain well, rinse, and drain again.

Preheat the oven to 300 degrees.

Place the beef and marinade, onions, pork lardons, calf's foot, if using, tomatoes, carrots, and mushrooms, if using, into the stew pot and mix well. Add the spice bag. If the wine doesn't cover the meat, add more or just enough water to cover. Cover with a lid and bring up to a boil on top of the stove. Then cook in a low oven (300 degrees) for 3 to 4 hours, or until the beef is meltingly tender. Discard the spice bag and remove the calf's foot. Add any meat clinging to the bone to the stew. Skim off excess fat, add the olives, if using, and adjust the seasoning. Sprinkle with chopped thyme or parsley or a combination of the two.

Variation: For lamb daube you may use white wine; cooked white beans may be added at the end. Fresh rosemary is added to the bouquet garni.

Kitchen Conversation

The acidity of the wine cuts the richness of the meat, and mellows with the long cooking. Isn't it amazing how two strips of orange peel can subtly perfume a robust beef stew? Orange is a key seasoning. I like the way it works with beef and olives almost more than how it works with mushrooms, but you be the judge. Don't feel that you have to serve noodles with this stew. A potato gratin or mashed potatoes also would absorb the pan juices nicely. Did you wonder how the mushrooms survived such long cooking and still held some texture? One of the joys and mysteries of cooking!

Wine Notes

Pairing Pointers: *Rich, rib-sticking red wines are the call here—wines with intensity of flavor, texture, and lots of personality. The light orange note is playful and a nice complement to concentrated red wine fruit. Don't overlook some spiciness in the wine as an added flavor nuance. Olives or mushrooms will be enhanced by a bit of earthiness in the wine.*

Category: 6

Specific Recommendations:

6: *Cabernet/blends—powerful and dense—France, California* ■
Syrah/blends—unabashed and peppery—Southern France, Australia

Four Recipes for Leg of Lamb

Leg of lamb is so succulent and delicious, I wonder why more people don't cook it at home.
It is really easy to prepare and should not just be reserved for rare occasions. Leg of lamb is
less expensive than loin or chops. It takes beautifully to spice rubs. After boning, it can be stuffed
and rolled with ease. It makes enough for a family dinner, with the tantalizing possibility of fabulous
leftovers.

Leg of Lamb with a Moroccan Mechoui of Ginger, Garlic, Coriander, Cayenne, and Cumin

W*hile the term* mechoui *in Morocco refers to lamb grilled on a spit over an open fire,
I am using it here to describe the marinade and basting liquids that go with the
Moroccan grilled baby lamb. After all, it's the taste that counts. And what a taste it is!
Fragrant meat juices mingled with pungent spices pull you into the kitchen. This spice rub can be
used on lamb chops or an unrolled leg of lamb, but the flavor will permeate the meat more if it is
seasoned from within.*

Serves 6

Spice Mixture	Basting Butter
2 teaspoons ground ginger	**6 tablespoons unsalted butter,** melted
1 tablespoon minced garlic	**2 teaspoons ground ginger**
1 tablespoon ground coriander	**1 tablespoon paprika**
$^1/_2$ teaspoon cayenne pepper	**$^1/_4$ teaspoon saffron filaments,** crushed
1 tablespoon ground cumin	**1 teaspoon freshly ground black pepper**
2 tablespoons unsalted butter, softened	Sauce
Salt and pepper	**1$^1/_2$ cups Lamb Stock** (page 117)
1 5-pound leg of lamb, boneless and butterflied, excess fat trimmed	**2 to 3 tablespoons basting butter**

Combine all of the ingredients for the spice mixture. Combine all of the ingredients for the basting butter. Salt and pepper the inside of the boned, butterflied leg of lamb, then spread with the spice mixture. Roll and tie the lamb. Sear on a grill or in a large skillet. Roast in a 350 degree oven for 45 to 50 minutes, or until a thermometer reads 120 degrees, basting 3 times with the basting butter. Let rest for 10 minutes before slicing.

To make the sauce, reduce the lamb stock by half over high heat. Add the basting butter and salt and pepper to taste. Slice the lamb and serve it with the sauce.

☛ Note: You can use this spice rub on a butterflied leg of lamb without rolling and tying it, or on a leg of lamb with the bone in, basting as you cook it. However, rolling and tying keeps more of the spices inside so they can permeate the meat.

Kitchen Conversation

All of these traditional Moroccan spices have a bitter edge, but the meat can stand up to them. The butter cuts their intensity somewhat. If you don't have lamb stock to make a jus, it's not the end of the world. So the meat won't have a sauce. Do what they do in Morocco: Dip the meat into ground cumin and salt as you eat it. Quite a tasty option! Serve with couscous and a vegetable ragout (page 278) or one of the carrot dishes (pages 304 and 306) for contrast.

Wine Notes

Pairing Pointers: *As a marinade/rub, mechoui is more intense than most. The roasting process will caramelize the spices somewhat, so choose a wine with some oak. The spiciness is tempered by the richness of the meat, which demands a wine of character.*

Category: 5

Specific Recommendations:

5: *Pinot Noir—full, spicy, generous—California, Oregon* ▪ *Tempranillo—fruity, gutsier style—Central Spain* ▪ *Carignan/blends—medium rich/ripe with ample tannin—Southern France*

Leg of Lamb in a Greek Marinade of Yogurt, Aniseed, and Cinnamon

*T*he robust flavor of lamb takes wonderfully to the sweet and fragrant anise-scented mari-nade. The Greeks love to use tart yogurt as a marinade. And it tenderizes the meat. The spices take on a sweet smokiness after grilling. Again, if you are cooking for two, the mari-nade works well on lamb chops. So adjust the proportions accordingly, and cut amounts by a third.

Serves 6

1 leg of lamb, boned and butterflied, about 5 pounds

1 large onion, chopped

3 cloves garlic, chopped fine

1 tablespoon aniseed, toasted and ground

1 teaspoon cinnamon

1 teaspoon ground coriander

1 teaspoon freshly ground black pepper

1¹⁄₂ cups yogurt

¹⁄₄ cup ouzo

Olive oil

Salt and pepper

Trim all excess fat from the lamb. Place in a nonalu-minum container. Puree the onion, garlic, spices, yogurt, and ouzo in a food processor or blender. Pour the marinade over the lamb and refrigerate, covered, for at least 8 hours, preferably overnight.

Bring the meat to room temperature. Preheat the broiler or make a charcoal fire. Brush the leg of lamb with the olive oil, sprinkle with salt and pepper. Grill for 10 to 15 minutes per side. Some parts will be rare, others medium, as the leg varies in thickness. Slice across the grain.

Kitchen Conversation

Contrast, contrast. The grill or broiler tempers the tartness of the yogurt, builds a crust, and adds a wonderful smoky cast to the sweet anise and cinnamon. Sweet and sour can take a little more of the same if paired with a mild intermediary such as rice pilaf, bulgur wheat, or roast potatoes. As an accompaniment, choose a savory ragout of fennel, artichokes, and greens or celery root with dill (pages 294 and 296). Or spinach sweetened with toasted pine nuts and raisins. Or zucchini with mint or basil. Or green beans with tomatoes and oregano.

Wine Notes

Pairing Pointers: Yogurt marinades break down protein and add a velvety textural dimension. This means less tannin is needed in the wine. The anise and cinnamon are significant back notes that require some attention. If you were ever looking for an occasion to serve Pinot Noir, this is it!

Category: 5

Specific Recommendations:

5: *Pinot Noir—textured, complex, round—France, Oregon* ■ *Carignan/blends—moderately rich, supple, uncomplicated— Southern France* ■ *Zinfandel—softer, brambly with medium intensity—California*

Cosciotto di Castrato Sulle Tegole Leg of Lamb Sicilian Style

*W*hile doing research for a Sicilian dinner, I came upon a reference to a very old recipe where leg of lamb was cooked directly on tiles in a wood-burning oven. Deep slits were cut in the lamb leg and slices of garlic, rosemary, and strips of pancetta rolled in black pepper were inserted. The lamb was basted with olive oil and lemon juice until done. To intensify the seasoning for this recipe we made a stuffing for the leg of lamb using those ingredients. If you don't have time to let the butcher bone the leg and don't want to do it yourself, you could make this with leg of lamb on the bone, just as described in the original recipe.

Serves 6 to 8

4 ounces pancetta, diced

1 tablespoon finely minced garlic

2 tablespoons chopped fresh rosemary

2 tablespoons grated lemon zest

1 teaspoon freshly ground black pepper

1 6-pound leg of lamb, boned, trimmed, and butterflied

Garlic slivers

Additional black pepper and fresh rosemary

$^1/_2$ cup olive oil

$^1/_4$ cup fresh lemon juice

1$^1/_2$ cups reduced Lamb Stock (page 117)

In a medium sauté pan, render the pancetta over low heat until soft and partly cooked, about 3 minutes. It should not be allowed to crisp or brown. Drain the pancetta well and cool. Mix with the garlic, rosemary, lemon zest, and pepper. Rub this mixture on the inside of the leg of lamb, roll and tie. Stud the lamb with garlic slivers and, if you have the patience, with rosemary needles, or rub the outside with a little chopped rosemary and black pepper.

Preheat the oven to 375 degrees. Sprinkle the leg of lamb with salt and pepper. Roast for 1 hour to 1 hour and 10 minutes for medium rare. Baste occasionally with olive oil and lemon juice. When a meat thermometer registers 120 degrees, remove the lamb from the oven. Let rest 10 to 15 minutes, then slice the leg.

Serve with reduced lamb stock seasoned with a little garlic, chopped rosemary, and black pepper.

Kitchen Conversation

Be careful with salt, as the pancetta adds a little of its own to the meat. The lemon is a key ingredient that holds the bitter seasonings in check. But even bitter rosemary, garlic, and black pepper and sour lemon need some sweet relief. So, while little potatoes baked in the pan along with the lamb will soften some of the sharp edges (or Rosemary Roast Potatoes on page 287), sweet roast tomatoes, young green beans, peas, or glazed carrots will add a fine balance to this full-flavored dish.

Wine Notes

Pairing Pointers: *Classic, simple, and flavorful are the adjectives for this dish. The herbs are the key, as is the salty sweetness of the pancetta. If you like your lamb less rare, make certain that the wine you choose is sufficiently juicy to replace the moistness that is extracted in roasting. And don't forget the lemon; some acidity in the wine is needed for balance.*

Categories: 5, 6

Specific Recommendations:

5: *Nebbiolo—lighter, earthier, round—Northern Italy* ■ *Cabernet Sauvignon—soft, harmonious—South America, France*

6: *Merlot—herbal, olivey, rich—Pacific Northwest* ■ *Pinotage—complex, spicy—South Africa*

Kilis Kuslari Turkish Leg of Lamb Stuffed with Walnut Kofte

*T*his recipe is a variation on southern Turkish and Syrian recipes where slices of leg of lamb are pounded and stuffed with a kofte filling, rolled, browned, and braised in a tomato sauce. As most leg of lamb is fairly lean, there is a real danger of the meat becoming quite dry after a long braising. However, I like the idea of lamb stuffed with lamb, so I decided to stuff a boned leg of lamb with kofte (ground seasoned lamb), roll and tie it, and roast it in the oven. It remains very moist, and the meat can be cooked medium rare. Here is an updated version that I think you will enjoy.

Serves 6

Stuffing

2 tablespoons unsalted butter or **olive oil**

1¹/₂ cups onion, finely chopped

1 pound ground lamb

1 cup peeled, seeded, and chopped tomatoes

¹/₂ cup chopped toasted walnuts

4 tablespoons chopped parsley

1 teaspoon salt

¹/₂ teaspoon ground allspice

1 teaspoon cinnamon

1 teaspoon ground cumin

¹/₂ teaspoon freshly ground black pepper

Pinch cayenne pepper

1 leg of lamb, 5 to 6 pounds, boned

Garlic slivers (optional)

Sauce

1 cup reduced Lamb Stock (page 117)

¹/₂ cup tomato puree

2 cloves garlic, finely minced

2 bay leaves

Melt the butter or warm the oil in a medium sauté pan and cook the onion over moderate heat until tender, about 10 minutes. Add the ground lamb and sauté, stirring often, until the meat loses its redness, about 5 minutes. Add the tomatoes, walnuts, parsley, and spices, and cook for 4 minutes. Transfer to a bowl and cool the stuffing.

Trim the leg of lamb and pound it slightly between sheets of plastic wrap to a uniform thickness of about 1 inch.

Spread the prepared leg of lamb with the ground meat mixture. Roll the leg and tie with string.

Preheat the oven to 375 degrees. You may choose to stud the leg with small slivers of garlic if you like.

Place the leg of lamb in a roasting pan and roast for 1 hour to 1 hour and 10 minutes, or until a thermometer reads 120 degrees for medium rare. (The meat will continue to cook while it rests.)

While the lamb is roasting, combine the lamb stock, tomato puree, garlic, and bay leaves in a small saucepan, and simmer for 5 minutes. Baste the leg with the sauce a few times during roasting. Let the lamb rest for 15 minutes, then slice. Serve with the remaining sauce.

Kitchen Conversation

The richness of the meat responds well to the sweet spices, sweet tomato, and bitter walnuts. Serve with roast potatoes or rice or wheat pilaf, grilled eggplant with a little tomato sauce scented with cinnamon, eggplant with walnut sauce, or smoky grilled eggplant cream. To play up the sweetness, try green beans or carrots. Or, for a tart accent, serve sautéed spinach, but soften it with some plumped currants.

Wine Notes

Pairing Pointers: *This complex and flavorful dish is rich with wine possibilities. You can go purely on flavor, attempting to mirror the spice notes. You can work with the sharp contrasts of the bitter walnuts and the acidity of the tomatoes. Or you can try to do both at the same time.*

Categories: 5, 6

Specific Recommendations:

5: *Pinot Noir—spicy, opulent, fleshy—USA* ■ *Syrah/blends— peppery, jammy, round—Australia, France*

6: *Other Italian—full, leathery, smoky—Campania, Apulia* ■ *Carignan/blends—thick, coarse, uncomplicated*

Cordero al Chilindron Spanish Lamb Ragout with Roasted Peppers

his stew is part of a repertoire of Spanish recipes called al chilindron, *where sweet paprika and sweet peppers are contrasted with tart seasonings and rich meat. In Portugal sweet red peppers are ground into a paste with garlic and salt and rubbed on meat or poultry before cooking. And in Turkey sweet red peppers are combined with tomatoes and/or hot peppers for another savory spice rub. While tomatoes may be added to a* chilindron *dish, heat is not a necessary factor. This savory stew can be made the day before and reheated gently.*

Serves 6

3 pounds lamb shoulder, well trimmed of fat and sinew

Marinade

2 tablespoons paprika

2 teaspoons ground cumin

1 bay leaf, crumbled

¹/₂ cup mild olive oil

¹/₂ cup white wine

8 to 10 thin strips of lemon zest

¹/₂ cup olive oil

Salt and freshly ground black pepper

3 cups chopped onions

2 tablespoons paprika

2 teaspoons ground cumin

2 tablespoons finely minced garlic

¹/₂ cup white wine

1¹/₂ cups Lamb Stock (page 117) or **Basic Chicken Stock** (page 115)

1 cup diced tomatoes

Grated zest of 2 lemons

2 tablespoons fresh lemon juice or to taste

4 to 6 roasted red peppers, cut into wide strips

6 tablespoons finely snipped parsley for garnish

Place lamb in a nonaluminum container and toss well with the paprika, cumin, bay leaf, olive oil, wine, and strips of lemon zest. Cover the container and marinate overnight in the refrigerator.

Bring the lamb to room temperature. Heat ¹/₄ cup of the olive oil in a large sauté pan. Salt and pepper the lamb and brown it over high heat, then transfer with a slotted spoon to a stewpot. Pour off the fat.

Heat the remaining ¼ cup oil in the sauté pan and cook the onions over moderate heat for about 10 minutes until translucent and tender. Add the paprika, cumin, and garlic, and cook for a few minutes longer. Season with salt and pepper. Add the cooked onions to the lamb. Deglaze the pan with the white wine and add the pan juices to the lamb. Add the stock, diced tomatoes, lemon zest, and lemon juice to the stewpot and bring up to a boil. Reduce the heat and cover the pan. Simmer gently for about an hour, then add the roasted pepper strips. Simmer for about 30 minutes longer until lamb is tender. Adjust the seasoning. Does it need more lemon? If so, add a bit more. Garnish the stew with parsley and olives.

Kitchen Conversation

Bitter and sour are cautious partners. If you want to be daring, serve saffron rice and bitter greens. (Saffron can be bitter too, so go easy.) Want to be safe? Stay with bitter and sweet. Serve sweet little roast potatoes and green beans with tomatoes and mint or fresh coriander.

If you'd like to fool around with this dish, instead of marinating the lamb in wine, make a spice rub of 2 tablespoons sweet paprika, 2 teaspoons cumin, 3 pureed roasted peppers, and 4 finely minced cloves of garlic, mixed with a little olive oil and a bit of lemon juice or grated lemon zest. Marinate the lamb in this for 24 hours. Instead of browning the meat, just add it to the cooked onions and proceed with the stew. Or use the spice rub on lamb chops and broil them.

Wine Notes

Pairing Pointers: *The process of stewing takes away all the fat, which throws out preconceived pairing notions of red wine/red meat, white wine/white meat. Match the wine to the other ingredients: the roasted peppers, lemon peel, paprika, and garlic. Full-bodied whites are equally as enjoyable as a medium-intensity red.*

Categories: 3A, 5

Specific Recommendations:

3A: *Chardonnay—rich, citrusy, and round—France, Spain* ■
Marsanne/blends—dusty, earthy, and mouth-coating—France

5: *Tempranillo—piquant, youthful, and lightly oaked—Spain* ■
Merlot—juicy, plump, and rustic—Northeast Italy, South America

Abbacchio or Agnello alla Cacciatora Spring Lamb Hunter's Style

*A*bbacchio is the Roman name for milk-fed lamb, a month or two old. The meat is pale rose in hue, and incredibly tender, so all the parts can be quickly sautéed and the meat will still be meltingly soft. Alas, most of us do not have access to baby lamb, so to achieve similar tenderness we must braise lamb shoulder slowly until it is well cooked and almost falling apart. Please don't be afraid of the anchovy; here it acts as salt. The heat is a subtle buzz on the tongue, not a blast. You can add it in stages if you are not sure how hot your pepper flakes are.

Serves 6

4 tablespoons olive oil

3 pounds lamb shoulder, trimmed and cut into 2-inch cubes

2 to 3 onions, chopped

2 tablespoons garlic, finely minced

1 to 2 teaspoons hot pepper flakes

2 tablespoons dried oregano or **chopped fresh rosemary**

1 cup white wine

$^1/_2$ cup Lamb Stock (page 117) or **Basic Chicken Stock** (page 115)

2 tablespoons pureed anchovy

Freshly ground black pepper

A bit of vinegar added to the wine if wine is not tart enough (optional)

Heat the oil in a heavy sauté pan; salt and pepper the lamb and brown over high heat. Remove from the pan with a slotted spoon and set aside.

Add the onions to the oil remaining in the pan and sauté over moderate heat until soft, about 10 minutes. Add the garlic, most of the hot pepper flakes, oregano or rosemary, and sauté for 2 minutes longer.

Return the lamb and its accumulated juices to the pan, add the wine and stock, and simmer, covered, over low heat until the lamb is very tender, about 1 1/2 hours. Skim off excess fat. Stir in the anchovy puree and add the black pepper, the rest of the hot pepper flakes if needed, and vinegar to taste. Simmer a few minutes longer to blend flavors.

Kitchen Conversation

To work with the salty anchovy, bitter garlic and herbs, tart wine, and little buzz of heat, you will need a mild foil such as simple roast, richer mashed, or pan-fried potatoes. Or, for a real treat, Potato Gnocchi (page 152). Asparagus, favas, fennel, peas, and artichokes are all at their best when spring lamb appears, so pick a vegetable that sings along with the season.

Wine Notes

Pairing Pointers: *Surprisingly pungent and powerful, this lamb dish demands a bold wine. The herbs, heat, and wine/vinegar are strong in concert. No wimpy wine here! Texture is still important, and as this is a long-cooked dish, low on fat, a less tannic wine is fine.*

Categories: 5, 6

Specific Recommendations:

5: *Barbera—sharp, full flavored, dense—Italy, California* ■ *Various Portuguese—pungent, rustic, harmonious—Dão*

6: *Other Italian—tangy, pronounced, ripe—Central and Southern Italy*

Avgolemono Stews

What follows are two stews with an avgolemono, egg and lemon thickener, added at the end of cooking. One has rich lamb and greens as the base; the other has sweeter pork and celery. The first dish is to celebrate spring and the second is right for a winter repast.

Arni Frikasee Avgolemono Greek Lamb Ragout with Greens, Egg, and Lemon

T his classic Greek lamb ragout would be equally at home in Apulia, the southern Italian province where the Greeks landed many centuries ago. (In Apulia this stew might be called caldariello, *after the cooking utensil.) Wild greens are added during the last minutes of cooking, and then the mixture is thickened with eggs and lemon. When in season, blanched asparagus can be used in place of or in addition to the greens. Dill or mint is ideal as an additional flavor accent to this very tasty spring stew. Sprinkle with crumbled feta cheese if you like.*

Serves 4 to 6

¹/₂ cup olive oil or as needed

3 pounds lamb shoulder, trimmed well and cut into 1¹/₂-inch cubes

2 large onions, cut into medium dice, about 3 cups

3 cloves garlic, minced fine

1¹/₂ cups wine, water, Basic Chicken Stock (page 115) or **Lamb Stock** (page 117)

2 pounds (about 6 to 8 cups) coarsely chopped assorted greens such as Swiss chard, dandelion, spinach, etc., or **1¹/₂ pounds asparagus,** trimmed, cut in 2-inch lengths, blanched

¹/₃ cup chopped fresh dill or **mint**

Salt and freshly ground black pepper to taste

3 eggs, at room temperature

¹/₃ cup fresh lemon juice

1 cup crumbled feta cheese (optional)

Heat ¹/₄ cup of the olive oil in a large sauté pan over high heat. Add as many lamb cubes as will comfortably fit in the pan without crowding. You want the meat to brown, not steam. Sprinkle with salt and pepper, and brown it on all sides. With a slotted spoon transfer the meat to a large stewpot or casserole. Repeat with the remaining lamb cubes, adding a tablespoon or two of oil, as needed, for each batch.

Heat 2 tablespoons of olive oil in the same sauté pan over medium heat. Add the onions and cook until translucent, about 10 minutes. Add the garlic, salt, and pepper, and cook a minute or two, then add to the lamb. Pour the wine, water, or stock into the pan and boil a minute or two, scraping the browned bits on the bottom. Add to the stewpot. Bring the meat, onions, and pan juices up to a boil, reduce the heat, cover, and simmer very slowly until the meat is tender. You may prepare the stew ahead of time up to this point.

Fifteen minutes before serving time, bring the stew up to a simmer. In a large pan, steam the greens in a bit of water until they wilt. Add them to the stew, stir to mix well and simmer, covered, for about 10 minutes. This would also be the time to add the blanched asparagus. During the last 5 minutes of cooking, stir in the dill or mint. Adjust the seasoning. Beat the eggs and lemon juice in a medium-sized bowl until very frothy. Gradually whisk in a few ladles full of the lamb stew juices, about 1 cup. Remove the lamb stew from the heat and stir in the egg and lemon mixture, and feta if using. Serve at once.

Kitchen Conversation

The egg and lemon mixture not only adds flavor, but helps thicken the sauce and gives it a velvety texture. With this stew we are playing with a balance of rich meat, sour lemon, and bitter greens or less sour asparagus. We have to watch that the dish doesn't get too sour. And that there is enough sweet mint and not too much tart dill to skew the balance. Certainly you're safe serving rice or potatoes, as they will counteract any excess tartness or bitterness. If you decide to add feta cheese, be sure not to oversalt the stew. The salty feta will help mask excessive sourness.

Wine Notes

Pairing Pointers: *Ironically, I find that this red meat dish is better with sharp whites, bright rosés, and crisp, angular reds. The lemon, dill, and greens are the dominant ingredients, and they are more white wine friendly than red. The egg neutralizes the hard edges in the dish, but can soften the wine.*

Categories: 2, 4

Specific Recommendations:

2: *Sauvignon Blanc—sharp, zesty, herbaceous—France, New Zealand* ■ *Rosé/blends—tangy, fragrant, spicy—Southern France, Spain, Italy*

4: *Pinot Noir—lean, herbal with some tannin—France, Australia, USA* ■ *Corvina—fresh, simple, clean—Northern Italy*

Hirino me Selino Avgolemono Pork with Celery, Egg, and Lemon

While this classic Greek stew is usually made with pork, veal can be used too. And of course sweet fennel or celery root would be a nice alternative to the simple mild celery. Some versions of this stew use sweet onions as the base; others use the more sour-edged leeks.

Serves 4

¹/₃ cup olive oil

2 pounds lean pork shoulder, cut in 1¹/₂-inch cubes

Salt and freshly ground black pepper

1 large onion, chopped, or **2¹/₂ cups chopped leeks,** white parts only, well washed

2 cups hot water

1 cup white wine

3 cups celery, strings removed, cut in 2-inch lengths (or **fennel,** cut in half, cored, and cut in strips or small wedges)

¹/₄ cup celery leaves (or fennel fronds reserved and chopped)

2 egg yolks

3 to 4 tablespoons fresh lemon juice

Warm half the oil in a heavy stewpot and quickly brown the pork over high heat. Sprinkle with salt and pepper. Remove with a slotted spoon to a bowl and set aside. Heat the remaining oil in the pot and cook the onion or leeks until soft, 8 to 10 minutes. Season with salt and pepper. Return the pork to the pot, add the water and wine, and bring up to a boil. Reduce the heat and cover the pan.

Simmer for 35 minutes. Then add the celery or fennel, cover the pan, and simmer until the pork and celery or fennel are tender. Remove the pork and celery from the pan with a slotted spoon and transfer to a warm serving bowl or platter. Cover and keep warm. Skim the excess fat from the pan juices. Boil the juices down to about 1¹/₂ cups. Adjust the seasoning.

In a separate bowl, beat the egg yolks and lemon juice until frothy. Gradually add a few spoonfuls of the hot pan juices to the eggs and lemon juice to temper them gradually, then add a bit more. Pour the mixture into the pot, stir well off the heat, and pour the sauce over the pork and celery. Sprinkle with chopped celery leaves or fennel fronds.

Kitchen Conversation

We're playing with sweet and sour, with the accent on sour. (The pork is sweet, as is the fennel or celery. The lemon juice, wine, and leeks are sour.) Simple rice pilaf, more robust cracked wheat, or sweeter roast potatoes are needed to relieve the tartness. If you still feel that the dish is too tart, add chopped mint or parsley or fennel fronds to the celery leaves.

Wine Notes

Pairing Pointers: *The addition of celery or fennel amplifies the tart profile of avgolemono. Pork also adds a note of sweetness, but as it is braised for a long time, it defers to the pungency of the sauce.*

Categories: 2, 4

Specific Recommendations:

2: *Vernaccia—earthy, grassy, refreshing—Italy* ■ *Chardonnay—austere, steely, unoaked—Italy, France, USA*

4: *Merlot—herbaceous, smooth—South America, Eastern Europe* ■ *Sangiovese—tart, pure in style—California, Central Italy*

Pork Loin "Agrodolce"

*S*hades of ancient Rome or the Italian Renaissance. This sweet-and-sour "agrodolce" pork dish was originally prepared with cinghiale, *wild boar. As we cannot easily step up to the butcher's counter and ask for wild boar, we are going to use a more accessible relative, pork loin. The sweet-and-sour contrast is set up with a savory mulled red wine marinade and a rich sauce of dried fruits cooked in red wine.*

Serves 8

6 pork tenderloins, 3^1/$_2$ to 4 pounds in total weight, or **1 4-pound boneless pork loin**

Marinade

1 cup red wine (for the tenderloins; you may need a bit more liquid to cover a loin)

^{1}/$_2$ teaspoon ground cloves

1 tablespoon grated orange zest

^{1}/$_4$ cup fresh orange juice

2 tablespoons chopped fresh thyme

^{1}/$_2$ teaspoon freshly ground black pepper

Agrodolce Sauce

2 tablespoons olive oil

2^1/$_2$ cups diced onions

^{1}/$_2$ teaspoon salt

3 cups red wine or a bit more as needed

1 cup diced pitted prunes

1 cup brown raisins

^{1}/$_2$ cup toasted pine nuts

Grated zest of 1 orange and 1 lemon

3 tablespoons fresh lemon juice

^{3}/$_4$ cup fresh orange juice

Pinch cloves

Salt and freshly ground black pepper

For the marinade, warm the wine, cloves, zest, orange juice, thyme, and pepper in a small saucepan over moderate heat. Remove from the stove and let the mixture steep for 30 minutes. Place the pork in a nonaluminum container. When the marinade is completely cool, pour it over the pork. Cover and marinate overnight or up to 18 hours in the refrigerator.

To make the sauce, warm the olive oil in a large, deep sauté pan or saucepan. Add the onions and salt, and cook over moderate heat until onions are quite soft, about 15 minutes. Add the red wine and reduce by half. Add the fruits, pine nuts, and zests, and cook for 5 to 10 minutes until fruits are tender. Add the juices and cloves, and season to taste with salt and pepper. Keep warm. You will have about 4 cups of chunky sauce. (And you won't mind that, as the sauce is almost the best part. Any that is left over can be used for pork chops on another day.) **B**ring the pork to room temperature. Preheat the broiler or make a charcoal fire. Remove the pork from the marinade, brush lightly with oil, and sprinkle with salt and pepper. Broil for about 5 minutes on each side for tenderloins, 10 minutes per side for a larger boneless loin. Slice the meat on the diagonal across the grain. Spoon the warm sauce atop the meat.

☛Note: You also can roast the pork in a 400 degree oven for 25 minutes for tenderloins, 45 minutes for a boneless loin, or until the meat tests 147 degrees on an instant-read thermometer. Let rest before slicing.

Kitchen Conversation

Sweet and sour requires both bland and bitter for balance. So whether you serve roast potatoes or mashed, you will want the contrast of a green like spinach, chard, red or green cabbage, Brussels sprouts. You get the idea. You could also serve the Sicilian pumpkin squash gratin (page 280), even though that would tip the scale in favor of sweetness. In this case, serve the bitterest greens for contrast.

Wine Notes

Pairing Pointers: *The juxtaposition of sweet and sour sometimes stops people in their tracks when it comes to selecting a wine. If you make sure that the sharpness of the wine is on a par with that of the sauce, you're okay. Also, while your wine can have the perception of sweetness through ripe fruit, don't go overboard on sweetness. Crisp off-dry whites are lovely here.*

Categories: 1B, 2, 4

Specific Recommendations:

1B: *Riesling—fresh, floral, balanced—Germany, Pacific Northwest*

2: *Albariño—zesty, fragrant, unoaked—Spain*

4: *Rosé Champagne—sharp, spicy, balanced—France*

Pork Souvlaki

*M*any years ago, on my first visit to Greece, at a roadside kebab house in a very small town I was served a delicious peppery kebab. The meat was light in color, very tender, and quite sweet. I thought it was pork, but now I realize that the meat was very young milk-fed lamb. As we cannot get lamb that tender and sweet, pork tenderloin may be the closest alternative. This recipe is my attempt at capturing that taste memory. Thread the cubes of meat on skewers, alternating with thin wedges of red onion and bay leaves. Incidentally, this marinade also is wonderful with chicken.

Serves 6

2 pounds pork tenderloin, cut into 1½-inch cubes

2 tablespoons finely minced garlic

2 tablespoons cracked black pepper

3 tablespoons cracked coriander seed

½ teaspoon ground allspice

2 tablespoons dried oregano

4 tablespoons red wine vinegar

2 tablespoons honey

½ cup olive oil

Salt and freshly ground black pepper

Onion wedges

Bay leaves

Grilled red pepper strips (optional)

Marinated Onion Salad (optional)

Place the cubed pork tenderloin in a nonaluminum container.

Combine the garlic, spices, vinegar, honey, and oil in a bowl, and pour this marinade over the pork. Roll the meat in the marinade until well coated. Cover and refrigerate overnight.

To cook, preheat the broiler or make a charcoal fire. Thread the meat on 6 skewers, alternating with onion wedges and bay leaves. Brush lightly with oil and sprinkle with salt and a little pepper. Broil or grill until the meat is browned but still juicy, 5 to 6 minutes per side. Baste occasionally with remaining marinade.

Serve with rice pilaf and grilled eggplant. Or stuff the meat into pita bread with some grilled red pepper strips and the onion salad:

Onion Salad

2 large red onions, quartered, sliced paper thin

1 teaspoon salt

8 tablespoons chopped flat-leaf parsley

Sprinkle the onions with salt and let stand for 10 minutes. Rinse and squeeze dry. (The salt draws out the sharpness.) Toss with the parsley and

2 teaspoons dried oregano

2 teaspoons sugar dissolved in 2 tablespoons vinegar (optional)

oregano. Taste the onions and if they are very sharp, combine the sugar and vinegar and pour over the onions. Let sit for 5 minutes before serving.

Alternate Pork Brochette Marinade

1¹/₂ cups honey

¹/₂ cup fresh lemon juice

¹/₄ cup chopped fresh thyme

Warm the honey and mix with the other ingredients. When cool, pour over 2 pounds cubed,

1 tablespoon freshly ground black pepper

1 teaspoon ground cloves

trimmed pork. Marinate overnight. Broil or grill as for souvlaki.

Kitchen Conversation

This is a very subtle play of sweet (pork, allspice, coriander, honey, and red pepper strips, if using) and sour (vinegar in the marinade and in the onion salad) with just the right amount of bitter (garlic, black pepper, and oregano) to hold them in balance. Of course a pilaf is a nice neutral partner, but in this instance the bread, sweet peppers, and sweet-tart onion salad make for a more interesting taste adventure.

Wine Notes

Pairing Pointers: *Your choice of wine will depend upon whether you grill or broil. Grilling will add char (bitter), caramelize the marinade (sweet/bitter), and play down the overt flavors of the marinade. If so, stick with a rich red wine. If you broil, you'll get more of a sweet glaze of marinade on the surface of the meat, and the marinade flavors will remain more true, in which case stay with light reds and rosés.*

Categories: 2, 5

Specific Recommendations:

2: *Rosé/blends—spicy, generous, balanced—Southern Europe ■ White/blends—aromatic, pungent, earthy—Greece, Spain*

5: *Syrah/blends—lighter, jammy, round—California, Australia ■ Tempranillo—flowery, ripe, vanilla scented—Spain (Rioja)*

Nocette di Maiale alla Salsa di Senape
Pork Tenderloin in Mustard Sauce

*T*he success of this dish is determined by the bite of the mustard you use. If bottled Dijon seems a little flat, mix some dry mustard powder with a little white wine and add it to the mustard. Heat and bitter sharpness are needed to play off the herbs, the tart wine, and the richness of the meat.

Serves 4

Marinade

3 tablespoons Dijon mustard

5 tablespoons white wine

2 tablespoons finely minced garlic

2 tablespoons chopped fresh sage

1 tablespoon chopped fresh rosemary

2 tablespoons olive oil

2 pounds pork tenderloin, well trimmed of excess fat and sinews

Sauce

3 tablespoons Dijon mustard

1 cup strong chicken or beef stock

1 tablespoon chopped fresh sage

1 tablespoon chopped fresh rosemary

Salt and freshly ground black pepper

Combine the ingredients for the marinade in a non-aluminum container. Toss the pork in the marinade, cover, and refrigerate for a day.

To make the sauce, combine the mustard, stock, and herbs in a small saucepan, and bring up to a simmer. Season with salt and pepper.

Preheat the broiler or make a charcoal fire. Bring the meat to room temperature. Remove the pork from the marinade. Sprinkle with salt and pepper, and brush with olive oil. Broil for about 10 minutes until medium cooked but still quite moist, turning once, and slice across the grain. Spoon the sauce over the meat. Serve at once.

Kitchen Conversation

As this dish is spicy and a little bitter, you will want to serve it with mashed potatoes, potato croquettes, and sweet braised fennel or carrots. Or choose sweet, creamy, mild polenta, or mashed yams or sweet potatoes (or a combination of the two, as on page 158), and Braised Bitter Greens (page 298).

Wine Notes

Pairing Pointers: Given the combination of sweet, mild pork and pungent, earthy mustard, I prefer white wines to reds. If you choose red wine, be advised that the bitter edge of mustard can clash with tannins. As there is no cream in this dish to balance the tannins, opt for suppler reds.

Categories: 3A, 5

Specific Recommendations:

3A: *Pinot Gris—floral, earthy, spicy—France, Oregon* ■
Grenache Rosé—dry, earthy, peppery—Southern France

5: *Pinot Noir—rustic, smoky, ripe—California, Germany* ■
Dolcetto—supple, refreshing, lightly tannic—Italy, California

Grilled Veal Loin Chop with Mustard and Cracked Pepper Crust

his is such a simple recipe that it's almost silly to write it down. Everyone loves it, especially when it is paired with Risotto Pancakes filled with fontina and sage (page 150) and garlicky grilled mushrooms. So I suspect that it will become a favorite of yours as well, especially because it is so very easy to prepare. And so good. ☛*Now, a veal chop is not a "diet" plate. However, every once in a while we have a craving for caveman cuisine, but with a little contemporary sophistication. That's where the mustard and black pepper crust comes in. The meat is robust enough to stand up to the bitter flavors, which become smoky after grilling. You could probably make this with a thick steak if you cannot find excellent free-range veal. While no sauce is needed, a little veal or beef stock drizzled on after cooking would be a juicy refinement.*

Serves 4

Strong Dijon mustard

All-purpose flour

Coarsely cracked black pepper

4 veal loin chops, each about 14 ounces with
the bone

Olive oil

Salt

²/₃ cup reduced beef or veal stock (optional)

Put the Dijon mustard in a wide, shallow bowl and mix it well with a fork so that it becomes loose in texture.

Place the flour on a plate. Place the cracked peppercorns on another.

Dredge the veal chops in the flour on both sides. Brush liberally with the Dijon mustard. (I use a wide pastry brush.) Then dip the chops in cracked pepper, as much as you think you can stand. (Some will fall off on the grill.) Refrigerate the chops for a few hours to set the crust.

Preheat the broiler, but preferably make a charcoal fire. Brush the chops lightly with olive oil and sprinkle with salt. Grill for 4 to 5 minutes on each side for medium rare.

If desired, heat the reduced stock and a little salt in a small pan. Spoon the stock over each chop.

Kitchen Conversation

Smoky, bitter, hot. What this needs is something mild and a little salty to create a harmonious plate. Risotto cakes stuffed with cheese (salt) fill the bill. Play this combination off sweet glazed carrots or green beans. Or, as the grill is already hot, you might want to introduce the less sweet element of grilled mushrooms basted with garlic oil and a sprinkling of thyme. Creamy mashed potatoes would also work well, but then you will have to consider adding a generous sprinkle of Parmesan or crumbled Gorgonzola to the mushrooms to provide salt for balance.

Wine Notes

Pairing Pointers: *The nature of black pepper forces your hand. A spicy blockbuster of a wine is necessary to both stand up to and, ironically, tame the peppercorns. The mustard adds a spicy, earthy element when grilled. Big and balanced is the theme.*

Category: 3

Specific Recommendations:

3: *Syrah/blends—peppery, extracted, round—Southern France, USA, Australia* ■ *Malbec—thick, coarse, assertive—France* ■ *Corvina—inky, rich, ripe—Italy*

JOYCE GOLDSTEIN KITCHEN CONVERSATIONS
VEGETABLES

VEGETABLES

Vegetables

Vegetables used to be the shortest section in a cookbook, the most overlooked or haphazard part of a home-cooked meal, and on the average restaurant menu were identified as "sides." How things seem to be changing! Vegetarian entrees are selling like steak used to, and to people who are not vegetarians. What is going on?

At first glance you could call this new focus on vegetables a momentary fad and chalk it up to the public's addiction to trends. But interest in vegetables runs deeper than that. Many diners have discovered that a dish of vegetables built around grains can be a wonderful, sustaining, and truly satisfying meal.

I love vegetables and I've always tried to show them off in their natural environment. If it's a Greek dish, all of the vegetables on the plate reflect that heritage. If it's French, let the gratins and glazed carrots abound. Let the ethnic signature spices ring true and consistent. No curried vegetables with Moroccan spices and couscous, no Italian pesto with Turkish eggplant. No charmoula and romesco on the same plate. Try to love your vegetables in the style of their home country.

This chapter is not about vegetables as an afterthought. And it isn't a chapter about "sides." It is about centers. Butternut-squash gratin can be the center of a plate of braised greens and grilled eggplant. You can be very happy with Pugliese Potato Pie served with grilled eggplant and Brussels sprouts. Why not serve spinach and chick-peas alongside Middle Eastern Spiced Carrots and a wheat or rice pilaf?

Be sure to cook the vegetables for as long as it takes to maximize their flavor. Not every vegetable is meant to be al dente. Some need longer cooking to shine and reveal their flavor. Green beans, cauliflower, and broccoli profit from a few extra minutes in the pan. Undercooked eggplant is bitter and tough. Fennel is either best served raw or braised to a melting tenderness. Carrots are fine to munch on when raw, but as a cooked vegetable they don't develop sweetness until they've simmered for a while. On the other hand, Brussels sprouts taste less cabbagy with briefer cooking.

Some of your greatest dining pleasures will come from a perfectly seasoned beet, a slice of broiled eggplant with esme, a lovingly prepared bowl of greens with rice and piri piri. Heaven is in the details. Almost anyone can grill a steak, but it takes a cook to reveal the subtleties and fine flavors of vegetables. Here are some very succulent vegetable dishes that can become stars on your plate.

Calcots y Esparragos con Romesco
Grilled Green Onions and Asparagus with Romesco

*I*n spring when fat green onions appear in the market, Catalonians fire up the grill and whisk up a batch of savory romesco sauce. While we don't have the same specially cultivated mammoth calcots, or Spanish green onions, we can gather the fattest ones available or substitute baby leeks. Traditionally the calcots are grilled 2 hours before serving, wrapped in plastic wrap to steam so the burned skin loosens and the insides become buttery and soft. If you don't want to grill the vegetables 2 hours ahead of time to ensure tenderness, blanch the green onions and precook the leeks before grilling. And steam some fat spears of asparagus to grill along with the green onions.

Serves 4

16 fat green onions or **very small leeks,** ½ to ¾ inch in diameter if possible

16 large spears asparagus

4 tablespoons olive oil

Salt and freshly ground black pepper

Hazelnut Romesco Sauce (page 316)

Wash the small leeks or green onions, trim off the hairy roots but keep the bulb heads intact. Trim off all but 4 inches of green. Blanch in boiling salted water until the heads feel tender and crack slightly when you pinch them with your fingers. Green onions will take about 5 minutes; leeks, depending upon size, can take up to 10 minutes. Drain and refresh in cold water. Drain again. Put 4 green onions or leeks on a skewer for easier handling. **B**reak off the tough part of the asparagus. Peel them halfway up the spear. Cook in boiling salted water until firm cooked. Drain and refresh with cold water. Put on four spears per wooden skewer.

Make a charcoal fire. Brush the green onions and asparagus with the olive oil. Sprinkle with salt and pepper. Grill until well browned and even a little charred. Serve with bowls of romesco sauce.

☛Note: Roast potatoes warmed on the grill or cooked beets make a nice addition to the vegetable platter and romesco accompaniment.

Kitchen Conversation

Make sure the leeks are really tender. Pinch the head of the blanched leek between your fingers; it should crack. If it doesn't cut easily, cook it a little longer. The smoky, tart leeks or the sweet, smoky asparagus are more interesting to eat with a good dollop of Hazelnut Romesco Sauce.

Moroccan-Inspired Vegetable Ragout for Couscous

*A*lmost any combination of vegetables will work for this fragrant ragout to serve with couscous. You might add potatoes, sweet potatoes, or pumpkin squash to the assortment. The raisins add sweetness and the preserved lemons (not the classic Moroccan-style salted preserved lemons) add a wonderful sweet and tart quality to brighten the vegetables' inherent sweetness.

Serves 6

3 tablespoons unsalted butter or **olive oil**

1 large onion, chopped

2 cloves garlic, minced

1 teaspoon salt

2 teaspoons paprika

1/2 teaspoon freshly ground black pepper

1 teaspoon ground ginger

2 teaspoons ground cumin

1/2 teaspoon cayenne pepper

4 tomatoes, peeled, seeded, and chopped

4 ounces chick-peas, soaked overnight in cold water (see note)

4 carrots, peeled and cut into 2-inch lengths

2 turnips or **rutabagas,** peeled and cut into 2-inch pieces

6 small new potatoes, cut into 2-inch pieces, or **3 sweet potatoes,** or **peeled pumpkin,** or **butternut squash,** cut into 3-inch chunks

4 small zucchini, cut into 2-inch lengths

1/2 cup raisins, plumped in hot water

2 Sweet Preserved Lemons, cut in fine slivers

Harissa or **hot sauce** to taste (optional)

Chopped parsley, fresh coriander, or **mint** (optional)

Heat the butter or oil in the bottom of a large stew-pot and cook the onion over moderate heat until tender and translucent. Add the garlic, spices, and tomatoes, and cook for 2 to 3 minutes longer. Add the chick-peas and 4 cups water or stock. Bring up to a boil, lower the heat, cover the pan, and simmer for 30 minutes. Add the carrots and cook for 15 minutes, then add the turnips, potatoes or sweet potatoes or pumpkin, and simmer for 10 minutes longer. Add the zucchini, raisins, and preserved lemons, and simmer for 15 minutes longer, or until all the vegetables are cooked. Adjust the seasoning. Serve with couscous (and harissa if desired). Sprinkle with herbs if desired.

☛Note: 1 cup canned chick-peas can be added during the last 15 minutes of cooking. Drain and rinse well before using.

Sweet Preserved Lemons

3 cups water

6 lemons, quartered lengthwise or cut into eighths if large

³/₄ cup sugar

Bring the water to a boil. Add the lemons and simmer for 5 minutes. Drain and soak the lemons in cold water for a few hours to eliminate excessive bitterness.

Make a sugar syrup with ³/₄ cup sugar and ³/₄ cup water. Drain the lemons and add to the sugar syrup. Simmer for 5 minutes. Let plump in syrup overnight. Refrigerate. These will keep for a week.

To use, scrape off all lemon pulp and cut the peel into fine julienne.

Kitchen Conversation

The overall flavor of the vegetables is earthy, the spices bitter. Traditional Moroccan salted preserved lemons would add a salty tart accent but still not give the bright counterpoint this dish needs. That is why the sweetened lemons are important for those little sweet-and-sour notes that seem to make the vegetables taste brighter and lighter. Don't forget to salt the stew; you can add as much black pepper as you'd like for contrast. You also might want to experiment with the herb garnish. Mint will repeat the sweetness of the carrots, pumpkin, raisins, and sweetened lemons. Fresh coriander will pick up the bitter tones of the turnips and spices. Parsley will be neutral and clean-tasting, adding brightness without altering the balance of flavors.

Zucca al Forno Baked Pumpkin Squash

Unlike our native pumpkin, Mediterranean pumpkin squashes have a dark, bumpy green peel and a bright red-orange flesh. Their closest relation in flavor is butternut squash. This squash gratin is Sicilian in inspiration and makes a wonderful accompaniment for roast chicken, duck, or pork, especially if they are served with a slightly sweet sauce.

Serves 4

2 pounds butternut squash

3 to 4 tablespoons olive oil or as needed to cook all of the squash

1 tablespoon finely minced garlic

2 tablespoons sugar

1 to 2 tablespoons balsamic vinegar

Salt and freshly ground black pepper

5 tablespoons chopped fresh mint

¹/₂ cup toasted slivered almonds

Peel the squash with a potato peeler. Cut the squash in half and scoop out the seeds. Cut the squash into ¹/₄-inch slices and cut the slices in half again. You should have 4 to 4¹/₂ cups sliced squash. (Alternately, you may cut the squash into 1-inch dice. This is an aesthetic decision.)

Warm the olive oil in a very large sauté pan. Cook the squash in batches over moderate heat, stirring occasionally, until crisp tender, 5 to 8 minutes. Add more oil if needed. Add the garlic, sugar, balsamic vinegar, salt and pepper, and cook for a minute or two longer. Toss in 3 tablespoons of chopped mint.

Transfer the squash to a lightly oiled gratin dish or individual ramekins. (Of course you can prepare the gratins up to this point and refrigerate them before baking.)

Preheat the oven to 400 degrees.

Add ¹/₄ to ¹/₃ inch of water to the gratin dish, cover with foil, and bake for 25 to 30 minutes, or until the squash is tender. Sprinkle with the remaining mint and the toasted almonds.

Kitchen Conversation

Sweet and sour, but not really very sour, as the balsamic vinegar has more sweetness than acidity. The almonds add sweetness and texture; the mint also accents the sweetness of the squash. Don't forget to add enough salt. Salt brings up all the flavors, especially the sweetness. Test for tenderness along the way. Some squashes cook more quickly than others.

Use of Fresh Herbs

I realize that not everyone has room for a garden or even a window box, but there is a vast difference in taste between fresh and dried herbs. Fortunately, most supermarkets are now stocking fresh herbs in the produce section, reducing the need for using dried herbs. If you are a student of flavor, perform some experiments. Buy fresh basil and then taste contrast it with dried. Or sage. Or mint. Or dill. You will be amazed at the different tone and presence of each fresh herb, the vibrancy of flavor and perfume, the lack of grassiness or musty undertones.

Gratin of Fennel and Endive with Gorgonzola

I first ate a version of this gratin at a classic old Roman restaurant called Al Moro. The combination of ingredients was an eye-opener and a palate surpriser. What a medley of sweet, bitter, and salt. Would they work together? Yes indeed, if they are sweet fennel, bitter endive, and salty Gorgonzola cheese. While you could make this succulent gratin with just fennel or just endive, they are especially harmonious together. Go easy on the salt, as the cheese can be salty. You may braise the vegetables, or for a slightly smoky taste, precook (blanch) and then grill the endive and fennel. This dish can be fully assembled ahead of time, brought to room temperature, and then put under the broiler to brown or baked in a hot oven.

Serves 4

2 large or 4 small heads fennel

2 large or 4 small heads Belgian endive

4 tablespoons olive oil or butter

About 1 cup water, vegetable stock, or Basic Chicken Stock (page 115)

Salt and freshly ground black pepper

1/2 cup crumbled mild Gorgonzola dolcelatte

Toasted Bread Crumbs (page 133) (optional)

Cut the fennel into quarters and remove the central cores. Trim away any bruised outer leaves. (If the heads are large you can cut the fennel into eighths.) Cut the endive in half lengthwise, but keep the root end intact.

You may now either braise the vegetables or grill them. The grill adds a certain smokiness that works well with the cheese, but I certainly understand that you might not want to light it just for this gratin. However, if you have the grill going for another dish, by all means try the grilling option.

To braise the vegetables, warm 2 tablespoons olive oil or butter in a sauté pan and add the fennel. Cook over moderate heat for 5 minutes until golden. Season lightly with salt and pepper, then add a little water or stock and cover the pan. Cook until really tender, about 10 minutes. Set aside.

Warm 2 tablespoons olive oil or butter in the sauté pan and sauté the endive for a few minutes until golden, season lightly with salt and pepper, then add some water or stock, cover the pan, and cook until very tender, about 8 minutes. Set aside.

To grill the vegetables, blanch the fennel (cut in halves or quarters or thick slices) in boiling salted water and cook until tender. Drain. Blanch the endive until tender. Drain.

Lightly oil the vegetables and grill or broil them briefly until they color.

To assemble the gratin, combine the endive and fennel. Place in 1 large gratin dish or 4 individual small ones. Sprinkle with pepper and top with the crumbled Gorgonzola. (Bread crumbs are a nice but not essential touch.) Glaze the gratin under the broiler until golden and bubbly. Serve at once. Or bake in a preheated 450 degree oven until the cheese is melted.

Kitchen Conversation

Please, no al dente vegetables here! Be sure that they are tender, not crunchy. The aroma of the melting Gorgonzola is pungent, yet the taste is delicate when paired with the bitter endive and sweet fennel. I prefer Gorgonzola dolcelatte for this dish, as it is milder than regular Gorgonzola. I love the smoky taste of the grilled vegetables as they push the salty assertiveness of the cheese back a bit. If you find that Gorgonzola is too intense for your palate, try grated fontina or a mixture of fontina and Parmesan. Fresh goat cheese would also work.

Sicilian Vegetables with Savory Bread Crumbs: Cauliflower Gratin, Grilled Eggplant Rolls, Stuffed Artichokes, and a Pasta Sauce Too

*T*his is the story of a savory mixture of bread crumbs, garlic, grated cheese, and parsley used three ways, or how to get the most out of your labor. Sicilian style. Use the mixture as a topping on cooked cauliflower and bake the cauliflower until it is meltingly tender and the topping is crusty and golden. Or spread the crumb mixture onto eggplant slices, roll them up, and grill or bake them with tomato sauce. Or stuff artichoke halves with the savory bread and cheese mixture and braise them in white wine or water. Incidentally, this makes a wonderful "sauce" for cooked pasta too.

Serves 6

1 large cauliflower, broken into florets, or **3 medium eggplants,** or **6 large artichokes**

Olive oil as needed

Savory Bread Crumbs

4 to 6 cloves garlic, finely minced

1/2 cup chopped parsley

1 cup bread crumbs (oven-dry or toasted)

1 cup grated cacciocavallo or **pecorino cheese**

Freshly ground black pepper to taste

Cauliflower Gratin

Preheat the oven to 400 degrees.

Cook the cauliflower in boiling salted water until tender. Drain and place in an oiled baking dish. Combine the garlic, half the parsley, half the bread crumbs, half the cheese, and the pepper and sprinkle over the cauliflower. Drizzle with 1/2 cup olive oil. Bake for 25 minutes. For two 1-pound heads of cauliflower you will probably use all of the ingredients.

Grilled Eggplant Rolls

Preheat the broiler or make a charcoal fire. Or preheat the oven to 350 degrees.

Peel the eggplants and slice them about ⅓ inch thick. Sprinkle with salt and let drain in a colander for an hour. Rinse and pat dry. Fry the eggplant slices in the olive oil to soften and cook through, but don't brown. Drain on paper towels. Warm a few tablespoons of olive oil in a sauté pan and cook the garlic for about 2 minutes. Combine it with the bread crumbs, cheese, and parsley. Season with pepper. Spread the mixture on the eggplant slices. Roll them up and then thread the eggplant rollatini on wooden skewers. Grill or broil until golden. You may serve these with tomato sauce.

Or sauté the eggplant slices, stuff and roll them, and arrange in a gratin dish. Spoon tomato sauce over the top and bake until heated through and bubbly. Sprinkle with additional chopped parsley.

☛Note: Some versions of this dish add chopped salame or mortadella to the filling.

Stuffed Artichokes

Combine all the ingredients for the stuffing mixture. **T**o stuff 6 large artichokes, trim off the outer leaves, cut in half, and scoop out the choke. Stuff with the filling and place in a baking dish. Drizzle with ¼ cup olive oil and ½ cup white wine, cover the dish with foil, and braise in a 350 degree oven (or in a heavy saucepan on the stove) for 30 to 45 minutes, or until tender. Check after 25 minutes and if the bread crumb mixture seems dry, add additional liquid.

Pasta Sauce

Cook spaghetti or another long, thin pasta until al dente. Warm 6 tablespoons olive oil in a large sauté pan. Add the garlic and sauté for 2 minutes. Toss in bread crumbs and parsley, then toss in the cooked pasta, and mix well. Sprinkle with cheese.

Kitchen Conversation

Speechless, eh? What a lot of mileage one can get out of a few simple ingredients we usually have at home: bread crumbs, grated cheese, olive oil, garlic, and parsley. Just stop at the market and decide on your vegetable options. The bread crumb mixture certainly plays down the cabbagy quality of the cauliflower. It cuts any bitterness in the eggplant and makes the tomato sauce seem sweeter. It adds a nice salty tang to the artichokes and cuts their bitterness. And it makes for a delicious, really fast, and cheap pasta dinner. What more can you ask?

Use of Bread Crumbs

In the Mediterranean, bread is never wasted. What isn't made into croutons is ground into crumbs. Crumbs are used fresh, dried, or toasted to thicken sauces or in place of or in conjunction with grated cheese as an enrichment for pasta. The farther south you go in Italy, the more bread crumbs are used in pasta dishes.

Rosemary Roast Potatoes

*T*hese are so easy to make, you'll wonder why you didn't think of it yourself. Take little new potatoes, bake them halfway, cut a slit in each potato, and gently tuck in a sprig of rosemary leaves. Bake until tender. You will have the most savory and aromatic potatoes that ever accompanied roast lamb, chicken, fish, or a good steak.

Serves 6

2 pounds little new potatoes, well scrubbed and dried

Extra virgin olive oil

Salt and freshly ground black pepper

6 to 12 cloves garlic, unpeeled and lightly smashed

Sprigs of fresh rosemary

Preheat the oven to 350 to 400 degrees. **P**ut the potatoes in a roasting pan, rub them with the olive oil, and sprinkle them with salt and pepper. Intersperse a few unpeeled garlic cloves and sprigs of rosemary among the potatoes. Roast until almost tender, about 35 minutes, depending upon the size of the potatoes. Shake the pan a few times while baking so the potatoes roll around and cook more evenly. Remove the potatoes from the oven and when they are cool enough to handle, cut a small slit in each one. Tuck in a small sprig of rosemary into each slit. Continue baking until the potatoes are quite tender.

Kitchen Conversation

Didn't you love the way the rosemary perfumes the potatoes? The goal is to get the potatoes tender on the inside and their skin slightly crackly on the outside. Texture, texture! Test a potato from time to time (you can cook a few extras as testers). Don't forget the salt and pepper.

Tortiera di Patate e Funghi Gratin of Potatoes and Mushrooms

ortiera *is the name of a baking dish. This gratin could also be called* tiella, *a name that reflects the Spanish influence on the food of Apulia during the days when the Aragonese were in power in the region. This Pugliese potato gratin can be simple and satisfying, or more refined and elegant if you use full-flavored brown mushrooms—crimini, portobellos, or chanterelles.*

Serves 6

2 pounds potatoes (about 4 large)

1 pound brown mushrooms (preferably portobellos or crimini)

1¹/₂ cups fresh bread crumbs

¹/₂ cup chopped parsley

¹/₂ cup grated pecorino cheese

Salt and freshly ground black pepper

Olive oil as needed

Peel the potatoes, wash them, and slice them ¹/₂ inch thick.

Wipe the mushrooms with a damp towel and slice them ¹/₂ inch thick, keeping part of the stems if they are not tough.

Combine the bread crumbs, parsley, and pecorino.

Preheat the oven to 350 degrees.

Oil a large baking pan or gratin dish. Place a layer of potatoes in the pan, sprinkle with salt and pepper, then the crumb mixture, then mushrooms, then potatoes, salt and pepper, and the crumb mixture. Pour olive oil over the top and bake in a moderate oven for an hour. (If after a half hour the potatoes still seem too firm, or you have used waxy new potatoes, add about 1 cup water to the pan. Baking potatoes or russets may not need any water, especially if the mushrooms give off some liquids.) If the potatoes are browning too fast, cover the pan with foil.

Variation: For a *tortiera* or *tiella di patate e carciofi,* use trimmed, sliced artichokes in place of mushrooms. Drizzle with 1 cup liquid along with the olive oil. Sprinkle with lots of pecorino cheese. Bake as above.

Kitchen Conversation

Earthy, tender, and better than just potatoes and mushrooms cooked separately. You could add stock in place of water to the baking pan for deeper flavor. The cheese adds the salt that is needed to liven the dish.

Pitta di Patate Pugliese Potato Pie

Looking for a way to use leftover mashed potatoes with a big payoff? After you taste this pie you'll want to make mashed potatoes just so you can enjoy it. Called pitta in Pugliese dialect (probably revealing some Greek ancestry; in Greece pitta is the name for pie), this layered potato pie makes an ideal side dish for meat, poultry, or fish. Of course pitta di patate can be the center of a meal in itself, accompanied by other vegetable dishes.

Serves 6

3 pounds russet potatoes, peeled and cut into chunks if boiling

1/2 cup flour

3/4 cup grated Parmesan

2 eggs

1/2 cup milk or as needed

Salt and freshly ground black pepper

4 tablespoons olive oil plus some for drizzling

3 onions, sliced, about 1 pound

3 large tomatoes, peeled, seeded, and diced

2 tablespoons rinsed capers

4 to 6 tablespoons pitted black olives, coarsely chopped

1/2 cup Toasted Bread Crumbs (page 133)

Boil or bake the potatoes and while they are still hot, put them through a ricer. Knead in the flour and Parmesan, then add the eggs and milk, and season abundantly with salt and pepper. The mixture should be like a soft dough. Add milk as needed. Set aside. **H**eat the olive oil in a large sauté pan and cook the onions until tender, about 15 minutes. Add the tomatoes and cook for 15 minutes longer. Stir in the capers and olives. Set aside.

Oil a baking pan and sprinkle with half the bread crumbs. Place half the potatoes in the pan, patting them down for an even layer. Add the onion mixture, top with the remaining potatoes, patting them down over the filling. Drizzle with olive oil and the bread crumbs.

Preheat the oven to 400 degrees and bake for 45 minutes, or until golden. Cut into squares or rectangles and serve hot or warm.

Kitchen Conversation

This dish is really surprising. It offers yet another example where the whole is more than the sum of its parts. The potatoes take on a melting quality that contrasts nicely with the crunchy topping.

Sandwiched between the Parmesan-enriched mashed potatoes, the long-cooked tomatoes and onions taste even sweeter, almost as if you'd added sugar. Somehow you are not aware of the saltiness of the cheese.

What is also wonderful about this potato pie is that it can be prepared well ahead of time and heated as you need it. By the piece or all at once. For fun and contrast, serve the pie with some Braised Bitter Greens (page 298).

Spinach with Chick-peas

The combination of leafy spinach or greens with starchy chick-peas is quite popular in many Mediterranean cuisines. The chick-peas can be prepared a day or so ahead (or you may use the canned variety). Wash the spinach a few times to remove grit and sand.

Serves 6

¼ cup olive oil

1½ cups diced onions

2 cloves garlic, minced

½ teaspoon cinnamon

2 teaspoons ground cumin

½ teaspoon ground ginger

Pinch cayenne

2 cups diced, peeled, and seeded tomatoes

2 pounds spinach, stemmed, washed, and coarsely chopped

2 cups cooked chick-peas

Salt and freshly ground black pepper

Warm the olive oil in a large sauté pan. Saute the onions over moderate heat until tender and translucent, 8 to 10 minutes. Add the garlic, spices, and tomatoes, and cook for 2 minutes, stirring from time to time. Add the spinach in batches, stirring often to moisten the leaves, until all are barely wilted. Stir in the chick-peas and simmer for 5 minutes, stirring often. Season with salt and pepper.

Kitchen Conversation

The cinnamon and tomatoes add sweetness, the cumin a tart note that echoes the spinach. Chick-peas, which can be boring, become positively alluring due to the company they keep. The bitter greens brighten and lighten the starchy chick-peas (just as they would lentils or white beans).

Brussels Sprouts with Garlic and Parmesan

M any people have had a bad history with Brussels sprouts and consider them soggy, cabbagy old things. However, if you cut small sprouts in half, or cut larger halves crosswise
into narrow strips, cook them quickly and season them well, with lots of garlic,
Parmesan cheese and toasted pine nuts, Brussels sprouts will become a new favorite, and former
sprouts haters won't even recognize them.

Serves 4 to 6

2 pounds Brussels sprouts

2 tablespoons unsalted butter

3 tablespoons olive oil

4 to 6 large cloves garlic, finely minced

1¹/₂ cups Basic Chicken Stock (page 115) or
vegetable stock

Salt and freshly ground black pepper

¹/₂ cup grated Parmesan cheese

Trim the ends off the Brussels sprouts and cut them in half lengthwise. If you like, you can then cut them crosswise in thin strips.

Warm the butter and oil in one large sauté pan (or two if one is not large enough to hold all the sprouts). Add the garlic and cook over low heat for 2 to 3 minutes. Add the Brussels sprouts and stock, and cover the pan. Steam until crisp-tender, stirring occasionally, about 3 to 5 minutes for strips and 6 to 8 minutes for halves. Season with salt and pepper, and top with a generous sprinkling of grated Parmesan and toasted pine nuts. Serve at once.

Kitchen Conversation

Here's where long cooking is not recommended, as it brings up the worst cabbagy flavor of Brussels sprouts. Short cooking produces wonderful and surprising results. And by not cooking the sprouts whole in a lot of liquid for a long time, you've eliminated their sog-giness and off-putting color. The sprouts are a sprightly green, and their bitterness has been trans-formed by the sweet pine nuts, salty cheese, and pun-gent garlic.

Artichokes, Fennel, and Greens Avgolemono

A classic Mediterranean vegetable stew with the avgolemono (egg and lemon) thickener added as the grande finale to temper the bitter greens and to balance the sweetness of the fennel and artichokes.

Serves 6

4 large artichokes

2 large or **3 small heads of fennel**

Extra virgin olive oil

1 large bunch green onions (scallions),
sliced thin, about 1 cup

Vegetable or **Basic Chicken Stock** (page 115)
as needed

8 cups assorted greens, such as escarole, chard, dandelion

Salt and freshly ground black pepper

2 eggs

¼ cup fresh lemon juice

Chopped fresh dill or **mint**

Prepare a bowl of cold water with the juice of 1 lemon plus the squeezed lemon halves floating in it.

To prepare the artichokes, if the stems are tender, try to leave a 1-inch piece attached or cut all of it off if they appear withered or limp. Cut off the top inch or more of each artichoke, and tear off all of the outer leaves. Peel the stem end and pare the remaining leaf ends down to the heart. Carefully scoop out the choke with a sharp spoon or melon baller. Rub the artichoke with a cut lemon as you work. Trim all the artichokes and cut them in quarters, or eighths if they are very large. Put them into the lemon water to keep them from discoloring.

To prepare the fennel, cut in quarters, remove tough central core, and pull off any discolored or bruised outer leaves. If the fennel bulbs are large, cut them in eighths.

Warm the olive oil in a wide, deep sauté pan and add the green onions, and sauté over moderate heat for 4 minutes. Add the artichokes and toss in the oil for a few minutes. Add enough stock to just cover the artichokes. Cook, covered, for 10 minutes, then add the fennel. Cook for 10 minutes longer, or until both the artichokes and fennel are almost tender and cooked through. (You may stop now if you wish and complete the cooking later.)

Uncover the pan and add the greens, stirring and turning until they are wilted. Season with salt and pepper.

Beat the eggs and lemon juice in a small bowl until very frothy. Add a bit of the pan juices to warm them, then return the egg mixture to the pan. Remove from the heat. Stir well and sprinkle with dill or mint. Serve at once.

Kitchen Conversation

Sweet and bitter flavors are brightened and tamed by the lemon mixture, which also adds body to the pan juices. Artichokes are a most interesting vegetable in that they taste bitter when raw, become almost nutty after sautéeing, and yet turn amazingly sweet after steaming. If you've overlemoned them, they can keep a sour edge. In other words, artichokes present a chal-

lenge to work with in playing the game of flavor balance. Here the avgolemono cuts their sweetness, but doesn't dim the sweetness of the fennel. The lemon also tames the bitterness of the greens. If you want more sweetness, add mint. Want to accent tart? Use dill.

Zeytinyagli Kereviz Turkish Celery Root Ragout

I wonder why celery root is so underappreciated in the United States. The French make a superb celery root salad, dressed with the classic remoulade, a caper, onion, and mustard-tinged mayonnaise. When we serve this salad, I notice that guests are often surprised by it and ask, What's that vegetable? Occasionally batons of celery root are added to composed citrus-based salads, or used in soups with potato, but rarely do they star on the American menu. In Turkey celery root is a favorite, often combined with other vegetables in a light and fragrant broth. This dish resembles the more famous artichokes à la polita, or city style. It is usually served at room temperature, accompanied by lots of good bread, and can be part of a meze assortment.

Serves 4 to 6

2 pounds celery root

4 cups water

Juice of 1 lemon

2 onions, chopped

$^1/_3$ cup olive oil

3 to 4 cups hot water, vegetable stock, or
  Basic Chicken Stock (page 115) as needed to cover

3 carrots, peeled and diced

3 potatoes, peeled and diced

1 cup peas

1 tablespoon sugar

Salt and freshly ground black pepper

$^1/_2$ cup chopped dill

Peel the celery root, wash it well, and drain it. If you prep it ahead of time, keep it in lemon water as you would artichokes. Cut the celery root into $^1/_2$-inch slices. Cook for 10 minutes in boiling water acidulated with the juice of a lemon. Drain and set aside.

Heat the olive oil in a large sauté pan. Add the onions and cook for 8 minutes over moderate heat.

Add the hot water or vegetable stock, celery root, carrots, potatoes, sugar, and salt, and cook for 15 minutes. Add the peas and cook for 8 to 10 minutes longer until vegetables are tender and some of the liquids have evaporated. Add salt and pepper, and a little lemon juice to taste, if desired. Serve at room temperature, sprinkled with dill.

Kitchen Conversation

The key ingredient here is that little pinch of sugar, which heightens the sweetness of the carrots, celery root, peas, and potatoes. It's so small you'd think it wouldn't make a difference, but leave it out and the lemon takes over and the rest of the vegetables taste flat.

Verdure di Campagna Braised Bitter Greens

I n this world of al dente vegetables, we are somewhat shocked when we encounter one that has been cooked to total tenderness. In fact, many vegetables profit from longer cooking, as this helps their flavor to develop. ☛Recently I dined with a group of chefs in Rome. It was spring, so we ordered lots of primizie, the first young spring vegetables. They were served to us on platters and all were what one might consider "overcooked." They were not bright green, and even seemed a little gray. But how sweet and tender the vegetables were! What a culinary dilemma. How could we get our staff and our guests to accept that not every vegetable has to bite back, and let them understand that greenness could be sacrificed for flavor? ☛Green beans usually profit from longer cooking as do peas, asparagus, broccoli, and cauliflower. Here is another example of the joys of longer cooking, sweeter flavor.

Serves 6

3 pounds assorted bitter greens, such as escarole, chicory, beet greens, mustard greens, collards, mizuna, broccoli rabe, or endive, tough stems removed

Olive oil as needed

3 to 4 cloves garlic, minced

1 fresh, very hot pepper, finely minced, or

1 tablespoon hot pepper flakes (optional)

3 tablespoons minced anchovies (optional)

Salt and freshly ground black pepper

Wash the greens well and cut off any tough stems and trim or discard unsightly leaves. Cut or chop any large leaves into large bite-sized pieces.

Bring a large pot of salted water to a boil. Cook the greens, uncovered, for 10 to 15 minutes until soft. Drain well.

Heat the olive oil in a large sauté pan. Add the garlic, hot pepper, and anchovies if using. Mash them down in the oil over moderate heat for a few minutes. Add the greens and simmer for 5 minutes, stirring often. Season with salt and pepper.

Serve the greens at room temperature.

Kitchen Conversation

I know that these greens can be stir-fried or steamed and served slightly crisp! However, most bitter greens profit from longer cooking to reach their flavor potential. Especially if they are tough. Just give this method a try. Keep tasting along the way. You will notice the changes. And try a longer cooking method with green beans too. And broccoli. Cook them until they melt in your mouth and no longer offer resistance to your tooth. As a variation, add cooked white beans or chick-peas or well-cooked broccoli to the greens. Try tossing these cooked greens with pasta. For example, add both beans and greens to orecchiette (page 123).

Spinach with Garlic, Anchovy, and Lemon Zest

People were always raving about the spinach at Square One and asking what we did to make it so good. The answer is, very little—on purpose. Heat butter in a sauté pan, turn the spinach leaves around in it until they wilt, then season them simply with salt and pepper. Do not add water or any liquid and never cover the pan, which would steam the leaves and bring up a metallic taste. By cooking the spinach uncovered, with only a bit of moisture clinging to the leaves, you end up with a tender, bright green vegetable. Spinach is porous and can absorb quite a bit of butter. But you don't want to get carried away. (Brillat-Savarin writes of a legendary dish where 5 pounds of spinach absorbs 1 pound of butter over the course of 5 days!) Try this recipe if you want guests to rave about your spinach too.

Serves 4 to 6

4 tablespoons unsalted butter (see note)

2 tablespoons finely minced anchovies

1 tablespoon finely minced garlic

2 tablespoons grated lemon zest

2 pounds spinach, large stems removed, well washed

Freshly ground black pepper

Melt the butter in a very large sauté pan. Add the anchovies, garlic, and lemon zest, and cook for 2 minutes over moderate heat. Add the spinach and keep stirring and turning the leaves until they wilt and are tender. Taste one for tenderness. Season with pepper. The anchovies should have brought salt to the party.

☛Note: For those of you watching your fat intake, you can use olive oil, but it does not absorb into the spinach the way butter does. Since it stays on the surface of the leaves, don't use too much.

Kitchen Conversation

I have a confession to make. I cooked that Brillat-Savarin spinach recipe one time and it was extraordinary, but not like spinach as we know it. It was something else, out of this world. For the sake of my arteries, I will probably never do it again but I had to try it.

Now, let's talk about our spinach. First, you might just want to try cooking it simply, with salt, pepper, and butter. Just to practice the art of making perfect spinach. Then try it with anchovy, garlic, and lemon, as a savory variation on this simple theme. The anchovy replaces salt, the garlic flavors the butter with its pungent note, and the lemon zest puts all of it in balance. Salt and sour work in harmony and bring up the sweetness of the spinach.

Mercimekli Kabak Squash with Lentils

*T*his Turkish ragout of green lentils and summer squash can be served as a main dish, paired with rice or wheat pilaf and a dollop of tart yogurt. Chopped spinach may be added as well as to the summer squash. You may make this hours ahead and reheat it gently at serving time.

Serves 4 to 6

1¼ cups green lentils

3 tablespoons olive oil

2 onions, chopped

Salt

¼ teaspoon ground allspice

2 tablespoons tomato paste or ¼ cup tomato sauce

4 medium summer squash, such as green or gold zucchini or pattypan, cut in 1-inch dice

1 pound spinach, chopped and well washed (optional)

1 tablespoon finely minced garlic

2 to 4 tablespoons fresh lemon juice

6 tablespoons chopped fresh mint or
3 tablespoons dried mint

Toasted nuts (optional)

Yogurt (optional)

Soak the lentils overnight in 1½ cups cold water to cover. Drain and cover with fresh cold water and simmer until firm cooked, not soft and falling apart, or about 35 minutes. Drain, reserve the liquids, and set aside.

Heat the olive oil in a large sauté pan and cook the onions over moderate heat until tender, about 10 minutes. Season the onions with salt, add the lentil liquids, allspice, and tomato paste, and stir well.

Then add the lentils. Bring up to a boil, add the squash, cover the pan, and simmer for about 15 minutes. (If using spinach, add it halfway through cooking the squash.) Add the garlic and simmer for 3 minutes longer. Then add the lemon juice and season with salt and pepper. Remove from the heat and sprinkle with mint. Top with a dollop of yogurt or toasted nuts if desired. Serve hot.

Kitchen Conversation

Another variation on the theme of legumes and veg-etables, this dish is not only a study in texture con-trasts, but also of foreground and background, of top and bottom. The squash benefits from this combina-tion, as often it can taste thin and watery, all high notes. The lentils provide some bottom or low notes for the delicate flavor of the squash, and the allspice and tomato paste lend sweetness. Lemon juice brightens the starchiness of the lentils. Keep tasting as you sea-son. Don't forget to salt. Lentils will absorb it. Try adding toasted almonds or pine nuts to the mixture. Do their texture and sweetness enhance the dish? Or would you rather have tart yogurt as the accent?

Middle Eastern Spiced Carrots

*C*ooked carrots are reliable and comforting, but can be a little boring, although simple glazed carrots will never go out of style in my kitchen. However, here's a way to add excitement to this sweet and tender root vegetable when you are ready for a change.

Serves 6

¼ cup olive oil

1 cup chopped onions

1 to 2 tablespoons grated fresh ginger

1 teaspoon cinnamon

1 teaspoon ground toasted cumin seeds

3 tablespoons sugar or honey

2 pounds carrots, peeled, sliced ¼ inch thick (or cut into julienne strips on a mandoline)

Water or Basic Chicken Stock (page 115) as needed

Salt

3 tablespoons chopped fresh dill or fresh coriander (cilantro) or mint

Warm the olive oil in a large saucepan. Add the onions and cook until tender and translucent, about 8 to 10 minutes. Add the ginger, cinnamon, cumin, sugar or honey, and cook for 2 minutes longer. Add the carrots and enough water or stock to just barely cover the carrots. Simmer covered, stirring from time to time, until the carrots are tender and the liquid is reduced and syrupy. Season to taste with a little salt. Sprinkle with chopped herbs.

☞ Note: Since I refer to glazed carrots in other recipes I think I should give you directions for that old standby before we talk about this more exotic carrot recipe.

Simple Glazed Carrots

Sauté 2 pounds sliced carrots in 4 tablespoons unsalted butter, 1 cup stock or water (or as needed until carrots are tender), 1 teaspoon salt, and 4 tablespoons sugar. Carrots are done when most of the liquids are absorbed and sauce is syrupy.

Kitchen Conversation

Okay. Let's tackle the simple recipe first. Carrots are best when sweet, and they need some salt to bring up sweetness. Taste a raw carrot first. Is it sweet or starchy? Adjust the amount of sugar you add to the stock. One time try orange juice instead of stock or water. Another time use a full-flavored beef stock. All these subtle changes will give you a very different result. Cooked carrots do not taste the same as raw carrots. Cooking transforms them. They need to be tender for their full flavors to emerge.

On to our gingered carrot recipe. Fresh ginger would not really be used in the Middle East, partly because of geography, history, and the culinary tradition of using dried ginger. However, because fresh ginger is widely available here and is so much more aromatic and pungent than dried, I've taken the liberty of using it. The cinnamon echoes the inherent (we hope) sweetness of the carrots, and the honey or sugar helps them reach their full potential. The cumin adds a hint of bitterness for contrast. As would the fresh coriander. Or you can use the sweeter mint or more sour dill.

Mzoura Tunisian Spiced Carrots

T he Tunisians are enamored of a spice mixture called tabil, *which consists of garlic, caraway, coriander, and hot pepper. These spicy carrots are laced with* tabil *and make an excellent accompaniment for lamb, poultry, or mild fish. These carrots can be served hot or at room temperature.*

Serves 6

3 tablespoons olive oil

3 cloves garlic, minced

1/2 teaspoon cayenne

1 tablespoon each coriander and caraway seeds, toasted and coarsely ground

2 pounds carrots, peeled and cut into rounds or julienne strips

1/2 cup water

3 tablespoons vinegar or **fresh lemon juice**

Salt

Pinch sugar if needed to balance the flavors

Chopped fresh parsley, mint, or **fresh coriander**

Heat the olive oil in a large sauté pan. Add the garlic and spices, and stir over moderate heat for a minute or two. Add the carrots and water and cook over medium heat, covered, until the carrots are half done, or 6 to 8 minutes. Add the vinegar or lemon juice, salt to taste, and sugar if carrots are overly starchy. Cook for another 5 to 7 minutes until the carrots are tender and the liquids are almost all absorbed. Adjust the seasoning and sprinkle with herbs.

Kitchen Conversation

The first thing you should have noticed is that this is not a sweet dish. Unlike the previous carrot recipes, here the carrots, even if they were inherently sweet, are up against some strong flavor accents and heat. They rarely play in this turf. The pinch of sugar is for balance but not for "sweetness." You use it the way you use salt to bring up the other flavors. Your choice of herb will also affect the final balance. If the heat or starchiness is too intense, try sweet mint. If you are enjoying the adventure in assertiveness training of carrots, use the bitter fresh coriander, as it's no shrinking violet.

Beets with Mustard, Honey, and Black Pepper

What makes this so good is the way the sweetness of the beets and honey plays against the bitter heat of the mustard and spicy heat of the pepper. This dish can be assembled a few hours ahead of time without any loss of flavor. Just cook the beets by any method you prefer. Baking the beets intensifies their earthy quality. Boiling them makes them milder.

Serves 4

4 to 5 tablespoons unsalted butter

1 tablespoon or more **dry mustard**

¹/₄ teaspoon cinnamon

3 tablespoons honey (or brown sugar if you prefer)

Salt

Lots of freshly ground black pepper

1 pound cooked beets, peeled and quartered if small, cut into eighths if large, or sliced in half-moons, about ¹/₃ inch thick (see page 40)

Melt the butter over low heat in a saucepan or sauté pan. Add the mustard and cinnamon, and stir until they are completely dissolved. Add the honey or sugar, salt, and ample black pepper to taste. At this point you can add the cooked beets to the pan, toss until heated through in the hot sauce, and serve immediately. Or you may place the sliced beets in a baking dish and pour the sauce over them. Cover with foil. The beets can rest this way for a few hours at room temperature, and be baked later in a 350 degree oven until warmed through, 15 to 20 minutes.

Kitchen Conversation

Did you enjoy the contrast of sweet beets and bitter heat, mellowed by the sweetness of honey and butter? Or was it too assertive for you? I love the bite of dry mustard. If you found it too sharp, dissolve the mustard in a little water, orange juice, or balsamic vinegar, and add it gradually to the honey butter. However, dry mustard does something that prepared mustard does not do: It adds a kind of bitter heat, whereas most commercial mustards are just sour.

Finally, don't be shy with the black pepper. It will accent the sweetness of beets and honey. As a variation try making this without the mustard, just simple glazed beets with butter, honey, and black pepper. You might want to use maple syrup instead of honey another time. And if you are a turnip fan, combine turnips and beets and see how the turnips respond to the bittersweet sauce.

Eggplant with Walnuts and Coriander

*T*he spicy walnut sauce is a close relative to a Russo-Georgian sauce called bazha. *The sauce can be spooned over cooked fish, chicken, or vegetables. I particularly like it over grilled eggplant or stirred into roasted eggplant puree. You also can sauté eggplant, then add the sauce to the pan. The coriander garnish gives it a Balkan flavor, but you can try basil for a more Mediterranean taste.*

Serves 6

4 tablespoons olive oil plus as needed for cooking the eggplant

1 cup finely minced white onions

2 cloves garlic, finely minced

2 teaspoons ground coriander

¹/₄ to ¹/₂ teaspoon cayenne pepper

1 cup walnuts, toasted and finely chopped

2 tablespoons vinegar

¹/₂ cup water or **vegetable stock**

Salt and freshly ground black pepper

6 Japanese eggplants or **2 small globe eggplants**

¹/₂ cup chopped fresh coriander or **basil**

To make the sauce, heat the olive oil and sauté the onions over moderate heat for 8 minutes. Add the garlic, spices, walnuts, and vinegar, and cook for 2 minutes longer. Add the vegetable stock or water. Adjust the seasoning. You may want more vinegar for sharpness and more water or oil for spoonability. Don't forget to add salt.

To use as a sauce for broiled or grilled eggplant: With Japanese eggplant, cut in half lengthwise and score with the point of a knife. Broil or grill until tender and spoon the walnut sauce on top.

Or peel the globe eggplants and slice about 1 inch thick. Brush with olive oil and broil until tender. Spoon the sauce over the top. Sprinkle with chopped fresh coriander or basil.

To cook the eggplant in the sauce: Slice the eggplant 1 inch thick and cut into 1-inch dice. Sauté until golden on all sides, then add the sauce to the pan and warm through. Sprinkle with chopped fresh coriander or basil.

Kitchen Conversation

Bitter is as bitter does. The sweetness of the cooked onions plus that little bit of vinegar makes bitterness a pleasant experience. You can serve this with a lemon wedge in case it's not tart enough, or add a little grated lemon zest to the sauce.

JOYCE GOLDSTEIN KITCHEN CONVERSATIONS
SAUCES

311

SAUCES

After a hard day at work, most of us don't have the energy or desire for any elaborate or even semielaborate cooking. When you've staggered home, if you haven't succumbed to takeout or discovered interesting leftovers, you're probably willing to make just enough time for some bare-bones functional cooking. A pasta or a risotto. Some broiled fish or chicken.

Those are the times when it pays to have a few wonderful sauces or condiments up your sleeve or, better yet, in your pantry. They can enliven a simple piece of broiled chicken or fish. They can add pizzazz to vegetable and grain combinations. Or even to a soup mix! Having a few of these on hand will make you feel as if you did more than just throw dinner on the table.

Here are some of my favorite Mediterranean sauces and spice mixtures. Most can be prepared ahead of time; a few have a very long life in either the refrigerator or pantry. Please remember always to taste a sauce before using it. If some flavors have flattened out, you can bring them up in a minute.

Moroccan Charmoula for Fish

M any years ago when I put fish in charmoula marinade on our menu, no one knew what it was. But people sure have come to love it. We joke that if you marinate it in charmoula, you can sell anything. So what is it? Charmoula, also spelled chermoula, is a classic Moroccan paste rubbed on fish. It's a savory mixture of spices and herbs, sometimes sweet, sometimes bitter and sour. There is no one way to make it, and every cook has his or her own favorite spice blend. ☛Here are two charmoulas, one hot, one sweet. Whether you plan to bake, grill, fry, or steam the fish, marinating it in charmoula for 2 to 4 hours will only improve its flavor. After cooking, a little extra charmoula paste thinned with olive oil can be spooned over the fish.

Makes about 1 cup

Basic Charmoula

6 tablespoons chopped fresh coriander

5 cloves garlic, finely minced

1 tablespoon each paprika and ground cumin

1/2 or more teaspoon cayenne pepper

1/2 teaspoon saffron filaments, steeped in 1/4 cup water

3 tablespoons fresh lemon juice

6 tablespoons olive oil

1 1/2 teaspoons salt

1 teaspoon freshly ground black pepper

Combine ingredients in a bowl.

Sweet Charmoula

Makes about 1 1/2 cups

2 cloves garlic, finely minced

1/2 cup each chopped parsley and fresh coriander

1 teaspoon freshly ground black pepper

1/2 teaspoon cinnamon

1/2 teaspoon ground ginger

1/2 teaspoon saffron filaments, steeped in 4 tablespoons water

2 teaspoons ground cumin

1 tablespoon ground coriander

1 teaspoon paprika

1 1/2 teaspoons salt

6 tablespoons olive oil

Combine ingredients in a bowl.
Rub either charmoula paste on fish and refrigerate for 3 to 4 hours.

☛Note: Charmoula is also good on chicken, quail, lamb, etc.

Kitchen Conversation

You want the spices to be strong enough that you can taste each one. Salting the paste again at the last minute will bring them up. Keep adding salt until you can taste each spice. If you've gone too far, and the sauce seems too salty, a squeeze of lemon juice will push the salt back.

Marinades and Spice Rubs

The role of a marinade is to tenderize while infusing with flavor. A spice rub adds the flavors but not the tenderizing effect. Rubs are good on meat or fish that are to be simply grilled or sautéed.

Hazelnut Romesco Sauce

Romesco is a rich and flavorful nut-thickened sauce, a specialty of the city of Tarragona in the province of Catalonia, Spain. It is served as a condiment for cooked shellfish, fish, lamb chops, and such vegetables as beets, potatoes, asparagus, green beans, grilled baby leeks, or green onions. Traditionally it is not a "hot" sauce. However, given the present American love affair with heat and strong, assertive flavors, we've gradually intensified the heat, as our guests prefer it that way. Romesco can be made the day before you need it (it keeps for at least 3 to 4 weeks in the refrigerator, if you don't use it all at one time). ☞This version of romesco is made with hazelnuts, but you could use almonds, or part almonds and part hazelnuts. The recipe doubles or triples with ease, just in case you are planning a party or summer barbecue!

Makes 2 cups or enough for 8 to 10

2 dried ancho chiles

2 red bell peppers

1 cup hazelnuts

4 cloves garlic, chopped

4 teaspoons sweet paprika

¹/₂ teaspoon cayenne pepper or more to taste (see note)

2 tablespoons tomato paste (see note)

4 tablespoons red wine vinegar or to taste

²/₃ cup olive oil

Salt to taste

Put the ancho chiles in a small saucepan and cover with water. Bring up to a boil, then turn off the heat, and let steep for 20 minutes. Roast the red bell peppers on an open flame or under the broiler. When the skin is charred all over, place the peppers in a plastic container and cover the container, or put them in a paper bag. Let the peppers rest for 20 minutes.

Put the hazelnuts on a baking sheet and toast in a 350 degree oven for 10 minutes. Rub the hot nuts in a dish towel until most of the skins are removed. Set the nuts aside.

Drain the ancho chiles and remove the stems and seeds. Chop coarsely or tear into pieces. Place the ancho chile pieces in a small bowl. Peel the roasted peppers, remove the seeds and thick membranes, and cut the peppers into medium-sized pieces. Add to the ancho chiles.

Put the garlic and hazelnuts in the container of a blender or food processor and process on and off until finely ground. Add the ancho chile peppers, spices, tomato paste, and vinegar, and process to combine.

Gradually beat in the olive oil until the mixture emulsifies. Add salt to taste and a little more vinegar as wanted for balance. Refrigerate until needed.

Bring to room temperature before serving.

☛Note: Tomato paste comes in tubes, so you can use as little as you like and refrigerate the rest. If you can only find tomato paste in small cans, use what you need, and place the rest in a plastic container and keep in the freezer until the next time you need it.

Kitchen Conversation

The key to balancing the flavors in romesco sauce is the vinegar. The nuts are quite rich and sweet, the peppers also sweet, even the tomatoes pick up on the sweetness. The heat is present as a subtle buzz in the background. Check for sufficient acidity to bring the sugar and heat into balance. Some vinegars are milder than others, so the amount suggested cannot be precise.

☛*Note: Cayenne has a tendency to increase in heat after a few hours. At first bite you get a buzz, then a mild burn, then fire! If this sauce doesn't seem hot enough at first, let it rest awhile before adding more heat. Remember, you can put it in, but you can't take it out!*

Mzgaldi North African Onion and Honey Jam

*T*his savory onion jam is seasoned with a Moroccan spice mixture called ras al hanout, *which means "top of the shop." It can contain as few as ten and as many as two dozen spices. You can make your own blend using whole spices and grinding them in a spice mill, or you can combine fresh ground spices for this fragrant mixture. Serve this aromatic onion-honey jam with lamb.*

Makes about 3 cups

3 tablespoons olive oil

1 pound onions, sliced thin, about 6 cups

2 tablespoons Ras al Hanout

1 teaspoon salt

4 tablespoons honey

Heat the olive oil in a large sauté pan. Add the onions and cook, stirring often, over medium heat until the onions become very soft and translucent, about 15 minutes. Add ras al hanout and salt, and continue to cook and stir over low heat until the onions are golden and have the consistency of jam, about 25 to 35 minutes. Stir in the honey and cook for a few more minutes.

Makes 2 tablespoons

Ras al Hanout

¹/₄ teaspoon grated nutmeg

¹/₂ teaspoon cayenne

1 teaspoon each ground ginger, cinnamon, cumin, and coriander

¹/₄ teaspoon ground cardamom

¹/₈ teaspoon ground cloves

1 teaspoon freshly ground black pepper

Combine all the spices.
You can make this spice blend in large batches as it keeps well.

Kitchen Conversation

The onion mixture is very perfumy. However, if the onions are sweet and the spices seem too sweet, increase the salt for better balance. Remember that you are not eating this by itself. It is a condiment for full-flavored meat, so it can be pretty intense.

Toasting Spices

We all know it's not wise to store spices for over a year. They lose their intensity and eventually their life. Even if you store them for a reasonable time in a dark, cool pantry, they go dormant. Warming them over low heat in a dry sauté pan will revive them because heat releases their volatile oils. This is especially true of curry blends, cumin, and paprika. For maximum flavor intensity, whenever possible, toast whole spices, then grind them in a spice mill.

Hlou Moroccan Pumpkin Squash and Apricot Puree

Usually served at the end of Ramadan, hlou is a wonderful sweet-tart accompaniment for poultry or lamb. Some Moroccans make this squash puree without the apricots, using honey for sweetness and omitting the onions. In Spain they make a sweet pumpkin conserve called cabello de angel, or "angel's hair," because of its golden color. It is used as a filling for tarts. And in Italian Jewish cooking, there is a similar dish called zucca disfatta, which contains fresh citron instead of apricots.

Make about 3 cups

½ pound dried apricots, cut into small pieces

½ cup sugar

½ cup olive oil

2 onions, finely chopped

1 pound butternut squash, peeled and cut into ½-inch dice

2 cups water

¼ cup fresh lemon juice or to taste

1 teaspoon cinnamon

Soak the apricots in hot water for an hour to soften them.

Heat the sugar and oil in a saucepan until the sugar is melted and pale caramel in color. (Don't worry if the mixture looks odd and some sugar solidifies. It will melt as the onions cook.) Add the onions and cook, stirring occasionally, until tender, about 10 minutes. Add the squash and water, and cook until the squash is tender. Add the apricots, lemon juice, and cinnamon, and cook over low heat until you have a slightly chunky puree. You may need a pinch of salt to round out the flavor.

Kitchen Conversation

The sweetness of the squash, sugar, and cinnamon predominates, but the apricots and lemon add a tartness that holds the sweetness back, so the mixture is not cloying. Just keep playing with sugar and lemon until this puree comes into balance.

Molho de Piri Piri Portuguese Chili Pepper Hot Sauce

T his is a quintessential hot sauce. Its name comes from a very, very hot pepper that was brought to Portugal via Angola, the piri piri. Once prepared and ripened, this sauce keeps for many months in the pantry. Serve piri piri with grilled or broiled shellfish, Feijoada de Mariscos (page 210), broiled chicken, or anything that needs a flavor jolt.

Makes about 1¹⁄₂ cups

¹⁄₂ cup coarsely chopped fresh hot red chili peppers

3 to 4 cloves garlic, finely minced

1 teaspoon salt

1 cup olive oil

¹⁄₄ cup vinegar (optional)

Combine all the ingredients except vinegar in a jar and let rest in a cool, dark place for about a week before using. This sauce keeps well for about a month. Shake before using and add vinegar to taste.

☞Note: The Russo-Georgians also make a fresh hot red pepper sauce called *ajika* that is seasoned with fresh coriander and basil leaves. However, for every 6 hot red peppers they add 2 sweet red peppers.

Kitchen Conversation

Please don't forget to wash your hands well after handling chiles, so you don't pepper yourself. This is hot stuff! The major taste component here is bitter, which comes from the heat of the peppers and the garlic. If the flavor is too intense, balance it with a little vinegar.

Esme Turkish Roasted Tomato Relish

I first tasted this wonderful tart and spicy tomato relish at a small restaurant in Istanbul that specialized in the regional food of Gaziantep (near the Syrian border). Esme was part of an extensive meze course. It was served with puffed poorilike flatbread and was also used as a condiment for lamb sausage. Once the host realized that I was a chef, he dared me to guess the ingredients in the sauce and was surprised when I told him I believed there was pomegranate as well as lemon juice in it. ☛If you can't find pomegranate syrup, use vinegar or lemon juice for tartness with a pinch of sugar for balance. If pasilla chiles are unobtainable, use long green anaheims, but increase the amount of hot pepper. I can't think of a more interesting alternative to ketchup.

Makes about 1½ cups

1 pound ripe tomatoes

1 large or **2 small fresh (pasilla) poblano chiles**

Olive oil as needed

1 tablespoon minced garlic

4 finely chopped green onions or **4 tablespoons grated raw onion**

½ teaspoon cayenne or to taste, depending on heat of chiles

1 teaspoon sweet paprika

1 tablespoon pomegranate syrup or more to taste or **vinegar** or **lemon juice** to taste and a bit of honey

Salt

Very coarsely chopped Italian parsley

Roast the tomatoes on a griddle or in a cast-iron frying pan until the skins are cracked and charred. Roast the pasilla chile on the griddle or a direct flame until the skin is black and charred. Place the pasilla chile in a paper bag or small plastic container and let it steam for 15 minutes. Peel, seed, and finely chop the pasilla chile. Peel and core the tomatoes, and squeeze out most of the seeds. Chop the tomatoes coarsely. If they are very watery, place them in a strainer and drain. Or you may place chopped tomatoes in a medium sauté pan with a little olive oil and cook on low heat for about 5 minutes to reduce the liquids. Add the garlic, green onions, cayenne, paprika, and chopped pasilla chile. Season with the pomegranate syrup or vinegar or lemon juice and salt to taste.

Place the relish in a shallow bowl or saucer and top with chopped parsley. Serve with pita bread or as a condiment for lamb, chicken, and fish.

Kitchen Conversation

This relish is a study in the balance of sour (lemon or vinegar or pomegranate), bitter (hot peppers, garlic, raw onion), and sweet (tomatoes, paprika, and pomegranate), with sour winning out. Be sure that the heat is just a mild buzz on the tongue and that the tart elements dominate, with the sweetness of tomato as a secondary theme. Test by dipping a piece of bread into the sauce to determine if the sauce is well seasoned. If it is not, add a little salt to see if it brings everything into balance.

Balkan Ayvar Green Tomato and Walnut Relish

This green tomato relish is tart and accented by bitter walnuts. The green ayvar is traditionally served with roast, fried, or grilled fish, and with grilled meat. However, like the Yugoslavian eggplant and pepper Ajvar (page 58), it makes an excellent appetizer spread for bread or served as a condiment along with slices of feta, fresh curd cheese or goat cheese, and haloumi bread. It makes a wonderful accompaniment for Saganaki, fried kasseri, or haloumi cheese with oregano and lemon. Let the relish sit a few hours before serving so the flavors can develop. The ayvar can be made a day or two ahead of time. Keep refrigerated but bring to room temperature for serving.

Makes about 3 cups

2 pounds green tomatoes

$\frac{1}{2}$ cup toasted chopped walnuts

1 teaspoon finely minced garlic

$\frac{1}{2}$ cup olive oil

3 to 4 tablespoons wine vinegar to taste, depending upon tartness of tomatoes

$\frac{1}{4}$ cup chopped flat-leaf parsley

Salt and freshly ground black pepper

Olives for garnish

Roast the tomatoes over a flame. Peel, core, and chop coarsely. Mix with the walnuts, garlic, olive oil, and vinegar. Fold in the parsley and season generously with salt and pepper. Place in a serving bowl and top with olives.

Saganaki Fried Cheese à la Grecque
Serves 4

¹/₂ pound kasseri or **haloumi cheese**

About ¹/₄ cup flour

1 teaspoon freshly ground black pepper

About ¹/₄ cup olive oil

1 tablespoon dried oregano

2 tablespoons fresh lemon juice plus lemon wedges

Cut the cheese into slices that are ¹/₂ inch thick and about 3 inches long and 2 inches wide. Place the flour seasoned with the black pepper on a plate. Wash the cheese and pat dry. Dip in the seasoned flour on both sides. Heat ¹/₂ inch of olive oil in a heavy sauté pan on high heat, but do not let smoke.

Fry the cheese for about 2 minutes on each side until golden brown. Place the cheese on a warm plate, sprinkle with the oregano, squeeze a little lemon juice over the cheese, and serve at once, accompanied by lemon wedges and a large spoonful of green tomato ayvar and bread.

Kitchen Conversation

If the tomatoes are too sour, add a pinch of sugar. If they are bitter, increase the garlic and olive oil, and maybe add a pinch of cayenne or some jalapeño for heat. The tartness of the tomatoes requires salt to bring out their flavor. Remember that this relish is not eaten by itself, but is served with meat, fish, bread, or as an accompaniment to salty, creamy cheese and bread.

Or you can serve it with Saganaki.

Zaatar

Zaatar is not a sauce but a Middle Eastern dry spice mixture known as a dukkah. *Flatbread is dipped in olive oil, then into this spice mix. There are many variations of zaatar, some with sumac and sesame seeds, some without the seeds, and some without sumac, a lemony dried spice common to Persian cooking and found in markets specializing in Middle Eastern food. Some zaatar mixtures are based only on herbs (marjoram, thyme, mint, savory), and seasoned with salt and pepper. (*Zaatar *in Arabic translates as a species of wild thyme.)* ☞*All three variations here make nice toppings for pita bread (brush the top of the pita with oil, sprinkle zaatar, and warm in the oven). Or zaatar can be sprinkled on cooked vegetables as you'd use, pardon the expression, "seasoned salt." Add some olive oil or yogurt to zaatar to make a fragrant marinade for fish or chicken.* ☞*You may be surprised to discover, in this era of "fresh is best," that the zaatar mixture is made with dried not fresh herbs. Sesame seeds are toasted in a dry pan, and the seeds and herbs are ground to a powder in a spice mill; powdered sumac may be added. When I make a marinade, I prefer to use fresh herbs, but for a longer shelf life, you may use dried herbs. Store the* dukkah *in an airtight container.*

Version 1

½ cup dried thyme or **a combination of thyme, mint, or savory**

¼ cup sumac

3 tablespoons sesame seeds, toasted and ground

Salt to taste

Olive oil to make a paste

For a marinade, use fresh herbs and add olive oil or yogurt as needed. As a rule of thumb, double the amount of herbs when using fresh.

Version 2

3 tablespoons dried thyme or marjoram
or **6 tablespoons fresh herbs**

2 tablespoons sumac

2 tablespoons toasted and ground sesame seeds

Salt and freshly ground black pepper

For a marinade, use the fresh herbs and add olive oil as needed.

Version 3

3 tablespoons dried or **6 tablespoons fresh mint,** chopped

3 tablespoons dried or **6 tablespoons fresh thyme,** chopped

1 tablespoon salt

2 tablespoons pepper

Kitchen Conversation

The best way to test the zaatar is to dip some bread in olive oil and then into the herb mixture. That way you'll know if the zaatar is in balance or if it needs salt to bring up the tastes. Also, if you are planning to use it as a marinade, warm the zaatar in a little olive oil in a sauté pan so you can get an idea of how it will hold up on cooked food. Usually salt will be the deciding factor.

The sumac has a lemony taste that you may find a bit odd at first, but it grows on you. If at first it seems too strange, you may use lemon juice, but keep giving sumac a try.

Sour Plum Sauce

This resembles a Russo-Georgian sauce called tkemali, *but it has a sweeter edge. Walnuts may be added as well as raisins to turn the sauce into a conserve. Serve with lamb, poultry, and even salmon.*

Makes about 2 pints

3 to 4 pounds tart plums, Santa Rosa preferred (prune plums okay)

Water to cover

Fresh lemon juice to taste (optional)

Sugar to taste (optional)

2 tablespoons ground coriander

1 teaspoon cinnamon

¹/₂ teaspoon ground allspice

1 to 2 teaspoons cayenne pepper

6 cloves garlic, finely minced

Grated zest of 2 lemons

1 teaspoon salt or to taste

¹/₂ cup chopped fresh coriander (cilantro) or ¹/₄ cup coriander and ¹/₄ cup chopped fresh mint

1 cup raisins, plumped in hot water and drained, liquids reserved

Up to 1 cup chopped toasted walnuts (optional)

Cut the plums in half and remove the pits. Put in a saucepan with enough water to cover and simmer, covered, until tender. This can take 15 to 40 minutes, depending upon the ripeness of the plums. Puree in a food processor or blender.

Taste the plums. If they are very tart and need sugar, add some to taste. If they are sweet, add a little lemon juice. Return the pureed plums to the pot and add the spices, garlic, lemon zest, salt, and chopped fresh coriander or coriander and mint. Add the raisins, if using. Bring up to a boil, reduce the heat, and simmer until thickened, 15 to 30 minutes, stirring frequently. If the mixture seems too thick, add raisin liquid or water. Keep stirring as the mixture thickens. Don't let it scorch! Taste again and adjust the sweet-and-sour ratio, adding sugar or lemon. If you like, stir in the walnuts at this time. And salt to bring up the flavors. This will keep in the refrigerator for a few weeks.

Kitchen Conversation

The tartness of this sauce will subside over a week's time. And the bitter tastes of fresh coriander and walnut also will recede a bit. If you want this to be more sour than sweet, don't add sugar. The amount of heat is up to you.

JOYCE GOLDSTEIN KITCHEN CONVERSATIONS

DESSERTS

COMPOTES, CUSTARDS & CAKES

DESSERTS: Compotes, Custards & Cakes

Desserts: Compotes, Custards & Cakes

In Mediterranean countries, dessert, if served at all, is usually fruit or a piece of cheese. Elaborate sweets are reserved for coffee hours, or for special family events and holidays. Here is a selection of delectable Mediterranean-inspired desserts, occasional treats that make for festive meals. There are simple fruit compotes, and fruits combined with custard, somewhat richer than a compote. Add a little bread to the fruit and you up the ante of richness. This section contains a few cakes, and tarts filled with custard, cheese, nuts, or fruit. Also a trifle and a rich little cookie to accompany a fruit compote or a good cup of coffee. In most of the Kitchen Conversations about desserts, let's take it for granted that the dominant taste component is *sweet*. There may be fleeting accents of *sour*, usually from lemon or fresh fruits, or *bitter*, mostly in the form of walnuts, bittersweet chocolate, and, occasionally, bitter honey. Saltiness is not a factor, but a pinch of salt usually makes the sweet taste sweeter.

Dolce del Principe Milanese Prince's Dessert

This recipe raises Mastrich (page 360) to the next level, a dessert designed for royalty. It is a decadent Italian "trifle" based on yet another nineteenth-century Milanese recipe. Layers of anise-scented génoise, called in Italy pan di Spagna (in the original recipe, pan d'anes), are soaked in anise-scented Sambuca, then spread with mascarpone-enriched zabaglione, and served with apricot sauce. This sensual dessert suited for a prince is not to be eaten in huge portions, but a small slice will deliver huge satisfaction. It would make a great wedding or birthday cake!

Serves 10

Pan D'Anes (Génoise)

6 large eggs

1 cup sugar

1 teaspoon vanilla extract

2 tablespoons Sambuca or another anise-flavored liqueur

1 cup cake flour, sifted

6 tablespoons unsalted butter, melted

Zabaglione Filling

⅓ cup plus 1 tablespoon Sambuca

Apricot Sauce

Preheat the oven to 350 degrees. Lightly butter a 9-inch round cake pan and line with baker's parchment.

Whisk the eggs and sugar together in the bowl of an electric mixer. Set over hot water and whisk by hand until warm. Remove from the heat and beat on high speed until the mixture holds a 3-second ribbon. Beat in the vanilla and Sambuca. Then sift half the flour over the mixture and fold in. Fold in the melted butter and then the remaining flour. Pour batter into the prepared cake pan and smooth top.

Bake until a toothpick inserted in the cake comes out clean and the cake springs back when touched. This will take about 30 minutes. Cool for 5 minutes in the pan, then turn out onto a cake rack.

Zabaglione Filling

7 large egg yolks

6 tablespoons sugar

1 cup dry Marsala

1½ cups mascarpone at room temperature

Whisk the eggs in a bowl until blended, then whisk in the sugar and Marsala. Strain into a large shallow heatproof bowl. Set the bowl over boiling water and whisk constantly until the mixture is light and airy and forms a ribbon when the whisk is lifted from the bowl. This will take about 15 minutes. Chill thoroughly in a bowl of ice water. Fold the mascarpone into the zabaglione.

To assemble the cake, slice the génoise horizontally into 3 rounds with a serrated knife. Place the bottom layer in a parchment-lined 9-inch springform pan and sprinkle the cake with Sambuca. Spread one half the filling atop the cake. Place another cake layer atop the filling. Sprinkle with Sambuca. Top with the remaining filling. Top with the last layer of cake and sprinkle with Sambuca. Cover with plastic wrap and refrigerate overnight. It is imperative that this cake rest overnight in the refrigerator so that the alcohol dies down and the mascarpone filling sets.

Apricot Sauce

1¹⁄₂ cups apricot jam

¹⁄₂ cup water

Combine the jam and water in a small saucepan and stir over low heat until the jam is melted and a saucelike consistency is achieved.

To serve cake, remove the sides of the springform pan. Dust the top of the cake with powdered sugar.

Warm the apricot sauce. Slice the cake and spoon on a bit of the sauce atop the cake. ☛Note: As a variation, spread the cake layers first with apricot puree before layering with zabaglione. Then serve additional apricot sauce on the side.

Kitchen Conversation

Not for the faint of heart. Or those on a low-fat diet! This dessert is rich and proud of it. You'll find that the tartness of the apricot sauce relieves the sweetness and some of the richness of the cake, especially if you've brushed it between all the layers. This is a festive party dessert to be consumed with moderation, but without embarrassment.

Wine Notes

Pairing Pointers: *The anise is the paramount factor in finding the right wine for this dessert. Apricot is malleable in this context, and the mascarpone provides contrast and richness. There's a wealth of different flavors going on here, so it's fun to experiment. You could even offer more than one choice!*

Category: 7

Specific Recommendations:

7: *Fortified Muscat—Beaumes de Venise, for example* ■
  Madeira—a luscious Malmsey or a very, very sweet Bual ■
  Port style—Australian stickies—Semillon or Muscat

Peaches and Nectarines in Red Wine "Sangria"

This fruit compote is a really refreshing finale to a late-summer dinner. You probably recognize it as a dessert variation on a classic Spanish drink, sangria. Only instead of lots of wine with fruit, here's lots of fruit in a tangy wine punch. You may add berries to this "sangria." What is most important is that the fruit be ripe and fragrant.

Serves 8

2 cups red wine

2 tablespoons brandy

1 cup fresh orange juice

1 cup sugar

1 small cinnamon stick

2 long strips lemon zest and 2 long strips orange zest

8 large ripe peaches or nectarines

Berries (optional)

Bring the wine, brandy, juice, sugar, and cinnamon up to a boil in a nonaluminum saucepan. Simmer for 5 minutes. Set aside in a serving bowl.

Dip the peaches in boiling water to remove the skins. Cut the peaches in half, remove the pits, and cut the fruit into 1/2-inch slices. If using nectarines you don't have to peel them.

Add the fruit to the wine mixture and refrigerate until well chilled. Add the berries, if using, just before serving. The fruit should macerate for at least 5 hours, but you can make this the day before serving it. The fruit will have darkened from the wine, but the flavor will be even more intense.

Kitchen Conversation

If the wine has a bitter edge, or if the orange juice is tart rather than sweet, you may want to eliminate the lemon zest. You may also want to try this compote with a sweet white wine or a sparkling wine such as Champagne. Taste the wine and if it is sweet, cut back on the sugar. Many sparkling wines have a tart edge, except for Italian Prosecco. You may not want a wine with this dessert, but there are some nice options.

Wine Notes

Pairing Pointers: This refreshing dessert is not overly sweet, and from a wine point of view is dependent upon the quality of your fruit. If the fruit is not super-ripe, the macerating liquid becomes the focal point. Ripe peaches and nectarines are very intensely flavored, as are cinnamon and orange. So you will be pairing the wine with those flavors. If you choose to macerate the fruit in a dessert-style wine, serve the same wine as an accompaniment.

Category: 7

Specific Recommendations:

7: *Port—light ruby port, fresh and fruity* ■ *Champagne—citrus notes forward—extra dry* ■ *Muscat—orange Muscat, not too sweet—USA, Tunisia*

Apricot Compote with Almond

Each year the season for fresh apricots seems to grow shorter, and my yearning for them more poignant. When apricots are fresh and ripe they are an even more precious treat, with their fragrant, sweet tartness and pillowy tenderness. So when they are in season and are ripe and full flavored, make this dessert. The poached apricots will keep in the syrup for about a week under refrigeration, so you might want to double the recipe. The first time you make this compote use almonds as garnish. The next time add fresh raspberries as a variation.

Serves 4

1 cup sugar

1 cup water

1 cup white wine

Strip lemon zest

A few cardamom seeds (optional)

1 pound apricots, cut in half and pitted (about 3 apricots per person)

¹/₂ teaspoon almond extract, or **1 teaspoon vanilla,** or **1 tablespoon orange-flower water**

Toasted slivered almonds (optional)

Fresh raspberries (optional)

Combine the sugar, water, and wine in a large non-aluminum saucepan. Put the lemon zest and cardamom seeds in a spice ball or tie in cheesecloth. Add to the liquids and bring the mixture to a boil. Reduce the heat and simmer for 8 minutes. Slip in the apricots, simmer gently for 4 minutes. Remove from the heat. Remove the apricots with a slotted spoon to a serving bowl, discard the lemon zest and cardamom seeds. Reduce the syrup a bit if you find it is too thin. Taste the syrup at this point and decide if you want to add the vanilla or almond extract. Or the orange-flower water. Stir in the flavoring of choice and pour the syrup over the apricots. Refrigerate until cold. Sprinkle with almonds at serving time.

Kitchen Conversation

I must confess to a personal bias. I love almond with apricots and peaches. To me, the two flavors are soul mates. The perfume of almond extract lingers and improves as the compote sits. The aroma and flavor of orange-flower water are more subtle and dissipate more quickly. Vanilla is safe, but it is almost too prosaic for this special summer treat. Cardamom has its own lemony perfume, and it often pairs with orange-flower water or apricots in Middle Eastern sweets. I'd serve this with some sort of almond cookie for the echo effect.

Wine Notes

Pairing Pointers: *A caveat for all dessert wines: Always be sure that the sweetness level of the wine exceeds that of the dessert. Botrytised wines work wonders with apricots. If you add a significant quantity of almonds, you can match them directly. If not, stick to pairing with fruit.*

Category: 7

Specific Recommendations:

7: *Chenin Blanc, botrytised—rich, unctuous—Loire Valley, South Africa* ∎ *Riesling—botrytised, beerenauslese level—Germany, USA* ∎ *Sparkling wine—rosé styles with some sweetness in the dosage*

Spiced Figs with Lemon, Fennel, and Cloves

Figs are quite fragile when ripe. But ripe is the only way to eat them. You can make a light syrup and poach whole figs very gently, then cool them in the syrup. However, there's always the danger of overcooking, having them rupture and lose their sexy shape. One alternative is to make a syrup and pour it over fresh figs that have been cut in quarters, as if you were serving a macedonia or fruit salad. Or leave the figs whole (really the prettiest way to serve them) and bake them. If you can find lemon verbena, the leaves will perfume the figs in a most exotic way. If not, use lemon zest (or if you are feeling in an experimental mood, try lemongrass). Instead of water you may use port for a more intense syrup.

Serves 4

1 pound figs, 2 large or 3 small per person

1/4 cup sugar or **honey**

2/3 cup water (or **part** or **all port**)

2 strips lemon zest, or **4 lemon verbena leaves,** or **1 1/2 inches lemongrass,** sliced paper thin and chopped coarsely

1/2 teaspoon fennel or **aniseed** (optional)

2 to 3 whole cloves

Toasted pine nuts or **walnuts** (optional)

Cut the stems off the figs and prick lightly with a fork in a few places so that the figs will absorb the syrup.

Combine the sugar or honey and water or water and port in a medium saucepan. Put the lemon zest, lemon verbena leaves, or lemongrass and spices in a spice ball or tie in cheesecloth and add to the saucepan. Bring up to a boil, reduce the heat, and simmer for 5 to 6 minutes.

Pour over the figs and bake in a 350 degree oven for 15 to 20 minutes. Or poach the figs gently in this syrup for 5 to 8 minutes. Cool in the syrup. Discard the spice ball. Serve garnished with toasted pine nuts, walnuts, or lemon verbena leaves, if desired.

Kitchen Conversation

If you used port in your syrup, the dessert is considerably richer and more intense than if you used water. With port all of the spices will be muted. However, with a water-based syrup the dessert will seem lighter and the spices and lemony herbs more prominent. The fennel, anise, and cloves add a complex undertone to the syrup. If you used port, garnish with walnuts if crunch is desired. Pine nuts will be overpowered by the port-based syrup. If you used water, the pine nuts will add sweetness to play off the lemon.

Wine Notes

Pairing Pointers: *Despite the use of fresh figs (as opposed to dried) I find this dessert works better with fortified wines, especially Madeira, fortified Muscats, and Muscat ports (Australia). The nature of the spices mandates a wine with some oomph!*

Category: 7

Specific Recommendations:

7: *Muscat—luscious and fragrant—Australian port, Southern France* ■ *Madeira—Malmsey style* ■ *Vin Santo—rich, syrup version*

Torta Sabbiosa or Torta di Sabbia Venetian Pound Cake

This Venetian recipe for "sand torte" dates from the 1880s and produces a cake much like our American pound cake. The use of potato starch instead of flour gives it an exquisite texture. I think it's best made the day before eating, but then you may want to eat it right away! Please let it rest for at least 4 hours before slicing. This cake keeps at room temperature, well wrapped, for about 5 days. (Not that it will be around that long.) Slice it thin and serve with berries and a dollop of mascarpone, or with berries or sliced peaches macerated in wine. Or with any fruit compote.

Serves 8 to 10

½ pound unsalted butter

1 cup sugar

Grated zest of 2 lemons

4 to 5 eggs, separated

2 tablespoons brandy

1 teaspoon vanilla

1¼ cups potato starch

2 teaspoons baking powder

Cream the butter, sugar, and zest with a paddle until fluffy, no less than 15 minutes. Whisk the egg yolks in a bowl with the brandy and vanilla. Gradually dribble the egg yolks into the butter mixture and beat 10 minutes longer. Sift the potato starch with the baking powder. Fold the potato starch and baking powder gently into the batter. Beat the egg whites until soft peaks form. Carefully fold into the batter. Pour into a standard loaf pan, buttered and lined on the bottom with baker's parchment.

Bake at 325 degrees for 45 to 50 minutes. Then test the cake for doneness by inserting a wooden skewer or toothpick, and if it comes out clean, the cake is done. If not, bake the cake for another 10 minutes. Cool in the pan on a rack for 10 minutes, then turn the cake out of the pan onto the rack and cool. When cold, enclose in plastic wrap and then in foil and let rest at room temperature for at least 4 hours.

☛Note: Some versions of this recipe add a little anisette. See page 334 for Pan D'Anes, a relative of Torta Sabbiosa.

Kitchen Conversation

The lemon zest is a key ingredient that gives the cake a citrusy perfume. The brandy is elusive; it doesn't jump at you, but it adds a certain fullness of flavor. Careful but swift folding of starch and egg whites is important for an even texture. Does it need the garnish of fruit or mascarpone?

Wine Notes

Pairing Pointers: This Venetian pound cake can be looked at in two ways: By itself it's a blank canvas and any dessert wine will do. With fruit or sauce, a modest dessert wine to mirror the fruit would be best.

Category: 7

Specific Recommendations:

7: *Sherry—brown or cream sherries are lovely* ■ *Tawny port—10- or 15-year-olds are best* ■ *Port—a youthful ruby or LBV for berry accompaniments* ■ *Semillon/blends—Sauternes style for peaches, apricots, pears*

Apricot or Peach Clafouti

Sort of a pudding, sort of a pancake. The dominant taste is fruit. Only muted a bit. Traditionally clafouti is a dessert from the Limousin region of France, and the fruit used is the cherry, often unpitted! However, other fruits work well. Here it's peaches or apricots. But pears are fine too. ☛Clafouti is a great dessert to serve when entertaining. Warm desserts seem especially festive. Even though the baking is last minute, the fruit can be macerated and the batter ingredients readied to whirl in a blender or processor just before serving the last course. Serve warm, sprinkled with confectioners' sugar or with additional macerated fruit.

Serves 6

3 large peaches, peeled, cut into large dice (about 4½ cups), or **18 apricots,** cut in half, pits removed, peeling optional

1 tablespoon grated lemon zest

¼ cup sugar

¼ cup amaretto (optional)

2 tablespoons unsalted butter

3 eggs

1 cup milk

½ cup cream

Salt

1 teaspoon vanilla

¼ teaspoon almond extract (optional)

⅓ cup sugar

1 cup flour

Combine the fruit with the lemon zest, sugar, and optional amaretto, and let macerate for about 1 hour.

Preheat the oven to 375 degrees.

Butter a shallow pie plate or gratin dish. Place fruit on the bottom of the plate.

Combine the eggs, milk, cream, vanilla, or almond extract, if using, sugar, and flour in the container of a blender or food processor and pulse to combine, scraping down the sides to incorporate all of the flour. Make sure there are no lumps. Let the batter rest for 5 minutes.

Pour the batter over the fruit and bake until puffed and golden brown, about 35 minutes. Dust with confectioners' sugar and serve warm.

Kitchen Conversation

If the fruit is very sweet, you may want to cut back on the sugar in the maceration, and increase the lemon a bit. The amaretto-almond addition is up to you. You know I'm a sucker for this combination. But surely the clafouti can take it, as the batter cuts the intensity of the fruit. Please don't overbake or the pancake will be dry. A little quiver is a good sign when testing for doneness.

Wine Notes

Pairing Pointers: *Here the combination of custard/cake with ripe fruit provides an interesting juxtaposition of sweet and rich with a faint level of tart acidity from the fruit. Again, botrytised wines work splendidly. If you do add amaretto, something with a nutty component is not out of the question. If your clafouti is more cakey than custardy, fortified wines are a best choice.*

Category: 7

Specific Recommendations:

7: *Semillon/blends—botrytised and youthful* ■ *Various Italian— a lush Recioto di Soave is sublime* ■ *Chenin Blanc, botrytised—succulent, sweet fruit, and balanced acidity*

Visneli Ekmek Tatlisi Turkish Bread Pudding with Cherries

Turkey prides itself on the quality of its sour morello cherries, and there are many variations on the theme of cherry bread pudding. In one you toast the slices of bread lightly, sauté them in butter, and then simmer them in hot morello or sour-cherry compote. The mixture cools in the pan and is served with kaymak, very thick clotted cream, or whipped cream. Another version toasts the bread, places it in a baking dish, and covers it with a custard mixture containing cherries. ☛Here's yet another variation, which is my favorite. Of course, fresh sour cherries are best for this dessert, but we don't get to see them at our markets very often. Sometimes they're around for just a week! Bing cherries will work, but they are almost too sweet, so make adjustments in the sweet and tart ratios.

Serves 8

2 tablespoons unsalted butter

6 slices white bread, about 1 inch thick, crusts removed

1 teaspoon grated lemon zest

2 cups scalded milk

4 eggs

¹/₂ cup sugar

1 teaspoon vanilla

Pinch cinnamon

6 ounces pitted and halved morello or **sour cherries** (drained canned cherries are acceptable)

Butter a 1¹/₂-quart baking dish.
Preheat the oven to 300 degrees.
Cut the bread into cubes, place on a baking sheet, and toast in the oven until golden, about 15 minutes. In a medium saucepan over moderate heat add the lemon zest to the milk and bring up almost to a boil. Beat the eggs and sugar until frothy. Beat in the vanilla and cinnamon. Then carefully and gradually whisk in a little hot milk, a bit at a time, to the eggs. Add the rest of the hot milk when the eggs are warm and there is no danger of curdling. Toss the cherries with the bread cubes and fold in the custard. Pour the mixture into the baking dish. Place the dish in a pan of warm water and bake for 45 to 60 minutes, or until just set.

Kitchen Conversation

If you decided to use Bing cherries, did you increase the grated lemon zest? Or macerate the cherries in a little lemon juice before baking? And cut back a bit on the sugar? This cherry bread pudding should not be too firm; in fact, it should be a little quivery when you take it out of the oven.

Wine Notes

Pairing Pointers: *The cherries in this bread pudding are the focal point. The texture of the custard and the vanilla are background. Avoid ports, although it's tempting to try to match the cherry fruit. If you do elect to go that route, the simpler and fresher the better.*

Category: 7

Specific Recommendations:

7: *Muscat—medium-sweet black Muscat* ▪ *Various Italian— sweet, light red, Recioto della Valpolicella* ▪ *Sparkling wine—extra dry, California*

Greek-Inspired Peach and Honey "Bread Pudding"

This is not really a bread pudding in the traditional sense. It is neither baked, nor is it custardy. But it does center around bread. You'll be amazed that something so homey can be so sensual at the same time. That's because this dessert isn't overly sweet and it's served warm. In Spain it is called torrijos and is served with a simple syrup. In France it is called pain perdu and is served with a compote of sautéed apples. In this Greek-inspired version of dessert "French toast," the bread is topped with honeyed peaches. While you also might enjoy this dish for Sunday brunch, it makes a truly wonderful ending to a meal.

Serves 6

6 thick pieces of firm white bread (standard loaf old-fashioned white bread, brioche, or challah), crusts removed, cut in rounds or squares

1½ cups milk, depending upon thickness of bread

1 teaspoon almond extract or **1 tablespoon orange-flower water**

1 cup dry bread crumbs

1 teaspoon cinnamon

2 tablespoons sugar

1 to 2 beaten eggs

8 tablespoons clarified unsalted butter

1½ cups warm flavorful honey

4 large peaches, peeled, pitted, and sliced

Soak the bread in the milk and almond extract until the bread has absorbed all the liquid. Combine the dry bread crumbs with cinnamon and sugar. Dip the pieces of bread in beaten eggs, then in bread crumbs. Fry in the clarified butter until golden brown and slightly crusty on both sides, like French toast.

Put the honey in a sauté pan and warm it over moderate heat. Add the peaches and turn them in the warm honey for a few minutes, but don't cook them. Spoon them over the bread. Serve at once with a dollop of thickened cream or drained thickened yogurt.

Kitchen Conversation

This is sexy comfort food at its best! Not too many decisions need to be made here. If the peaches are sweet, and you'd like a little tart contrast, spoon yogurt over the top. But if you prefer extra richness, add the whipped cream.

Wine Notes

Pairing Pointers: Simple and soulful desserts are often the most fun. This dish is a relatively clean slate, dependent upon the flavor intensity of the fruit. Play off the honey by selecting botrytised wines, where honey is almost always the dominant flavor.

Category: 7

Specific Recommendations:

7: *Sauvignon Blanc, botrytised—unctuous, lush, honeyed—France, USA* ■ *Semillon/blends, botrytised—Australia too* ■ *Tokay—Hungarian delight—4 or 5 puttanyos (degrees of sweetness in Hungarian)*

Middle Eastern Custard

I'd describe this as a cross between a classic baked French custard or Spanish flan and a Middle Eastern pudding. The fragrance of cinnamon and cardamom and of rosewater or almonds gives it an exotic, Arabian Nights aura. The custard can be made the day before and refrigerated. Serve with berries, peaches, or apricots, or topped with chopped nuts or, if you're going for exoticism, candied rose petals.

Serves 6

2 cups half-and-half or **light cream**

¹/₂ cup honey

¹/₄ teaspoon ground cardamom

¹/₄ teaspoon cinnamon

2 eggs and 2 yolks or **3 whole eggs**

¹/₂ teaspoon vanilla

1 to 2 teaspoons almond extract or **1 to 2 teaspoons rosewater**

¹/₂ cup toasted almonds or **pistachios,** coarsely chopped (optional)

Candied rose petals (optional)

Preheat the oven to 300 degrees.

Heat the half-and-half with the honey, cardamom, and cinnamon in a small saucepan. Bring up to scalding but do not boil.

Mix the eggs lightly with a whisk and gradually add the hot cream, whisking constantly. Stir in vanilla and almond extract or rosewater. Strain the mixture into a pitcher and pour into 6 custard cups or ramekins and place cups in a baking pan. Pour hot water halfway up the sides of the cups. Cover the pan with foil. Bake for 50 to 60 minutes. Remove the custards from the pan, refrigerate until cooled, and cover well with plastic wrap. Bring to room temperature before serving.

☛ Note: A version of this recipe appeared in *Home Food,* a cookbook to raise funds for SOS. It was part of a Middle Eastern menu.

Kitchen Conversation

If you find that this is too intense or perfumy, serve it with fruit, like berries or peaches. The fruit will lighten the custard in your mind and mouth. Nuts or rose petals add greater taste complexity.

Wine Notes

Pairing Pointers: *Match to the exotics: cardamom, cinnamon, rosewater. Lighter, fragrant, and perfumed wines are best. If the wine demands too much center stage, the delicacy of the spices will be overshadowed.*

Category: 7

Specific Recommendations:

7: *Muscat—simple Muscat Canelli, Moscato Bianco, or orange Muscat* ■ *Asti Spumante—balanced and not too sweet*

Bougatsa Custard-Filled Filo Pie

*T*he bus stopped along the waterfront in Thessalonika and I followed the crowd to a tiny shop. A long line spilled out onto the sidewalk. Inside, on the counter, were warm custard filo pies. The women in the shop cut them and wrapped the slices in wax paper. Although this snack was supposed to suffice for a bus journey, I ate it before I left the port. And wished for more. And still do.

Serves 8

2¹⁄₂ cups milk

²⁄₃ cup sugar

3 eggs

²⁄₃ cup fine semolina or farina

2 teaspoons vanilla

³⁄₄ cup melted clarified unsalted butter

16 to 18 sheets filo dough, or about ²⁄₃ pound

1 teaspoon cinnamon

3 tablespoons confectioners' sugar

Preheat the oven to 350 degrees.

Combine the milk, sugar, eggs, and semolina in a medium saucepan and cook over very, very low heat, stirring constantly, until the mixture thickens. Stir in the vanilla. Remove from the heat, and brush a thin layer of melted butter on top of the custard to prevent a skin from forming and set aside.

Brush a thin layer of melted butter on a 15-inch pizza pan.

Lightly brush layers of filo with melted butter, overlapping the sheets so that the pan is covered and some of the excess buttered filo hangs over the edge. When you have used half the filo, spoon in the semolina custard. Bring up the overhanging filo pieces to partially cover the custard. Now proceed to cover the pie with the rest of the filo, buttering as you go. Tuck the overhanging buttered filo under the pie.

Bake for 35 minutes, or until golden. Combine the cinnamon and confectioners' sugar in a shaker and sprinkle over the pie. Serve warm, cut into wedges with a pizza wheel or very sharp knife.

☛ Note: You could also prepare this as individual filo pastries. Cut the filo into strips, brush with butter, add filling on the top corner, and fold as for large tiropetes (see Briouat Bil Kefta, page 71). Bake until golden. Serve with optional baklava syrup.

This is a variation in which a similar semolina custard is layered between sheets of filo:

Galatoboureko, Cream-Filled Baklava

Layer half the buttered sheets of filo in a rectangular baking pan (9×12×2, or about the size of the filo), add the custard, top with the remaining layers of buttered filo, chill for a bit to firm up the butter, then score the top layer of filo into squares. Bake at 350 degrees for 40 minutes, or until golden brown. Remove from the oven, cut it all the way through the score marks, and pour the following syrup over the hot baklava.

Baklava Syrup

In a saucepan place $1/2$ cup honey, $2/3$ cup sugar, $1 1/2$ cups water, 3 tablespoons lemon juice with a few thin strips of orange zest, and a small cinnamon stick. Boil for 10 minutes. Stir in 2 tablespoons orange-flower water.

Recut the baklava into squares. Sprinkle with cinnamon and confectioners' sugar after syrup is absorbed. Serve warm.

Kitchen Conversation

Bougatsa is a story of texture. Of a voluptuous but friendly custard (it tastes a bit homey, like a refined baby cereal) and crunchy, crispy filo. It's important not to be too lavish with the melted butter. Brush on a light film, even leaving spaces so that air can be trapped between the layers, for extra crispness. Bougatsa is sweet but not too sweet, perfumed with vanilla, and brightened with the cinnamon topping at the end. You could eat 2 pieces.

The same ingredients are transformed if you prepare them as galatoboureko. The baklava is denser than bougatsa because the custard melts into the filo pastry and the syrup makes the dessert heavier and sweeter. Of course it's delicious but not as delicate as bougatsa and lacks the latter's contrast of textures.

Wine Notes

Pairing Pointers: *The crunch and crackle of the filo add toasty elements that pair well with nutty wines such as older, more developed Sauternes, youthful tawny ports, and lighter dessert sherries. The custard is a textural sidebar and doesn't play too heavily into the wine suggestion. Fresh tropical dessert wines could be nice too.*

Category: 7

Specific Recommendations:

7: *Semillon/blends—mature, developed styles* ■ *Champagne— demi-sec* ■ *Sherry—toffeed, not too sweet dessert sherry*

Tarta Santiago Spanish Almond Custard Tart

*T*his voluptuous custard tart is scented with almonds. Steeping the nuts in the milk makes the almond flavor more pervasive, not just a surface taste. This is an ideal dessert for entertaining, as the crust can be baked ahead of time and the custard fully prepared and chilled. Just assemble and warm. Garnish the plate with berries if desired.

Serves 8

1³/₄ cups milk

¹/₃ cup sugar

1 cup toasted raw almonds, chopped fine

3 egg yolks

2 eggs

¹/₄ teaspoon salt

¹/₄ cup flour

2 tablespoons unsalted butter

1 teaspoon vanilla extract

1 teaspoon almond extract

²/₃ cup toasted sliced almonds

Prebaked 9-inch pie shell or puff pastry shell

Scald the milk and sugar in a medium saucepan. Add the almonds and steep for an hour. Strain and bring the almond milk to a boil. Mix the eggs, salt, and flour in a bowl. Gradually add some of the hot almond milk to the eggs to warm them. Return the egg mixture to the saucepan and cook over medium heat, stirring constantly with a wire whisk. The custard should boil for 2 to 3 minutes to remove the raw flour taste. Transfer the custard to a bowl set into a bowl of ice. Add the butter and extracts. Chill.

To serve, preheat the oven to 350 degrees. Pour the custard into the prebaked pie, or puff pastry shell. Bake for 5 minutes. Cover the top with toasted sliced almonds. Serve warm.

Kitchen Conversation

Crunch versus creamy! Creaminess cradled between two different crunches. This tart is an exercise in texture as well as taste. Puff pastry makes for a more interesting crust, with more complex layers. A regular pie crust almost seems demure. But both provide the vehicle for the creamy almond custard. What is essential is the toasted almond topping. Toasting the nuts is crucial for bringing up their sweet flavor. Please serve the dessert warm for maximum effect.

Wine Notes

Pairing Pointers: *The texture and flavor of almonds command attention. An interesting twist is to "add" raisiny flavors to this dessert via the wine selection, which is late harvested but* not *botrytised.*

Category: 7

Specific Recommendations:

7: *Tokay—mature, moderately sweet—3 to 4 puttanyos (degrees of sweetness in Hungarian) ▪ Sauvignon Blanc, late harvest—raisiny and sweet, lush texture ▪ Malaga—like sherry, but not as thick, with raisined character*

Brazo di Gitano (Gypsy's Arm) Custard-Filled Sponge Cake Roll

I don't know much about the gypsy or his arm, but I guess this cake is supposed to resemble it. Not too appealing to me, but it takes all kinds. In this Andalusian dessert, a classic *génoise, or sponge cake, is rolled around a sweet custard filling scented with cinnamon, orange, and sherry. The custard can be made the day before, refrigerated, and covered well with plastic wrap. The rolled cake can be assembled 4 to 6 hours ahead.*

Serves 8

Custard Filling

2¹⁄₂ cups milk

Cinnamon stick

Long strip orange zest

8 egg yolks

³⁄₄ cup sugar

¹⁄₂ cup flour

4 tablespoons sweet sherry

1 tablespoon unsalted butter

To make the custard filling, bring the milk to a boil in a medium saucepan with the cinnamon and orange zest. Lower the heat and simmer for 15 minutes.

Beat the egg yolks until pale. Gradually beat in the sugar and continue to beat until the mixture holds a 3-second ribbon. Stir in the flour and gradually add the hot milk. Return to the saucepan and cook over medium heat, stirring constantly, until the mixture thickens. Remove from the heat and stir in the sherry and butter. Transfer to a bowl set over a bowl of ice and cool, stirring from time to time. (If you've refrigerated the custard, bring it to room temperature before assembling the cake.)

Génoise, or Sponge Cake

5 eggs

¹⁄₂ cup sugar

1 teaspoon grated lemon zest

1 tablespoon grated orange zest

1 cup sifted all-purpose flour

4 tablespoons melted, unsalted butter

Powdered sugar and cinnamon for dusting

Preheat the oven to 375 degrees.

Butter and line a jelly roll pan (15×11) with baker's parchment. Place the eggs and sugar in a mixing bowl over a pan of hot water, whisking until warm. Transfer to the mixer and beat with the wire whisk attachment until very thick and pale. Add the grated lemon and orange zests. Alternately, fold in the flour, then fold in the melted butter. Pour the batter into the prepared cake pan and smooth the top. Bake for about 10 minutes, or until the cake is springy and golden. Turn out onto a sugar-sprinkled towel and roll up. Keep covered until ready to fill.

To assemble, when the custard is at room temperature, unroll the cake, spread with custard, and roll up. Sprinkle heavily with powdered sugar mixed with a little cinnamon. Cut slices on the diagonal with a sharp knife.

Kitchen Conversation

Please use a rich-sweet sherry for this dessert, as it is the primary flavor of the custard despite the accents of orange and cinnamon. If you like, serve some orange segments alongside to accentuate the orange undertones of the cake and the custard.

Wine Notes

Pairing Pointers: *The orange, sherry, and cinnamon play into the "local" angle. A sweet Muscat from Sitges, Spain, could not be a more charming match. You'll need some richness to match up with the custard filling, so don't go too light.*

Category: 7

Specific Recommendations:

7: *Muscat—orange-scented Muscat from Spain* ■ *Sherry—sweet Muscat sherries* ■ *Semillon/blends—sweet-tangy Australian versions*

Jennifer's Chocolate Budino

Jennifer Millar, beloved pastry chef, knows how to make you swoon with chocolate delirium. This most requested dessert is easier to make than a soufflé and just as delicious, a sort of warm, comforting, and sensual chocolate pudding (budino) for grown-ups. You can make it 2 to 3 hours ahead of time and reheat it gently, or make the batter, spoon it into custard cups, and refrigerate for up to 5 hours, then bake. Serve the budino topped with a dollop of whipped cream.

Serves 6

7 ounces unsalted butter

6 ounces bittersweet chocolate

¾ cup sugar (12 tablespoons)

1 teaspoon vanilla

Pinch salt

3 large eggs, separated

Preheat the oven to 375 degrees.

Brush six 5-ounce ramekins with 1 tablespoon melted butter and sprinkle with 1 tablespoon sugar. In the top of a double boiler melt the butter and chocolate. Add 8 tablespoons of the sugar, vanilla, and salt. Whisk the egg yolks and gradually add a bit of the chocolate mixture to warm them, then add the eggs to the chocolate. With the wire whisk attachment of an electric mixer, beat the egg whites and 2 tablespoons of the sugar until medium peaks are formed. Fold the whites into the chocolate mixture. Pour into ramekins. (You may stop now and refrigerate the budino mixture for a few hours.)

Sprinkle the budino with the remaining tablespoon of sugar. Place in a water bath and bake in the center of the oven for 20 to 30 minutes. The budinos should puff and form a crackly crust but still remain creamy on the inside. Serve warm.

Kitchen Conversation

Yum. Be careful when you rewarm the budini *not to overdo the process and let them dry out. They won't be quite as decadent as if you baked them at the last minute, but you won't mind suffering with less than perfection.*

Wine Notes

Pairing Pointers: *Serve this dessert warm with the right wine and you'll be in paradise. Chocolate desserts require wines with both bitterness (chocolate is inherently bitter) and sweetness. Fortified wines are better choices, as chocolate is usually accompanied by dense richness and the added alcohol assures that your match doesn't get lost. Port's traditional with chocolate, so why mess with a good thing?*

Category: 7

Specific Recommendations:

7: *Port—deep and concentrated vintage or single quinta port* ■ *Other fortified—Banyuls from Southwest France* ■ *Fortified Muscat—especially orange Muscat*

Mastrich Milanese Rum and Mascarpone Mousse with Bitter Chocolate Sauce

*G*iven the trendiness of mascarpone desserts and a virtual tidal wave of tiramisù, you may be surprised to learn that this Milanese dessert dates from the nineteenth century. It is quite rich, intense, and very sensual. You can spoon the mascarpone mousse in a 9-inch springform pan or into individual ring molds.

Serves 8

Mousse

1 pound mascarpone

1 cup sugar

2 egg yolks

4 tablespoons dark rum

2 teaspoons grated lemon zest

1 tablespoon gelatin sprinkled over ¼ cup water and dissolved over low heat

Whisk together all of the ingredients and spoon into a 9-inch springform pan oiled with almond oil and lined on the bottom with Génoise (see page 356, but omit orange zest). Let set for a day. Unmold and serve with a thick bitter chocolate sauce.

Bitter Chocolate Sauce

6 ounces bittersweet chocolate

¾ cup heavy cream

2 tablespoons unsalted butter

1 teaspoon vanilla extract

Melt the chocolate and heavy cream in a bowl over simmering water. Stir until smooth. Stir in the butter and vanilla. Serve warm.

Kitchen Conversation

This is all about texture, richness, and contrast. The rich creamy cheese mousse seems like a natural for simple berries and a berry sauce. And that's not a bad idea if you want a lighter dessert. The acidity of the fruit cuts some of the richness of the mascarpone. However, the decadent chocolate sauce is the richest and most sensual option. It plays up the contrast of sweet creaminess with bittersweet.

Wine Notes

Pairing Pointers: *Your choice of dessert libation is totally dependent upon how much of a chocoholic you are. If you drench this in sauce, you'd better select a wine to go with bittersweet chocolate, but your choices are limited. If you go light on the sauce, your options are greater.*

Category: 7

Specific Recommendations:

7: *Tawny port—coffee scented, 15 or 20 years old* ■ *Sauvignon Blanc, botrytised—if going easy on chocolate* ■ *Various Italian—a rich-textured Vin Santo*

Gelato al Forno Baked Ice Cream Cake

*T*his dessert was created by a Barese pastry chef, Felice Lippolis, who introduced it for the first time in 1931 at a state fair in Bari. Not only was this dessert a big hit then, it continues to be a hit today. Torrone or nougat ice cream is layered between sheets of lemon and cinnamon-scented Génoise (page 356) that has been spread with melted apricot or fig jam, then popped into a hot oven for a few minutes. We brush the assembled cake with a little of the jam and sprinkle with toasted sliced almonds (or meringue if you are a devotee of baked alaska). ☛*This is an ideal dessert for entertaining because it can be made 1 or 2 days ahead of time and kept in the freezer until ready to serve. (If you do not have a very cold freezer, please pass on this dessert.) Of course you can choose any ice cream flavor you like—vanilla, peach, banana, cinnamon, almond crunch—but remember that it has to be simpatico with the flavor of almonds.*

Serves 6

Génoise

See Pan D'Anes on page 334 but omit the Sambuca and add $1/2$ teaspoon cinnamon and 1 teaspoon grated lemon zest to the batter. Bake at 325 degrees in a buttered parchment-lined $15^{1}/_{2} \times 10^{1}/_{2}$-inch sheet pan for 10 to 15 minutes.

2 pints ice cream, good-quality vanilla (or any flavor of your choice that goes with almond), slightly softened in the refrigerator

4 ounces apricot or **fig preserves,** melted

1 cup toasted sliced almonds

Nougat

$1/8$ cup egg whites

$1/4$ cup sugar

1 cup raw almonds

1 teaspoon almond extract

Preheat the oven to 350 degrees. Whisk the egg whites and sugar until frothy. Add the almonds and almond extract, and toss well to coat. Pour the mixture into a parchment-lined baking pan and bake for 12 minutes until browned. Let cool, then grind to a chunky paste in a food processor.

To assemble cake, turn génoise out of the pan. Brush with the melted apricot jam. Cut the cake in half the short way into 2 strips $5^1/_4 \times 15^1/_2$ inches. On one half of the cake spread the ice cream. Sprinkle the nougat over the top. Freeze. When the ice cream is firm, place the remaining cake layer on top. Trim the cake.

Slice the cake into 6 pieces measuring about $2^1/_2$ inches, and keep them very cold. Brush the cake slices on all sides with the melted apricot jam and press in the toasted sliced almonds. Freeze overnight (or for a few days, well covered).

To serve, preheat the oven to 400 degrees. Place the frozen cake slices on a cookie sheet lined with baker's parchment. Bake for approximately 3 minutes. Serve immediately with whipped cream and berries. The cake and outside ice cream should be warm, and the ice cream in the center should be just starting to soften. The ice cream should not be melting.

☛ Note: You can serve this as an ice cream cake without the last warming step.

Kitchen Conversation

So the big question is, does this gain from being warmed and risking meltdown? The answer is yes. Yes for the drama of presentation. And the almond flavor is intensified by heating.

If you choose not to warm it, that's okay too. It is still a great ice cream cake, suitable for parties, birthdays, and general good times.

Wine Notes

Pairing Pointers: *The temperature factor is to be considered, as is the warmth of the cake. The shock of a cold wine with a warm dessert will not work. What flavor ice cream are you using? Everything else is secondary. You can literally plan the wine by the choice of ice cream. So choose the ice cream, go to the wine cellar and select the wine, then make the dessert!*

Category: 7

Specific Recommendations:

7: *With coffee or chocolate ice cream—tawny Port ▪ With nougat or vanilla ice cream—cream sherry ▪ With caramel ice cream—aged Sauternes, Semillon/blends*

Melopita Greek-Inspired Cheese Tart

I'm a sucker for cheese—in sandwiches, shaved into salads, or over pasta. But I also love cheese as a "dessert," served with a green salad or nuts and bread. And cheesecakes, cheese tarts, cheese pies, cheese danish are my weakness. This tart is a composite recipe, based on two from the Greek islands of Siphnos and Santorini. You can make 1 large tart or about 10 small tartlets if desired. Or you may enclose the filling in tart-dough circles, fold in half, seal, and deep-fry.

Serves 8 to 10

Crust

2¹/₂ cups flour

1 teaspoon baking powder

2 tablespoons sugar

¹/₄ teaspoon salt

Grated zest of 1 lemon

4 tablespoons unsalted butter

¹/₄ cup vegetable shortening (or ¹/₂ cup olive oil in place of butter and shortening)

2 tablespoons ice water

2 teaspoons orange-flower water

Filling

2 cups fresh ricotta or **mizithra cheese**

¹/₂ cup flavorful honey

5 tablespoons sugar

¹/₂ teaspoon cinnamon

3 eggs, lightly beaten

Grated zest of 1 large orange

A drop or two of orange-flower water (optional)

Sift the flour, baking powder, sugar, and salt into a medium-sized bowl. Add the lemon zest and cut in the butter and shortening until the mixture resembles cornmeal. Add the ice water and orange-flower water, and knead the dough until it holds together. (You can assemble this dough in a food processor.)

Wrap the dough in plastic and refrigerate for about an hour. Roll out the dough on a lightly floured surface and ease it gently into a 10-inch tart pan. (You could freeze the crust in the pan at this time. Just put it into a giant plastic bag and place it in the freezer until you need it.)

Preheat the oven to 350 degrees.

In a bowl mix together the cheese, honey, sugar, and cinnamon, then beat in the eggs and orange zest. If you are in the mood, add a bit of orange-flower water.

Pour the cheese mixture into the prepared tart pan and bake for 20 to 30 minutes until the filling is set and pale gold.

Tartlets: You can make individual tartlets with the dough (about 10 tartlets depending upon the size of your tins).

Turnovers: Roll the dough out into 4-inch circles, place a heaping tablespoonful of filling on half the circle, and fold over into a half-moon. Press together with damp fingertips to seal. Deep-fry. Sprinkle with confectioners' sugar.

Kitchen Conversation

This tart is not overly sweet. It's delicately scented with orange, but don't be afraid to add a bit more if you like that citrus accent. Be careful not to overbake and dry out the filling. It should be creamy and still wiggle a little when you take the tart out of the oven. To prevent the top from cracking, add 1 scant tablespoon of flour when mixing the filling.

Wine Notes

Pairing Pointers: *Cheesecake is the perfect vehicle to show off dessert wines. I like them on the richer side, but not so muscular as to overcome the subtle nuances of ricotta. Wines with botrytis seem to work best, as they provide creamy texture and explosive honeyed fruit. Look to enhance the orange-flower water, which is subtle but present.*

Category: 7

Specific Recommendations:

7: *Chenin Blanc, botrytised examples with an almost syrupy sweetness* ■ *Semillon/blends, botrytised—Sauternes or similar-style wines* ■ *Riesling, botrytised—a German eiswein is scrumptious*

Provençal Walnut and Honey Tart

*E*veryone loves nut tarts. In America it's pecan pie. In Spain it's likely to be one made with almonds. In Provence they use walnuts. Chewy and crunchy at the same time, this tart is bittersweet and very rich. If possible, make this with a Provençal lavender honey.

Serves 8 to 10

Crust

1¹/₂ cups flour

Pinch salt

1 tablespoon sugar

¹/₂ cup unsalted butter

2 to 3 tablespoons ice water

Filling

1¹/₄ cups sugar

¹/₂ cup water

1 cup heavy cream

¹/₂ pound shelled walnuts, about 3 cups

³/₄ cup unsalted butter

¹/₃ cup fragrant honey

To make the crust, place the flour, salt, and sugar in the container of a processor or in a mixing bowl. Cut in the butter until the mixture resembles cornmeal. Add the ice water and mix until the dough just holds together. Gather up into 2 balls, place in plastic wrap, and refrigerate for at least an hour.

Roll the dough out on a lightly floured surface. Press one circle of dough into a 9-inch pie pan or flan tin with a removable bottom. Place the other circle on wax paper and refrigerate until filling is made.

To make the filling, bring the sugar and water to a boil in a saucepan over high heat, stirring until the sugar has dissolved. Boil rapidly until the mixture starts to thicken and change color. When it becomes pale brown, remove from the heat and stir in the cream. Return the saucepan to the stove and simmer for 15 to 20 minutes, or until the mixture becomes very thick. Stir in the nuts, butter, and honey and remove from the heat. Cool this molten mixture until warm.

Preheat the oven to 375 degrees.

Working quickly, pour the warm filling into the prepared pan. Cover with the remaining dough circle and seal the edges. Cut a few decorative vents in the top crust and bake for 25 to 35 minutes, or until the top is lightly browned. Cool and remove from pie pan and transfer to a serving plate. Sprinkle the top with confectioners' sugar if desired.

Kitchen Conversation

Rich and sweet, but the sweetness is tempered by the underlying bitter edge to the walnuts and the neutral crust. If you are a supreme hedonist, and many are when it comes to dessert, an ice cream accompaniment is never out of the question. Vanilla or honey ice cream would not be an improper choice. Just perfect, in fact.

Wine Notes

Pairing Pointers: *A good bite of acidity is the perfect foil for this chewy, rich tart. Try a sparkling wine that has developed a nutty edge with age. Madeira, with its intrinsic citrusy bite, is also a flattering match. A "local" Muscat wine will work, if it's fortified and has some strength behind the fruit.*

Category: 7

Specific Recommendations:

7: *Champagne/sparkling wine—demi-sec level with some maturity* ■ *Muscat—fortified—Beaumes de Venise, Muscat de Frontignan* ■ *Madeira—Malmsey on the youthful side*

Melomakarona Honey-Dipped Walnut Cookies

*A*fter *suggesting fruit compotes or fresh fruit for dessert, I should probably give you a cookie to eat with them. These rich and crumbly little cookies are Phoenician in origin and are usually served at Christmas and New Year's. But why wait until then? Make them any time of year. Melomakarona can be stored for about a week in an airtight container.*

Makes about 2 dozen cookies

¹/₂ **pound unsalted butter,** melted

¹/₄ **cup vegetable oil**

¹/₄ **cup sugar**

¹/₄ **cup fresh orange juice**

¹/₂ **teaspoon almond extract**

3¹/₄ **cups flour** or **part fine semolina and part flour**

¹/₂ **teaspoon cinnamon**

2 **teaspoons baking powder**

Syrup

1 **cup honey**

¹/₂ **cup water**

3-inch strip orange zest

2-inch strip lemon zest

Cinnamon stick

Topping

¹/₂ **cup chopped walnuts**

1 to 2 tablespoons sugar

¹/₂ **teaspoon cinnamon**

Preheat the oven to 350 degrees.
Combine the butter, oil, sugar, orange juice, and almond extract in a mixing bowl. Stir in the flour, cinnamon, and baking powder. Knead the dough a little. Shape into oval cookies about 2¹/₂ inches long. Bake on parchment-lined or ungreased baking sheets for about 25 minutes, or until golden. When finished baking, cool until you can handle them, gingerly, then dip each cookie in hot honey syrup for 10 seconds (use chopsticks or a slotted spoon).

For the syrup, combine the honey, water, zests, and cinnamon stick in a saucepan and bring up to a boil over high heat. Reduce the heat and simmer for 15 minutes. Remove the zests and cinnamon stick.
For the topping, combine the chopped nuts with the sugar and cinnamon.
After the cookies are dipped in hot syrup, place on racks and top with the chopped nut mixture.

Greek Walnut Cake with Quince Puree and Sweetened Cheese

*I*n Portugal, Spain, and Greece, quince marmalade, fresh cream cheese, and crackers are often served in place of dessert. Sometimes I've served quince preserves and cheese with walnut bread instead of crackers because I love the combination of walnuts and quince, or walnuts and cheese. In Greece and Turkey, baked quinces are often stuffed with walnuts and topped with clotted cream. So, to give in to my predilections, I decided to make a walnut cake and filled it with quince puree and cream cheese for a wonderful Mediterranean-inspired dessert.

Serves 8 to 10

Walnut Cake

1/2 cup unsalted butter

2/3 cup sugar

6 eggs, separated

1/2 cup flour

2 teaspoons baking powder

Pinch salt

2 teaspoons cinnamon

1/2 teaspoon ground cloves

2 cups ground walnuts

1 tablespoon grated orange zest

Cheese Filling

1 cup fresh soft goat cheese

1 cup mascarpone

2 tablespoons sugar

2 cups Quince Preserves or **fig** or **apricot jam**

To make the walnut cake, preheat the oven to 350 degrees. Lightly butter and flour two 9-inch round cake pans with removable bottoms.

In the bowl of an electric mixer, cream the butter and sugar until light and fluffy. Add the egg yolks one at a time, beating well after each addition.

Sift the flour, baking powder, salt, cinnamon, and cloves. Fold into the egg mixture. Fold in the nuts and orange zest.

In another bowl beat the egg whites until medium stiff peaks form. Stir one third of the whites into the batter, then fold in the rest. Pour into the cake pans.

Bake until the cakes are brown and spring back when you touch them, about 45 minutes. Let the cakes cool on a rack and then remove them from the pans.

For the cheese filling, cream 1/2 pound mild, fresh goat cheese with 1 cup mascarpone and 2 tablespoons sugar.

continued

To assemble the cake, spread a layer of quince preserves atop bottom cake layer. Top with the cheese mixture. Put the cake together.

Quince Preserves

2 pounds quinces

4 cloves

1 cinnamon stick

Water to cover

4 cups sugar

4 to 6 tablespoons fresh lemon juice

Peel and core the quinces. Grate them and place in a nonaluminum saucepan. Tie the quince peels and seeds in cheesecloth along with the cloves and cinnamon stick. Add to the pan, push down, and cover with water. Bring up to a boil and cook until quince pulp is tender. This should take about 30 minutes. Strain the liquids into a bowl and measure. You will want about 2 cups liquid. Add the liquids to the pan. Bring up to a boil, add sugar, and boil for 2 minutes. Return the quince pulp and cheesecloth bag to the pan, and boil 5 minutes. Let the mixture

Glaze the top with some of the preserves, thinned with water and a little honey.

rest at room temperature for 2 hours. Bring up to a boil again and simmer for 15 minutes. Let rest another hour. Boil again. By now the quince pulp should be turning red. Add most of the lemon juice and boil for another 15 minutes. Let rest for an hour. Discard cloth bag, squeezing down to extract most of the liquid trapped within. Bring up to a boil and boil until thick and a candy thermometer reads 220 to 224 degrees. Add lemon juice to taste if desired. Pack in sterilized jars and seal. This makes 3 to 4 pints, but you will need about 2 cups for this recipe.

Kitchen Conversation

Yes! Yes! Yes! Isn't this a wonderful trio of tastes? The sweet and aromatic quinces, the bitter walnuts, and the slightly sour cheese make for a harmonious combination. The seeds and peel add flavor to the quinces and help them to redden a little sooner. If you used apricot preserves, you might need to sweeten the cheese a bit more, as the apricots are more tart than quinces or figs.

Wine Notes

Pairing Pointers: *The walnuts add oiliness of texture and bitter flavor notes to desserts. Quinces are very wine friendly, as they unite tart and sweet simultaneously. You need not go to the ultrasugary side here, since this dessert is both savory and sweet.*

Category: 7

Specific Recommendations:

7: *Various Italian—Recioto di Soave or sweet Marsala* ■
Tokay—4 to 5 puttanyos with exotic fruit, from a ripe year ■
Semillon/blends, late harvest—bright, balanced, especially Australian

INDEX